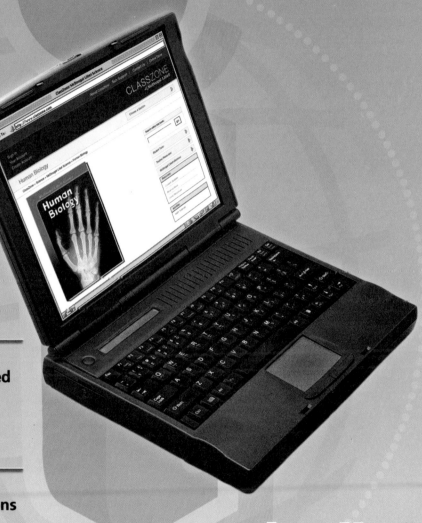

Human Biology

joint

tissue

HUMAN
(Homo sapiens)

skeletal
system

LIFE SCIENCE

A ▶ Cells and Heredity
B ▶ Life Over Time
C ▶ Diversity of Living Things
D ▶ Ecology
E ▶ Human Biology

EARTH SCIENCE

A ▶ Earth's Surface
B ▶ The Changing Earth
C ▶ Earth's Waters
D ▶ Earth's Atmosphere
E ▶ Space Science

PHYSICAL SCIENCE

A ▶ Matter and Energy
B ▶ Chemical Interactions
C ▶ Motion and Forces
D ▶ Waves, Sound, and Light
E ▶ Electricity and Magnetism

Acknowledgments: Excerpts and adaptations from *National Science Education Standards* by the National Academy of Sciences. Copyright © 1996 by the National Academy of Sciences. Reprinted with permission from the National Academies Press, Washington, D.C.

Excerpts and adaptations from *Benchmarks for Science Literacy: Project 2061.* Copyright © 1993 by the American Association for the Advancement of Science. Reprinted with permission.

ISBN: 0-618-33431-9   2 3 4 5 6 7 8 VJM 08 07 06 05 04

Internet Web Site: http://www.mcdougallittell.com

Science Consultants

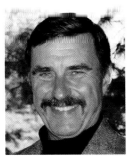

Chief Science Consultant

James Trefil, Ph.D. is the Clarence J. Robinson Professor of Physics at George Mason University. He is the author or co-author of more than 25 books, including *Science Matters* and *The Nature of Science.* Dr. Trefil is a member of the American Association for the Advancement of Science's Committee on the Public Understanding of Science and Technology. He is also a fellow of the World Economic Forum and a frequent contributor to *Smithsonian* magazine.

Rita Ann Calvo, Ph.D. is Senior Lecturer in Molecular Biology and Genetics at Cornell University, where for 12 years she also directed the Cornell Institute for Biology Teachers. Dr. Calvo is the 1999 recipient of the College and University Teaching Award from the National Association of Biology Teachers.

Kenneth Cutler, M.S. is the Education Coordinator for the Julius L. Chambers Biomedical Biotechnology Research Institute at North Carolina Central University. A former middle school and high school science teacher, he received a 1999 Presidential Award for Excellence in Science Teaching.

Instructional Design Consultants

Douglas Carnine, Ph.D. is Professor of Education and Director of the National Center for Improving the Tools of Educators at the University of Oregon. He is the author of seven books and over 100 other scholarly publications, primarily in the areas of instructional design and effective instructional strategies and tools for diverse learners. Dr. Carnine also serves as a member of the National Institute for Literacy Advisory Board.

Linda Carnine, Ph.D. consults with school districts on curriculum development and effective instruction for students struggling academically. A former teacher and school administrator, Dr. Carnine also co-authored a popular remedial reading program.

Donald Steely, Ph.D. serves as principal investigator at the Oregon Center for Applied Science (ORCAS) on federal grants for science and language arts programs. His background also includes teaching and authoring of print and multimedia programs in science, mathematics, history, and spelling.

Sam Miller, Ph.D. is a middle school science teacher and the Teacher Development Liaison for the Eugene, Oregon, Public Schools. He is the author of curricula for teaching science, mathematics, computer skills, and language arts.

Vicky Vachon, Ph.D. consults with school districts throughout the United States and Canada on improving overall academic achievement with a focus on literacy. She is also co-author of a widely used program for remedial readers.

Content Reviewers

John Beaver, Ph.D.
Ecology
Professor, Director of Science Education Center
College of Education and Human Services
Western Illinois University
Macomb, IL

Donald J. DeCoste, Ph.D.
Matter and Energy, Chemical Interactions
Chemistry Instructor
University of Illinois
Urbana-Champaign, IL

Dorothy Ann Fallows, Ph.D., MSc
Diversity of Living Things, Microbiology
Partners in Health
Boston, MA

Michael Foote, Ph.D.
The Changing Earth, Life Over Time
Associate Professor
Department of the Geophysical Sciences
The University of Chicago
Chicago, IL

Lucy Fortson, Ph.D.
Space Science
Director of Astronomy
Adler Planetarium and Astronomy Museum
Chicago, IL

Elizabeth Godrick, Ph.D.
Human Biology
Professor, CAS Biology
Boston University
Boston, MA

Isabelle Sacramento Grilo, M.S.
The Changing Earth
Lecturer, Department of the Geological Sciences
Montana State University
Bozeman, MT

David Harbster, MSc
Diversity of Living Things
Professor of Biology
Paradise Valley Community College
Phoenix, AZ

Richard D. Norris, Ph.D.
Earth's Waters
Professor of Paleobiology
Scripps Institution of Oceanography
University of California, San Diego
La Jolla, CA

Donald B. Peck, M.S.
*Motion and Forces; Waves, Sound, and Light;
   Electricity and Magnetism*
Director of the Center for Science Education (retired)
Fairleigh Dickinson University
Madison, NJ

Javier Penalosa, Ph.D.
Diversity of Living Things, Plants
Associate Professor, Biology Department
Buffalo State College
Buffalo, NY

Raymond T. Pierrehumbert, Ph.D.
Earth's Atmosphere
Professor in Geophysical Sciences (Atmospheric Science)
The University of Chicago
Chicago, IL

Brian J. Skinner, Ph.D.
Earth's Surface
Eugene Higgins Professor of Geology and Geophysics
Yale University
New Haven, CT

Nancy E. Spaulding, M.S.
Earth's Surface, The Changing Earth, Earth's Waters
Earth Science Teacher (retired)
Elmira Free Academy
Elmira, NY

Steven S. Zumdahl, Ph.D.
Matter and Energy, Chemical Interactions
Professor Emeritus of Chemistry
University of Illinois
Urbana-Champaign, IL

Susan L. Zumdahl, M.S.
Matter and Energy, Chemical Interactions
Chemistry Education Specialist
University of Illinois
Urbana-Champaign, IL

Safety Consultant

Juliana Texley, Ph.D.
Former K–12 Science Teacher and School Superintendent
Boca Raton, FL

English Language Advisor

Judy Lewis, M.A.
Director, State and Federal Programs for reading proficiency
and high risk populations
Rancho Cordova, CA

Teacher Panel Members

Carol Arbour
Tallmadge Middle School,
Tallmadge, OH

Patty Belcher
Goodrich Middle School,
Akron, OH

Gwen Broestl
Luis Munoz Marin Middle School,
Cleveland, OH

Al Brofman
Tehipite Middle School,
Fresno, CA

John Cockrell
Clinton Middle School,
Columbus, OH

Jenifer Cox
Sylvan Middle School,
Citrus Heights, CA

Linda Culpepper
Martin Middle School,
Charlotte, NC

Kathleen Ann DeMatteo
Margate Middle School,
Margate, FL

Melvin Figueroa
New River Middle School,
Ft. Lauderdale, FL

Doretha Grier
Kannapolis Middle School,
Kannapolis, NC

Robert Hood
Alexander Hamilton Middle School,
Cleveland, OH

Scott Hudson
Coverdale Elementary School,
Cincinnati, OH

Loretta Langdon
Princeton Middle School,
Princeton, NC

Carlyn Little
Glades Middle School,
Miami, FL

Ann Marie Lynn
Amelia Earhart Middle School,
Riverside, CA

James Minogue
Lowe's Grove Middle School,
Durham, NC

Joann Myers
Buchanan Middle School,
Tampa, FL

Barbara Newell
Charles Evans Hughes Middle School,
Long Beach, CA

Anita Parker
Kannapolis Middle School,
Kannapolis, NC

Greg Pirolo
Golden Valley Middle School,
San Bernardino, CA

Laura Pottmyer
Apex Middle School,
Apex, NC

Lynn Prichard
Booker T. Washington Middle Magnet
School, Tampa, FL

Jacque Quick
Walter Williams High School,
Burlington, NC

Robert Glenn Reynolds
Hillman Middle School,
Youngstown, OH

Stacy Rinehart
Lufkin Road Middle School,
Apex, NC

Theresa Short
Abbott Middle School,
Fayetteville, NC

Rita Slivka
Alexander Hamilton Middle School,
Cleveland, OH

Marie Sofsak
B F Stanton Middle School,
Alliance, OH

Nancy Stubbs
Sweetwater Union Unified School District,
Chula Vista, CA

Sharon Stull
Quail Hollow Middle School,
Charlotte, NC

Donna Taylor
Okeeheelee Middle School,
West Palm Beach, FL

Sandi Thompson
Harding Middle School,
Lakewood, OH

Lori Walker
Audubon Middle School & Magnet Center,
Los Angeles, CA

Teacher Lab Evaluators

Andrew Boy
W.E.B. DuBois Academy,
Cincinnati, OH

Jill Brimm-Byrne
Albany Park Academy,
Chicago, IL

Gwen Broestl
Luis Munoz Marin Middle School,
Cleveland, OH

Al Brofman
Tehipite Middle School,
Fresno, CA

Michael A. Burstein
The Rashi School,
Newton, MA

Trudi Coutts
Madison Middle School,
Naperville, IL

Jenifer Cox
Sylvan Middle School,
Citrus Heights, CA

Larry Cwik
Madison Middle School,
Naperville, IL

Jennifer Donatelli
Kennedy Junior High School,
Lisle, IL

Melissa Dupree
Lakeside Middle School,
Evans, GA

Carl Fechko
Luis Munoz Marin Middle School,
Cleveland, OH

Paige Fullhart
Highland Middle School,
Libertyville, IL

Sue Hood
Glen Crest Middle School,
Glen Ellyn, IL

William Luzader
Plymouth Community Intermediate School,
Plymouth, MA

Ann Min
Beardsley Middle School,
Crystal Lake, IL

Aileen Mueller
Kennedy Junior High School,
Lisle, IL

Nancy Nega
Churchville Middle School,
Elmhurst, IL

Oscar Newman
Sumner Math and Science Academy,
Chicago, IL

Lynn Prichard
Booker T. Washington Middle Magnet
School, Tampa, FL

Jacque Quick
Walter Williams High School,
Burlington, NC

Stacy Rinehart
Lufkin Road Middle School,
Apex, NC

Seth Robey
Gwendolyn Brooks Middle School,
Oak Park, IL

Kevin Steele
Grissom Middle School,
Tinley Park, IL

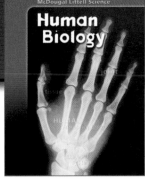

Human Biology

Unit Features

1 Systems, Support, and Movement 6

(the **BIG** idea)

The human body is made up of systems that work together to perform necessary functions.

2 Absorption, Digestion, and Exchange 34

(the **BIG** idea)

Systems in the body obtain and process materials and remove waste.

What materials does your body need to function properly? page 34

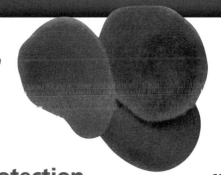

Red blood cells travel through a blood vessel. How do you think blood carries materials around your body? page 62

Features

Visual Highlights

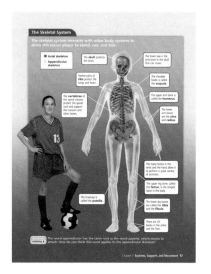

Internet Resources @ ClassZone.com

INVESTIGATIONS AND ACTIVITIES

EXPLORE THE BIG IDEA

Chapter Opening Inquiries

CHAPTER INVESTIGATION

Full-Period Labs

EXPLORE

Introductory Inquiry Activities

INVESTIGATE

Skill Labs

Standards and Benchmarks

Each chapter in **Human Biology** covers some of the learning goals that are described in the *National Science Education Standards* (NSES) and the Project 2061 *Benchmarks for Science Literacy*. Selected content and skill standards are show below in shortened form.The following National Science Education Standards are covered on pp. xii–xxvii, in Frontiers in Science, and in Timelines in Science, as well as in chapter features and laboratory investigations: Understandings About Scientific Inquiry (A.9), Understandings About Science and Technology (E.6), Science and Technology in Society (F.5), Nature of Science (G.2), and History of Science (G.3).

Content Standards

1 Systems, Support, and Movement

National Science Education Standards

C.1.a | Levels of organization for living systems include: cells, tissues, organs, organ systems, whole organisms, and ecosystems.
C.1.d | Specialized cells perform specialized functions in multicellular organisms.
C.1.e | The human organism has systems: digestion, respiration, reproduction, circulation, excretion, movement, control and coordination, and protection.

Project 2061 Benchmarks

6.A.1 | Like other animals, human beings have body systems for:
• obtaining and providing energy
• defense
• reproduction
• coordination of body functions
6.C.1 | Organs and organ systems
• are made of cells
• help to provide all cells with basic needs

2 Absorption, Digestion, and Exchange

National Science Education Standards

C.1.e | The human organism has systems: digestion, respiration, reproduction, circulation, excretion, movement, control and coordination, and protection.
F.1.e | Food provides energy and nutrients for growth and development.

Project 2061 Benchmarks

6.C.2 | For the body to use food energy and building materials, the food must first be digested into molecules that are absorbed and transported to cells.
6.C.3 | Respiratory, urinary, and digestive systems remove wastes from the body.

3 Transport and Protection

National Science Education Standards

C.1.d | Specialized cells perform specialized functions in multicellular organisms.
C.1.e | The human organism has systems: digestion, respiration, reproduction, circulation, excretion, movement, control and coordination, and protection.
C.1.f | Disease is a breakdown in structures or functions of an organism.

Project 2061 Benchmarks

6.C.3 | The circulatory system moves substances to or from cells where they are needed or produced. It responds to changing demands.
6.C.4 | Specialized cells and molecules they produce identify and destroy microbes.
6.E.4 | White blood cells engulf invaders or produce antibodies that fight them.

Control and Reproduction

National Science Education Standards

C.1.d	Specialized cells perform specialized functions in multicellular organisms.
C.1.e	The human organism has systems: digestion, respiration, reproduction, circulation, excretion, movement, control and coordination, and protection.
C.2.a	Reproduction is essential to the continuation of a species.
C.2.b	Females produce eggs, and males sperm, which unite to begin a new individual.
C.2.c	Every organism requires a set of instructions for specifying its traits.

Project 2061 Benchmarks

5.B.2	In sexual reproduction, a single specialized cell from a female merges with a specialized cell from a male.
6.B.1	Fertilization occurs when one of the sperm cells from the male enters the egg cell from the female.
6.B.3	After fertilization, cells divide and specialize as a fetus grows from the embryo following a set pattern of development.
6.C.5	Hormones are chemicals from glands that help the body respond to danger and regulate human growth, development, and reproduction.
6.C.6	Interactions among the senses, nerves, and brain make possible the learning that enables human beings to cope with changes in their environment.

Growth, Development, and Health

National Science Education Standards

C.1.e	The human organism has systems: digestion, respiration, reproduction, circulation, excretion, movement, control and coordination, and protection.
C.1.f	Disease is a breakdown in structures or functions of an organism.
C.3.a	Organisms must obtain and use resources, grow, reproduce, and maintain stable internal conditions.
C.3.b	Regulation of an organism's internal environment involves interactions with its external environment.
F.1.c	The use of tobacco increases risk of illness.
F.1.d	Alcohol and other drugs are often abused and can lead to addiction.
F.1.e	Food provides energy and nutrients for growth and development.

Project 2061 Benchmarks

6.B.5	Changes occur as humans age. Many factors affect length and quality of life.
6.E.2	Toxic substances, diet, and behavior may harm one's health.
6.E.3	Viruses, bacteria, fungi, and parasites may interfere with the human body.
6.E.4	White blood cells engulf invaders or produce antibodies that fight them.

Process and Skill Standards

	National Science Education Standards
A.1	Identify questions that can be answered through scientific methods.
A.2	Design and conduct a scientific investigation.
A.3	Use appropriate tools and techniques to gather and interpret data.
A.4	Use evidence to describe, predict, explain, and model.
A.5	Think critically to find relationships between results and interpretations.
A.6	Give alternative explanations and predictions.
A.7	Communicate procedures, results, and conclusions.
A.8	Use mathematics in all aspects of scientific inquiry.
A.9.a	Different kinds of questions suggest different kinds of scientific investigations.
A.9.c	Mathematics is important in all aspects of scientific inquiry.
A.9.d	Scientific explanations emphasize evidence, have logically consistent arguments, and use scientific principles, models, and theories.
E.6.b	Many different people in different cultures have made and continue to make contributions to science and technology.
G.1.a	Women and men of various social and ethnic backgrounds engage in the activities of science.
G.1.b	Science requires different abilities. The work of science relies on basic human qualities, such as reasoning, insight, energy, skill, and creativity.

	Project 2061 Benchmarks
1.C.1	Contributions to science have been made by different people, in different cultures, at different times.
12.A.1	Know why it is important in science to keep honest, clear, and accurate records.
12.A.2	Hypotheses are valuable, even if they turn out not to be true.
12.A.3	Different explanations can often be given for the same evidence.
12.C.3	Use appropriate units, use and read instruments that measure length, volume, weight, time, rate, and temperature.
12.D.1	Use tables and graphs to organize information and identify relationships.
12.D.2	Read, interpret, and describe tables and graphs.
12.D.3	Locate information in reference books and other resources.
12.D.4	Understand information that includes different types of charts and graphs, including circle charts, bar graphs, line graphs, data tables, diagrams, and symbols.

Introducing Life Science

Scientists are curious. Since ancient times, they have been asking and answering questions about the world around them. Scientists are also very suspicious of the answers they get. They carefully collect evidence and test their answers many times before accepting an idea as correct.

In this book you will see how scientific knowledge keeps growing and changing as scientists ask new questions and rethink what was known before. The following sections will help get you started.

What Is Life Science?

Life science is the study of living things. As you study life science, you will observe and read about a variety of organisms, from huge redwood trees to the tiny bacteria that cause sore throats. Because Earth is home to such a great variety of living things, the study of life science is rich and exciting.

But life science doesn't simply include learning the names of millions of organisms. It includes big ideas that help us to understand how all these living things interact with their environment. Life science is the study of characteristics and needs that all living things have in common. It's also a study of changes—both daily changes as well as changes that take place over millions of years. Probably most important, in studying life science, you will explore the many ways that all living things—including you—depend upon Earth and its resources.

The text and visuals in this book will invite you into the world of living things and provide you with the key concepts you'll need in your study. Activities offer a chance for you to investigate some aspects of life science on your own. The four unifying principles listed below provide a way for you to connect the information and ideas in this program.

- **All living things share common characteristics.**

- **All living things share common needs.**

- **Living things meet their needs through interactions with the environment.**

- **The types and numbers of living things change over time.**

(the **BIG** idea)

Each chapter begins with a big idea. Keep in mind that each big idea relates to one or more of the unifying principles.

All living things share common characteristics.

Birds nest among the plants of a reed marsh as sunlight shines and a breeze blows. Which of these is alive? Warblers and plants are living things, but sunlight and breezes are not. All living things share common characteristics that distinguish them from nonliving things.

What It Means

This unifying principle helps you explore one of the biggest questions in science, "What is life?" Let's take a look at four characteristics that distinguish living things from nonliving things: organization, growth, reproduction, and response.

Organization

If you stand a short distance from a reed warbler's nest, you can observe the largest level of organization in a living thing—the **organism** itself. Each bird is an organism. If you look at a leaf under a microscope, you can observe the smallest level of organization capable of performing all the activities of life, a **cell.** All living things are made of cells.

Growth

Most living things grow and develop. Growth often involves not only an increase in size, but also an increase in complexity, such as a tadpole growing into a frog. If all goes well, the small warblers in the picture will grow to the size of their parent.

Reproduction

Most living things produce offspring like themselves. Those offspring are also able to reproduce. That means that reed warblers produce reed warblers, which in turn produce more reed warblers.

Response

You've probably noticed that your body adjusts to changes in your surroundings. If you are exploring outside on a hot day, you may notice that you sweat. On a cold day, you may shiver. Sweating and shivering are examples of response.

Why It's Important

People of all ages experience the urge to explore and understand the living world. Understanding the characteristics of living things is a good way to start this exploration of life. In addition, knowing about the characteristics of living things helps you identify

- similarities and differences among various organisms
- key questions to ask about any organism you study

All living things share common needs.

What do you need to stay alive? What does an animal like a fish or a coral need to stay alive? All living things have common needs.

What It Means

Inside every living thing, chemical reactions constantly change materials into new materials. For these reactions to occur, an organism needs energy, water and other materials, and living space.

Energy

You use energy all the time. Movement, growth, and sleep all require energy, which you get from food. Plants use the energy of sunlight to make sugar for energy. Almost all animals get their energy by eating either plants or other animals that eat plants.

Water and Other Materials

Water is an important material in the cells of all living things. The chemical reactions inside cells take place in water, and water plays a part in moving materials around within organisms.

Other materials are also essential for life. For example, plants must have carbon dioxide from the air to make sugar. Plants and animals both use oxygen to release the energy stored in sugar. You and other animals that live on land get oxygen when you breathe in air. The fish swimming around the coral reef in the picture have gills, which allow them to get oxygen that is dissolved in the water.

Living Space

You can think of living space as a home—a space that protects you from external conditions and a place where you can get materials such as water and air. The ocean provides living space for the coral that makes up this coral reef. The coral itself provides living space for many other organisms.

Why It's Important

Understanding the needs of living things helps people make wise decisions about resources. This knowledge can also help you think carefully about
- the different ways in which various organisms meet their needs for energy and materials
- the effects of adding chemicals to the water and air around us
- the reasons why some types of plants or animals may disappear from an area

Living things meet their needs through interactions with the environment.

A moose chomps on the leaves of a plant. This ordinary event involves many interactions among living and nonliving things within the forest.

What It Means

To understand this unifying principle, take a closer look at the words *environment* and *interactions*.

Environment

The **environment** is everything that surrounds a living thing. An environment is made up of both living and nonliving factors. For example, the environment in this forest includes rainfall, rocks, and soil as well as the moose, the evergreen trees, and the birch trees. In fact, the soil in these forests is called "moose and spruce" soil because it contains materials provided by the animals and evergreens in the area.

Interaction

All living things in an environment meet their needs through interactions. An **interaction** occurs when two or more things act in ways that affect one another. For example, trees and other forest plants can meet their need for energy and materials through interactions with materials in soil and with air and light from the Sun. New plants get living space as birds, wind, and other factors carry seeds from one location to another.

Animals like this moose meet their need for food through interactions with other living things. The moose gets food by eating leaves off trees and other plants. In turn, the moose becomes food for wolves.

Why It's Important

Learning about living things and their environment helps scientists and decision makers address issues such as

- predicting how a change in the moose population would affect the soil in the forest
- determining the ways in which animals harm or benefit the trees in a forest
- developing land for human use without damaging the environment

The types and numbers of living things change over time.

The story of life on Earth is a story of changes. Some changes take place over millions of years. At one time, animals similar to modern fish swam in the area where this lizard now runs.

What It Means

To understand how living things change over time, let's look closely at the terms *diversity* and *adaptation*.

Diversity

You are surrounded by an astonishing variety of living things. This variety is called **biodiversity.** Today, scientists have described and named 1.4 million species. There are even more species that haven't been named. Scientists use the term *species* to describe a group of closely related living things. Members of a **species** are so similar that they can produce offspring that are able to reproduce. Lizards, such as the one you see in the photograph, are so diverse that they make up many different species.

Over the millions of years that life has existed on Earth, new species have originated and others have disappeared. The disappearance of a species is called **extinction.** Fossils, like the one in the photograph, provide evidence of some of the organisms that lived millions of years ago.

Adaptation

Scientists use the term **adaptation** to mean a characteristic of a species that allows members of that species to survive in a particular environment. Adaptations are related to needs. A lizard's legs are an adaptation that allows it to move on land.

Over time, species either develop adaptations to changing environments or they become extinct. The history of living things on Earth is related to the history of the changing Earth. The presence of a fishlike fossil indicates that the area shown in this photograph was once covered by water.

Why It's Important

By learning how living things change over time, you will gain a better understanding of the life that surrounds you and how it survives. Discovering more about the history of life helps scientists to

• identify patterns of relationships among various species
• predict how changes in the environment may affect species in the future

The Nature of Science

You may think of science as a body of knowledge or a collection of facts. More important, however, science is an active process that involves certain ways of looking at the world.

Scientific Habits of Mind

Scientists are curious. They are always asking questions. A scientist who observes that the number of plants in a forest preserve has decreased might ask questions such as, "Are more animals eating the plants?" or "Has the way the land is used affected the numbers of plants?" Scientists around the world investigate these and other important questions.

Scientists are observant. They are always looking closely at the world around them. A scientist who studies plants often sees details such as the height of a plant, its flowers, and how many plants live in a particular area.

Scientists are creative. They draw on what they know to form a possible explanation for a pattern, an event, or a behavior that they have observed. Then scientists create a plan for testing their ideas.

Scientists are skeptical. Scientists don't accept an explanation or answer unless it is based on evidence and logical reasoning. They continually question their own conclusions as well as conclusions suggested by other scientists. Scientists trust only evidence that is confirmed by other people or methods.

A white-tailed deer feeds on many plants, including the trillium shown here.

By measuring the growth of this tree, a scientist can study interactions in the ecosystem.

Science Processes at Work

You can think of science as a continuous cycle of asking and seeking answers to questions about the world. Although there are many processes that scientists use, scientists typically do each of the following:

- Observe and ask a question
- Determine what is known
- Investigate
- Interpret results
- Share results

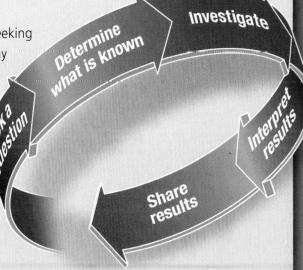

Observe and Ask a Question

It may surprise you that asking questions is an important skill. A scientific investigation may start when a scientist asks a question. Perhaps scientists observe an event or a process that they don't understand, or perhaps answering one question leads to another.

Determine What Is Known

When beginning an inquiry, scientists find out what is already known about a question. They study results from other scientific investigations, read journals, and talk with other scientists. A biologist who is trying to understand how the change in the number of deer in an area affects plants will study reports of censuses taken for both plants and animals.

Investigate

Investigating is the process of collecting evidence. Two important ways of collecting evidence are observing and experimenting.

Observing is the act of noting and recording an event, a characteristic, a behavior, or anything else detected with an instrument or with the senses. For example, a scientist notices that plants in one part of the forest are not thriving. She sees broken plants and compares the height of the plants in one area with the height of those in another.

An **experiment** is an organized procedure during which all factors but the one being studied are controlled. For example, the scientist thinks the reason some plants in the forest are not thriving may be that deer are eating the flowers off the plants. An experiment she might try is to mark two similar parts of an area where the plants grow and then build a fence around one part so the deer can't get to the plants there. The fence must be constructed so the same amounts of light, air, and water reach the plants. The only factor that changes is contact between plants and the deer.

Close observation of the Colorado potato beetle led scientists to a biological pesticide that can help farmers control this insect pest.

Forming hypotheses and making predictions are two other skills involved in scientific investigations. A **hypothesis** is a tentative explanation for an observation or a scientific problem that can be tested by further investigation. For example, since at least 1900, Colorado potato beetles were known to be resistant to chemical insecticides. Yet the numbers of beetles were not as large as expected. It was hypothesized that bacteria living in the beetles' environment were killing many beetles. A **prediction** is an expectation of what will be observed or what will happen and can be used to test a hypothesis. It was predicted that certain bacteria would kill Colorado potato beetles. This prediction was confirmed when a bacterium called *Bt* was discovered to kill Colorado potato beetles and other insect pests.

Interpret Results

As scientists investigate, they analyze their evidence, or data, and begin to draw conclusions. **Analyzing data** involves looking at the evidence gathered through observations or experiments and trying to identify any patterns that might exist in the data. Often scientists need to make additional observations or perform more experiments before they are sure of their conclusions. Many times scientists make new predictions or revise their hypotheses.

Computers help scientists analyze the sequence of base pairs in the DNA molecule.

Share Results

An important part of scientific investigation is sharing results of experiments. Scientists read and publish in journals and attend conferences to communicate with other scientists around the world. Sharing data and procedures gives them a way to test one another's results. They also share results with the public through newspapers, television, and other media.

Living things contain complex molecules such as RNA and DNA. To study them, scientists often use models like the one shown here.

The Nature of Technology

Imagine what life would be like without cars, computers, and cell phones. Imagine having no refrigerator or radio. It's difficult to think of a world without these items we call technology. Technology, however, is more than just machines that make our daily activities easier. Like science, technology is also a process. The process of technology uses scientific knowledge to design solutions to real-world problems.

Science and Technology

Science and technology go hand in hand. Each depends upon the other. Even designing a device as simple as a toaster requires knowledge of how heat flows and which materials are the best conductors of heat. Scientists also use a number of devices to help them collect data. Microscopes, telescopes, spectrographs, and computers are just a few of the tools that help scientists learn more about the world. The more information these tools provide, the more devices can be developed to aid scientific research and to improve modern lives.

The Process of Technological Design

Heart disease is among the leading causes of death today. Doctors have successfully replaced damaged hearts with hearts from donors. Medical engineers have developed pacemakers that improve the ability of a damaged heart to pump blood. But none of these solutions is perfect. Although it is very complex, the heart is really a pump for blood; thus, using technology to build a better replacement pump should be possible. The process of technological design involves many choices. In the case of an artificial heart, choices about how and what to develop involve cost, safety, and patient preference. What kind of technology will result in the best quality of life for the patient?

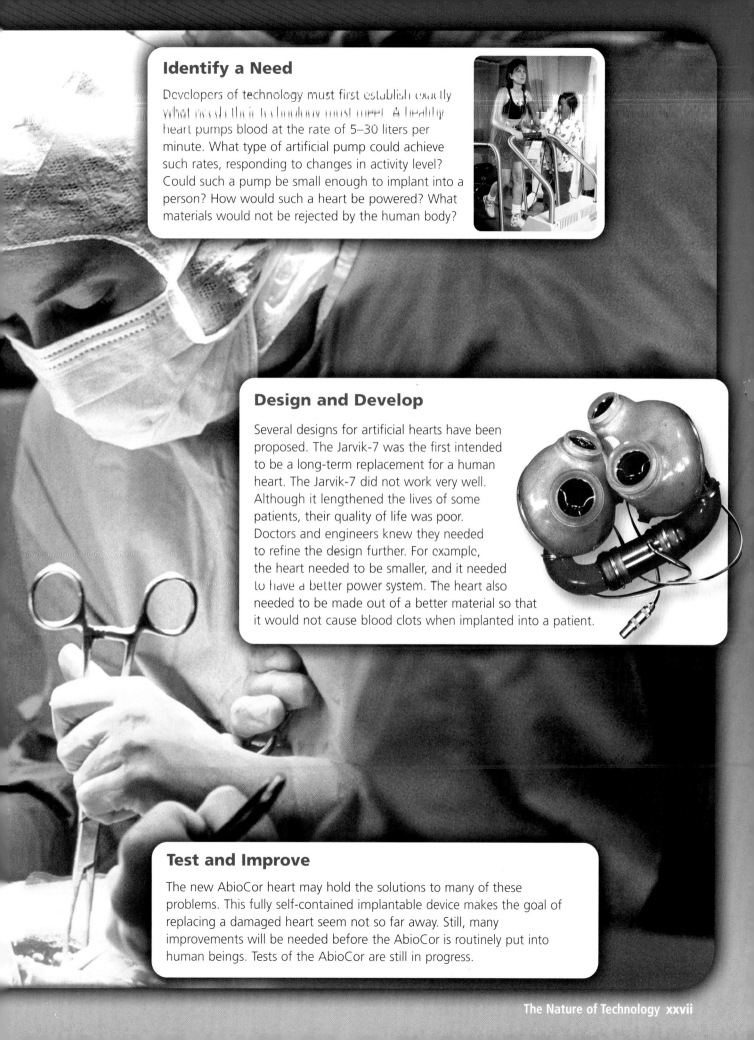

Identify a Need

Developers of technology must first establish exactly what needs the technology must meet. A healthy heart pumps blood at the rate of 5–30 liters per minute. What type of artificial pump could achieve such rates, responding to changes in activity level? Could such a pump be small enough to implant into a person? How would such a heart be powered? What materials would not be rejected by the human body?

Design and Develop

Several designs for artificial hearts have been proposed. The Jarvik-7 was the first intended to be a long-term replacement for a human heart. The Jarvik-7 did not work very well. Although it lengthened the lives of some patients, their quality of life was poor. Doctors and engineers knew they needed to refine the design further. For example, the heart needed to be smaller, and it needed to have a better power system. The heart also needed to be made out of a better material so that it would not cause blood clots when implanted into a patient.

Test and Improve

The new AbioCor heart may hold the solutions to many of these problems. This fully self-contained implantable device makes the goal of replacing a damaged heart seem not so far away. Still, many improvements will be needed before the AbioCor is routinely put into human beings. Tests of the AbioCor are still in progress.

Using McDougal Littell Science

Reading Text and Visuals

This book is organized to help you learn. Use these boxed pointers as a path to help you learn and remember the **Big Ideas** and **Key Concepts**.

Take notes.

Use the strategies on the **Getting Ready to Learn** page.

Read the Big Idea.

As you read **Key Concepts** for the chapter, relate them to **the Big Idea.**

CHAPTER

3 **Transp Protec**

the **BIG** idea

Systems function to transport materials and to defend and protect the body.

Key Concepts

SECTION 3.1 **The circulatory system transports materials.**
Learn how materials move through blood vessels.

SECTION 3.2 **The immune system defends the body.**
Learn about the body's defenses and responses to foreign materials.

SECTION 3.3 **The integumentary system shields the body.**
Learn about the structure of skin and how it protects the body.

 Internet Preview

CLASSZONE.COM
Chapter 3 online resources: Content Review, two Visualizations, four Resource Centers, Math Tutorial, Test Practice

E 62 Unit: **Human Biology**

CHAPTER 3

Getting Ready to Learn

◄ **CONCEPT REVIEW**

- The body's systems interact.
- The body's systems work to maintain internal conditions.
- The digestive system breaks down food.
- The respiratory system gets oxygen and removes carbon dioxide.

◄ **VOCABULARY REVIEW**

organ p. 11
organ system p. 12
homeostasis p. 12
nutrient p. 45

CONTENT REVIEW
CLASSZONE.COM
Review concepts and vocabulary.

► **TAKING NOTES**

MAIN IDEA AND DETAIL NOTES

Make a two-column chart. Write the main ideas, such as those in the blue headings, in the column on the left. Write details about each of those main heads in the column on the right.

VOCABULARY STRATEGY

Write each new vocabulary term in the center of a **frame game** diagram. Decide what information to frame it with. Use examples, descriptions, parts, sentences that use the term in context, or pictures. You can change the frame to fit each term.

See the Note-Taking Handbook on pages R45–R51.

SCIENCE NOTEBOK

MAIN IDEAS	DETAIL NOTES
1. The circulatory system works with other body systems.	1. Transports materials from digestive and respiratory systems to cells
	2. Blood is fluid that carries materials and wastes
	3. Blood is always moving through the body
	4. Blood delivers oxygen and takes away carbon dioxide

carries material to cells

moves continuously through body | **BLOOD** | carries waste away from cells

circulatory system

E 64 Unit: Human Biology

KEY CONCEPT

3.1 The circulatory system transports materials.

◀ **BEFORE, you learned**

- The urinary system removes waste
- The kidneys play a role in homeostasis

▶ **NOW, you will learn**

- How different structures of the circulatory system work together
- About the structure and function of blood
- What blood pressure is and why it is important

VOCABULARY

circulatory system p. 65
blood p. 65
red blood cell p. 67
artery p. 69
vein p. 69
capillary p. 69

EXPLORE The Circulatory System

How fast does your heart beat?

PROCEDURE

① Hold out your left hand with your palm facing up.

② Place the first two fingers of your right hand on your left wrist below your thumb. Move your fingertips slightly until you can feel your pulse.

③ Use the stopwatch to determine how many times your heart beats in one minute.

MATERIALS
stopwatch

WHAT DO YOU THINK?

- How many times did your heart beat?
- What do you think you would find if you took your pulse after exercising?

The circulatory system works with other body systems.

VOCABULARY
Add a frame game diagram for the term *circulatory system* to your notebook.

You have read that the systems in your body provide materials and energy. The digestive system breaks down food and nutrients, and the respiratory system provides the oxygen that cells need to release energy. Another system, called the **circulatory system,** transports products from the digestive and the respiratory systems to the cells.

Materials and wastes are carried in a fluid called **blood**. Blood moves continuously through the body, delivering oxygen and other materials to cells and removing carbon dioxide and other wastes from cells.

Chapter 3: **Transport and Protection** 65 **E**

Reading Text and Visuals

Read one paragraph at a time.

Look for a topic sentence that explains the main idea of the paragraph. Figure out how the details relate to that idea. One paragraph might have several important ideas; you may have to reread to understand.

Answer the questions.

Check Your Reading questions will help you remember what you read.

Study the visuals.

- Read the title.
- Read all labels and captions.
- Figure out what the picture is showing. Notice the information in the captions.

Exchanging Oxygen and Carbon Dioxide

Like almost all living things, the human body needs oxygen to survive. Without oxygen, cells in the body die quickly. How does the oxygen you need get to your cells? Oxygen, along with other gases, enters the body when you inhale. Oxygen is then transported to cells throughout the body.

The air that you breathe contains only about 20 percent oxygen and less than 1 percent carbon dioxide. Almost 80 percent of air is nitrogen gas. The air that you exhale contains more carbon dioxide and less oxygen than the air that you inhale. It's important that you exhale carbon dioxide because high levels of it will damage, even destroy, cells.

In cells and tissues, proper levels of both oxygen and carbon dioxide are essential. Recall that systems in the body work together to maintain homeostasis. If levels of oxygen or carbon dioxide change, your brain or blood vessels signal the body to breathe faster or slower.

The photograph shows how someone underwater maintains proper levels of carbon dioxide and oxygen. The scuba diver needs to inhale oxygen from a tank. She removes carbon dioxide wastes with other gases when she exhales into the water. The bubbles you see in the water are formed when she exhales.

CHECK YOUR READING What gases are in the air that you breathe?

Gas Exchange

This scuba diver breathes the same mixture of gases present in air.

Carbon dioxide is part of the mixture of gases the diver exhales.

Oxygen is in the mixture of gases the diver inhales.

Doing Labs

To understand science, you have to see it in action. Doing labs helps you understand how things really work.

① Read the entire lab first.

② Form a hypothesis.

③ Follow the procedure.

④ Record the data.

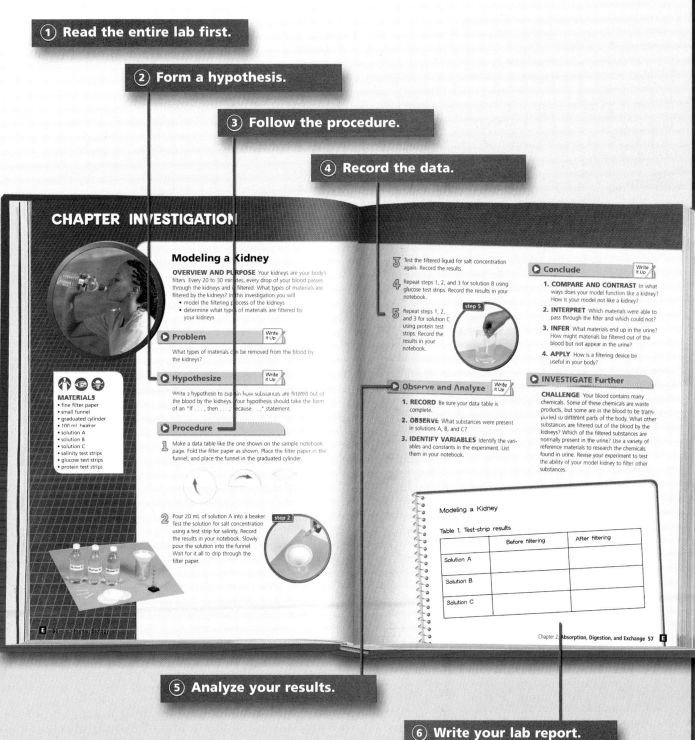

CHAPTER INVESTIGATION

Modeling a Kidney

OVERVIEW AND PURPOSE Your kidneys are your body's filters. Every 20 to 30 minutes, every drop of your blood passes through the kidneys and is filtered. What types of materials are filtered by the kidneys? In this investigation you will
- model the filtering process of the kidneys
- determine what types of materials are filtered by your kidneys

▶ Problem   Write It Up

What types of materials can be removed from the blood by the kidneys?

▶ Hypothesize   Write It Up

Write a hypothesis to explain how substances are filtered out of the blood by the kidneys. Your hypothesis should take the form of an "If . . . , then . . . , because . . ." statement.

▶ Procedure

MATERIALS
- fine filter paper
- small funnel
- graduated cylinder
- 100 ml beaker
- solution A
- solution B
- solution C
- salinity test strips
- glucose test strips
- protein test strips

1 Make a data table like the one shown on the sample notebook page. Fold the filter paper as shown. Place the filter paper in the funnel, and place the funnel in the graduated cylinder.

2 Pour 20 mL of solution A into a beaker. Test the solution for salt concentration using a test strip for salinity. Record the results in your notebook. Slowly pour the solution into the funnel. Wait for it all to drip through the filter paper.   *step 2*

3 Test the filtered liquid for salt concentration again. Record the results.

4 Repeat steps 1, 2, and 3 for solution B using glucose test strips. Record the results in your notebook.

5 Repeat steps 1, 2, and 3 for solution C using protein test strips. Record the results in your notebook.   *step 5*

▶ Observe and Analyze   Write It Up

1. **RECORD** Be sure your data table is complete.

2. **OBSERVE** What substances were present in solutions A, B, and C?

3. **IDENTIFY VARIABLES** Identify the variables and constants in the experiment. List them in your notebook.

▶ Conclude   Write It Up

1. **COMPARE AND CONTRAST** In what ways does your model function like a kidney? How is your model not like a kidney?

2. **INTERPRET** Which materials were able to pass through the filter and which could not?

3. **INFER** What materials end up in the urine? How might materials be filtered out of the blood but not appear in the urine?

4. **APPLY** How is a filtering device be useful in your body?

▶ INVESTIGATE Further

CHALLENGE Your blood contains many chemicals. Some of these chemicals are waste products, but some are in the blood to be transported to different parts of the body. What other substances are filtered out of the blood by the kidneys? Which of the filtered substances are normally present in the urine? Use a variety of reference materials to research the chemicals found in urine. Revise your experiment to test the ability of your model kidney to filter other substances.

Modeling a Kidney

Table 1. Test-strip results

	Before filtering	After filtering
Solution A		
Solution B		
Solution C		

⑤ Analyze your results.

⑥ Write your lab report.

Using Technology

The Internet is a great source of information about up-to-date science. The ClassZone Web site and NSTA SciLinks have exciting sites for you to explore. Video clips and simulations can make science come alive.

Look for red banners.

Go to **ClassZone.com** to see simulations, visualizations, resource centers, and content review.

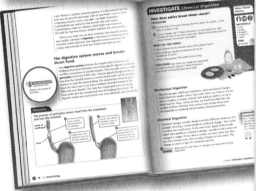

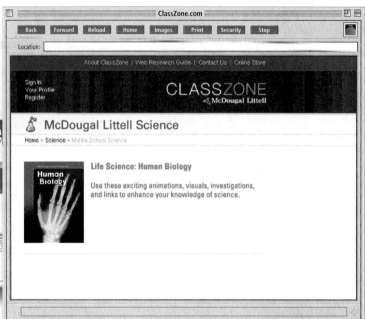

Watch the video.

See science at work in the **Scientific American Frontiers** video.

Look up SciLinks.

Go to **scilinks.org** to explore the topic.

Tissues and Organs **Code: MDL044**

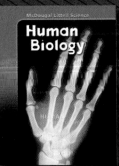

Human Biology
Contents Overview

Unit Features

the BIG idea

The human body is made up of systems that work together to perform necessary functions.

the BIG idea

Systems in the body obtain and process materials and remove waste.

the BIG idea

Systems function to transport materials and to defend and protect the body.

the BIG idea

The nervous and endocrine systems allow the body to respond to internal and external conditions.

the BIG idea

The body develops and maintains itself over time.

Surprising Senses

SCIENTIFIC AMERICAN FRONTIERS

Learn more about how the brain and senses work. See the video "Sight of Touch."

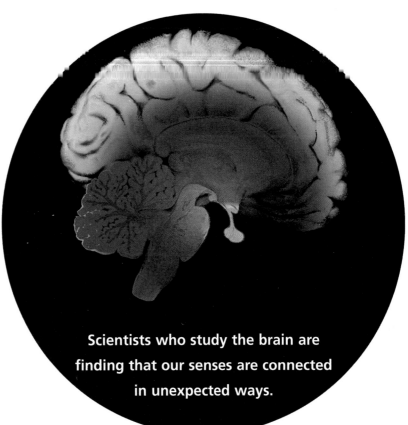

Scientists who study the brain are finding that our senses are connected in unexpected ways.

Senses and the Brain

One of the great mysteries still unsolved in science is what happens inside the brain. What is a thought? How is it formed? Where is it stored? How do our senses shape our thoughts? There are far more questions than answers. One way to approach questions about the brain is to study brain activity at times when the body is performing different functions.

Most advanced brain functions happen in the part of the brain called the cerebral cortex (suh-REE-bruhl KOR-tehks). That's where the brain interprets information from the senses. The cerebral cortex has many specialized areas. Each area controls one type of brain activity. Scientists are mapping these areas. At first, they studied people with brain injuries. A person with an injury to one area might not be able to speak. Someone with a different injury might have trouble seeing or hearing. Scientists mapped the areas in which damage seemed to cause each kind of problem.

Now scientists have even more tools to study the brain. One tool is called functional magnetic resonance imaging, or FMRI. Scientists put a person into a machine that uses radio waves to produce images of the person's brain. Scientists then ask the person to do specific activities, such as looking at pictures of faces or listening for specific sounds. The FMRI images show what parts of the person's brain are most active during each activity.

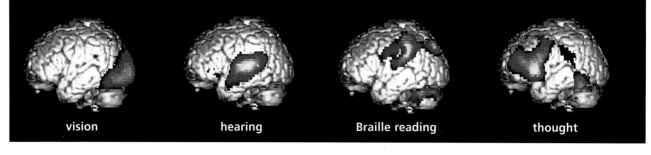

| vision | hearing | Braille reading | thought |

The PET scans show areas of the brain active during particular tasks. Braille is a textured alphabet read by the fingers. Braille reading activates areas associated with touch, vision, hearing, and thought.

Double Duty

Using FMRI and other tools, scientists have identified the parts of the cerebral cortex that are responsible for each of the senses. The vision area is located at the back of the brain. The smell, taste, touch, and hearing areas are all close together in the middle part of the brain.

People don't usually use just one sense at a time. Scientists have found some unexpected connections. In one study, Marisa Taylor-Clarke poked the arms of some volunteers with either one or two pins. Then she asked them how many pins they felt. Taylor-Clarke found that people who looked at their arms before the test did better than those who didn't. FMRI showed that the part of their brains responsible for touch was also more active when they used their sense of sight.

These connections in the brain show up even when one sense doesn't work. Many people who have hearing impairments read lips to understand what other people are saying. Scientists using FMRI discovered that these people use the part of the brain normally used for hearing to help them understand what they see. This is even true for people who have never been able to hear.

Scrambled Senses

Some people have more connections between their senses than most people have. They may look at numbers and see colors, or associate smells with shapes. Some even get a taste in their mouths when they touch something. All these are examples of synesthesia (sin-uhs-THEE-zhuh). About 1 in 200 people have some kind of synesthesia.

SCIENTIFIC AMERICAN FRONTIERS

View the "Sight of Touch" segment of your Scientific American Frontiers video to learn about another example of connections between the senses.

IN THIS SCENE FROM THE VIDEO ▶ Michelle, a research subject, reads Braille with her fingers after wearing a blindfold for three days.

SEEING BY TOUCHING Many blind people read using Braille, a system of raised dots used to represent letters. Some, such as Braille proofreader Gil Busch, can read Braille at astonishing speeds. Scientist Alvaro Pascual-Leone used MRI to study Gil's brain. The visual area of Gil's brain was active while he read Braille.

Gil has been blind since birth, so his brain has had a long time to adjust. Pascual-Leone wanted to know whether the brain could rewire itself in a shorter time. He asked volunteer Michelle Geronimo to wear a blindfold for a week. During that time, she learned to read Braille and experienced the world as a blind person does. At the end of the week, Pascual-Leone was able to demonstrate that Michelle's brain had rewired itself, too. Her visual center was active when she read Braille.

FMRI has made it possible for scientists to learn more about synesthesia. One group of scientists studied people who saw colors when they heard words. FMRI showed that the visual areas of their brains were active along with the hearing areas. (For most people, only the hearing area would be active.)

But why does synesthesia happen? Some scientists think that people with synesthesia have more connections between areas of their brains. Every person has extra connections when they're born, but most people lose many of them in childhood. Perhaps people with synesthesia keep theirs. Another theory suggests that their brains are "cross-wired," so information goes in unusual directions.

Some people with synesthesia see this colorful pattern when they hear a dog bark.

As scientists explore synesthesia and other connections between the senses, they learn more about how the parts of the brain work together. The human body is complex. And the brain, along with the rest of the nervous system, has yet to be fully understood.

? UNANSWERED Questions

Scientists have learned a lot about how senses are connected. Their research leads to new questions.

- How does information move between different areas of the brain?
- How and why does the brain rewire itself?
- How does cross-wired sensing (synesthesia) happen?

UNIT PROJECTS

As you study this unit, work alone or in a group on one of the projects below.

Your Body System

Create one or several models showing important body systems.

- Draw the outline of your own body on a large piece of craft paper.
- Use reference materials to help you place everything correctly. Label each part.

The Brain: "Then and Now"

Compare and contrast past and present understandings of the brain.

- One understanding is that each part of the brain is responsible for different body functions. This understanding has changed over time.
- Research the history of this idea.
- Prepare diagrams of then and now. Share your presentation.

Design an Experiment

Design an experiment that will test one of the senses. You should first identify a problem question you want to explore.

- The experiment may include a written introduction, materials procedure, and a plan for recording and presenting outcomes.
- Prepare a blank written experiment datasheet for your classmates to use.

CAREER CENTER
CLASSZONE.COM

Learn more about careers in neurobiology.

Systems, Support, and Movement

the **BIG** idea

The human body is made up of systems that work together to perform necessary functions.

Key Concepts

SECTION
1.1 The human body is complex.
Learn about the parts and systems in the human body.

SECTION
1.2 The skeletal system provides support and protection.
Learn how the skeletal system is organized and what it does.

SECTION
1.3 The muscular system makes movement possible.
Learn about the different types of muscles and how they work.

Internet Preview

CLASSZONE.COM

Chapter 1 online resources: Content Review, two Simulations, two Resource Centers, Math Tutorial, Test Practice

What systems make it possible for this racer to move so fast?

How Many Bones Are in Your Hand?

Use a pencil to trace an outline of your hand on a piece of paper. Feel the bones in your fingers and the palm of your hand. At points where you can bend your fingers and hand, draw a circle. Each circle represents a joint where two bones meet. Draw lines to represent the bones in your hand.

Observe and Think How many bones did you find? How many joints?

How Does It Move?

The bones in your body are hard and stiff, yet they move smoothly. The point where two bones meet and move is called a joint. There are probably many objects in your home that have hard parts that move against each other: a joystick, a hinge, a pair of scissors.

Observe and Think What types of movement are possible when two hard objects are attached to each other? What parts of your body produce similar movements?

Internet Activity: The Human Body

Go to **ClassZone.com** to explore the different systems in the human body.

Observe and Think How are the systems in the middle of the body different from those that extend to the outer parts of the body?

Tissues and Organs **Code: MDL044**

Getting Ready to Learn

◀ CONCEPT REVIEW

- The cell is the basic unit of living things.
- Systems are made up of interacting parts that share matter and energy.
- In multicellular organisms cells work together to support life.

◀ VOCABULARY REVIEW

See Glossary for definitions.

cell
system

CONTENT REVIEW
CLASSZONE.COM
Review concepts and vocabulary.

▶ TAKING NOTES

MAIN IDEA WEB

Write each new blue heading in a box. Then write notes in boxes around the center box that give important terms and details about that blue heading.

VOCABULARY STRATEGY

Write each new vocabulary term in the center of a **four square** diagram. Write notes in the squares around each term. Include a definition, some features, and some examples of the term. If possible, write some things that are not examples of the term.

See the Note-Taking Handbook on pages R45–R51.

SCIENCE NOTEBOOK

The cell is the basic unit of living things.

Tissues are groups of similar cells that function together.

The body has cells, tissues, and organs.

Organs are groups of tissues working together.

Definition	Features
Group of cells that work together	A level of organization in the body

TISSUE

Examples	Nonexamples
connective tissue, like bone	individual bone cells

The human body is complex.

BEFORE, you learned	NOW, you will learn
• All living things are made of cells • All living things need energy • Living things meet their needs through interactions with the environment	• About the organization of the human body • About different types of tissues • About the functions of organ systems

VOCABULARY

tissue p. 10
organ p. 11
organ system p. 12
homeostasis p. 12

THINK ABOUT

How is the human body like a city?

A city is made up of many parts that perform different functions. Buildings provide places to live and work. Transportation systems move people around. Electrical energy provides light and heat. Similarly, the human body is made of several systems. The skeletal system, like the framework of a building, provides support. The digestive system works with the respiratory system to provide energy and materials. What other systems in your body can you compare to a system in the city?

The body has cells, tissues, and organs.

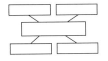

MAIN IDEA WEB
As you read this section, complete the main idea web begun on page 8.

Your body is made of many parts that work together as a system to help you grow and stay healthy. The basic level of organization in your body is the cell. Next come tissues, then individual organs, and then systems that are made up of organs. The highest level of organization is the organism itself. You can think of the body as having five levels of organization: cells, tissues, organs, organ systems, and the organism. Although these levels seem separate from one another, they all work together.

 What are five levels of organization in your body?

How do the systems in your body interact?

PROCEDURE

1. Work with other classmates to make a list of everyday activities.

2. Discuss how your body responds to each task. Record your ideas.

3. Identify and count the systems in your body that you think are used to perform the task.

4. Have someone from your group make a chart of the different activities.

WHAT DO YOU THINK?

- Which systems did you name, and how did they work together to perform each activity?

- When you are asleep, what activities does your body perform?

CHALLENGE How could you make an experiment that would test your predictions?

MATERIALS
large sheet of paper

TIME
20 minutes

Cells

The cell is the basic unit of life. Cells make up all living things. Some organisms, such as bacteria, are made of only a single cell. In these organisms the single cell performs all of the tasks necessary for survival. That individual cell captures and releases energy, uses materials, and grows. In more complex organisms, such as humans and many other animals and plants, cells are specialized. Specialized cells perform specific jobs. A red blood cell, for example, carries oxygen and other nutrients from the lungs throughout the body.

Tissues

A **tissue** is a group of similar cells that work together to perform a particular function. Think of a tissue as a brick wall and the cells within it as the individual bricks. Taken together, the bricks form something larger and more functional. But just as the bricks need to be placed in a certain way to form the wall, cells must be organized in a tissue.

 How are cells related to tissues?

The human body contains several types of tissues. These tissues are classified into four main groups according to their function: epithelial tissue, nerve tissue, muscle tissue, and connective tissue.

- Epithelial (ehp-uh-THEE-lee-uhl) tissue functions as a boundary. It covers all of the inner and outer surfaces of your body. Each of your internal organs is covered with a layer of epithelial tissue.

- Nerve tissue functions as a messaging system. Cells in nerve tissue carry electrical impulses between your brain and the various parts of your body in response to changing conditions.

- Muscle tissue functions in movement. Movement results when muscle cells contract, or shorten, and then relax. In some cases, such as throwing a ball, you control the movement. In other cases, such as the beating of your heart, the movement occurs without conscious control.

- Connective tissue functions to hold parts of the body together, providing support, protection, strength, padding, and insulation. Tendons and ligaments are connective tissues that hold bones and muscles together. Bone itself is another connective tissue. It supports and protects the soft parts of your body.

Organs

Groups of different tissues make up organs. An **organ** is a structure that is made up of two or more types of tissue that work together to carry out a function in the body. For example, the heart that pumps blood around your body contain all four types of tissues. As in cells and tissues, the structure of an organ relates to its function. The stomach's bag-shaped structure and strong muscular walls make it suited for breaking down food. The walls of the heart are also muscular, allowing it to function as a pump.

Levels of Organization

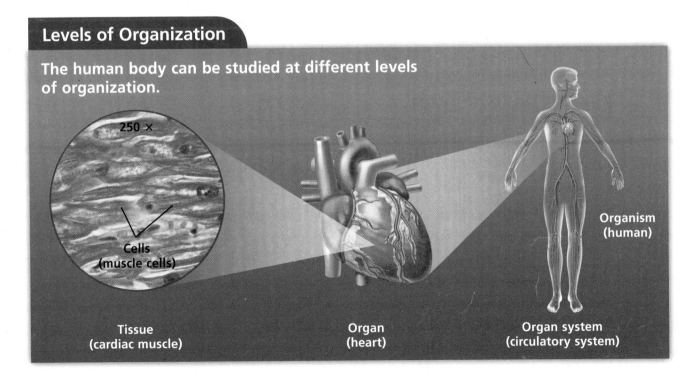

The human body can be studied at different levels of organization.

250 ×

Cells (muscle cells)

Tissue (cardiac muscle)

Organ (heart)

Organ system (circulatory system)

Organism (human)

Organ Systems

An **organ system** is a group of organs that together perform a function that helps the body meet its needs for energy and materials. For example, your stomach, mouth, throat, large and small intestines, liver, and pancreas are all part of the organ system called the digestive system. The body is made up of many organ systems. In this unit, you will read about these systems. They include the skeletal, muscular, respiratory, digestive, urinary, circulatory, immune, nervous, and reproductive systems. Together, these systems allow the human organism to grow, reproduce, and maintain life.

The body's systems interact with one another.

READING TiP

VOCABULARY
The word *homeostasis* contains two word roots. *Homeo* comes from a root meaning "same." *Stasis* comes from a root meaning "stand still" or "stay."

The ability of your body to maintain internal conditions is called **homeostasis** (HOH-mee-oh-STAY-sihs). Your body is constantly regulating such things as your body temperature, the amount of sugar in your blood, even your posture. The processes that take place in your body occur within a particular set of conditions.

The body's many levels of organization, from cells to organ systems, work constantly to maintain the balance needed for the survival of the organism. For example, on a hot day, you may sweat. Sweating keeps the temperature inside your body constant, even though the temperature of your surroundings changes.

INFER This student is drinking water after exercising. Why is it important to drink fluids after you sweat?

1.1 Review

KEY CONCEPTS

1. Draw a diagram that shows the relationship among cells, tissues, organs, and organ systems.

2. Make a chart of the four basic tissue groups that includes names, functions, and examples.

3. Identify three functions performed by organ systems.

CRITICAL THINKING

4. **Apply** How does drinking water after you sweat help maintain homeostasis?

5. **Compare and Contrast** Compare and contrast the four basic tissue groups. How would all four types of tissue be involved in a simple activity, like raising your hand?

⬤ CHALLENGE

6. **Apply** Describe an object, such as a car, that can be used as a model of the human body. Explain how the parts of the model relate to the body.

What Does the Body Need to Survive?

In 1914, Ernest Shackleton and 27 men set sail for Antarctica. Their goal was to cross the continent by foot and sled. The crew never set foot on Antarctica. Instead, the winter sea froze around their ship, crushing it until it sank. They were stranded on floating ice, over 100 miles from land. How long could they survive? How would their bodies respond? What would they need to stay alive?

You can make inferences in answer to any of these questions. First you need to recall what you know. Then you need new evidence. What was available to the explorers? Did they save supplies from their ship? What resources existed in the environment?

▶ Prior Knowledge

- The human body needs air, water, and food.
- The human body needs to maintain its temperature. The body can be harmed if it loses too much heat.

▶ Observations

Several of Shackleton's explorers kept diaries. From the diaries we know the following:

- The crew hunted seals and penguins for fresh meat.
- The temperature was usually below freezing.
- Tents and overturned lifeboats sheltered the crew from the wind.
- Their clothes were made of thick fabric and animal skins and furs.
- They melted snow and ice in order to have fresh water.

▶ Make Inferences

On Your Own Describe how the explorers met each of the needs of the human body.

As a Group How long do you think these 28 men could have survived these conditions? Use evidence and inferences in your answer.

CHALLENGE How might survival needs differ for sailors shipwrecked in the tropics compared to the Antarctic?

RESOURCE CENTER
CLASSZONE.COM

Learn more about Shackleton's expedition.

1.2 The skeletal system provides support and protection.

BEFORE, you learned

- The body is made of cells, tissues, organs, and systems
- Cells, tissues, organs, and organ systems work together
- Systems in the body interact

NOW, you will learn

- About different types of bone tissue
- How the human skeleton is organized
- How joints allow movement

VOCABULARY

skeletal system p. 14
compact bone p. 15
spongy bone p. 15
axial skeleton p. 16
appendicular skeleton p. 16

EXPLORE Levers

How can a bone act as a lever?

PROCEDURE

MATERIALS
sports bag

1. A lever is a stiff rod that pivots about a fixed point. Hold the bag in your hand and keep your arm straight, like a lever. Move the bag up and down.

2. Move the handles of the bag over your elbow. Again hold your arm straight and move the bag up and down.

3. Now move the bag to the top of your arm and repeat the procedure.

WHAT DO YOU THINK?

- At which position is it easiest to move the bag?
- At which position does the bag move the farthest?
- How does the position of a load affect the action of a lever?

Bones are living tissue.

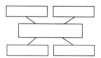

MAIN IDEA WEB
Make a web of the important terms and details about the main idea: *Bones are living tissue.*

Every movement of the human body is possible because of the interaction of muscles with the **skeletal system.** Made up of a strong connective tissue called bone, the skeletal system serves as the anchor for all of the body's movement, provides support, and protects soft organs inside the body. Bones can be classified as long bones, short bones, irregular bones, and flat bones. Long bones are found in the arms and legs. Short bones are found in the feet and hands. Irregular bones are found in the spine. Flat bones are found in the ribs and skull.

You might think that bones are completely solid and made up of dead tissue. They actually are made of both hard and soft materials.

Like your heart or skin, bones are living tissue. Bones are not completely solid, either; they have spaces inside. The spaces allow blood cells carrying nutrients to travel throughout the bones. Because bones have spaces, they weigh much less than they would if they were solid.

Explore the skeletal system.

Two Types of Bone Tissue

Every bone is made of two types of bone tissue: compact bone and spongy bone. The hard compact bone surrounds the soft spongy bone. Each individual bone cell lies within a bony web. This web is made up mostly of the mineral calcium.

Compact Bone Surrounding the spongy, inner layer of the bone is a hard layer called **compact bone.** Compact bone functions as the basic supportive tissue of the body, the part of the body you call the skeleton. The outer layer of compact bone is very hard and tough. It covers the outside of most bones.

Spongy Bone Inside the bone, the calcium network is less dense. This tissue is called **spongy bone.** Spongy bone is strong but lightweight. It makes up most of the short and the irregular bones found in your body. It also makes up the ends of long bones.

Marrow and Blood Cells

Within the spongy bone tissue is marrow, the part of the bone that produces red blood cells. The new red blood cells travel from the marrow into the blood vessels that run throughout the bone. The blood cells bring nutrients to the bone cells and carry waste materials away.

A Close Look at Bone

All bone, like the long bone shown here, is made up of compact bone tissue and spongy bone tissue.

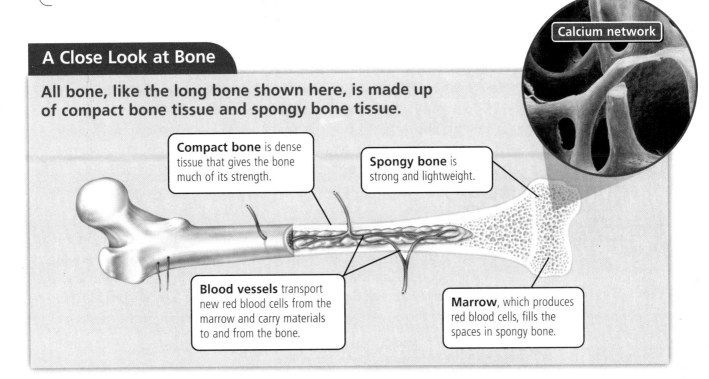

Calcium network

Compact bone is dense tissue that gives the bone much of its strength.

Spongy bone is strong and lightweight.

Blood vessels transport new red blood cells from the marrow and carry materials to and from the bone.

Marrow, which produces red blood cells, fills the spaces in spongy bone.

The skeleton is the body's framework.

Like the frame of a building, the skeleton provides the body's shape. The skeleton also works with other systems to allow movement. Scientists have identified two main divisions in the skeleton. These are the axial (AK-see-uhl) skeleton, which is the central part of the skeleton, and the appendicular (AP-uhn-DIHK-yuh-luhr) skeleton. Bones in the appendicular skeleton are attached to the axial skeleton. The diagram on page 17 labels some of the important bones in your skeleton.

The diagram on page 17 labels some of the important bones in your skeleton.

VOCABULARY
Remember to add four squares for *axial skeleton* and *appendicular skeleton* to your notebook.

The Axial Skeleton

Imagine a line straight down your back. You can think of that line as an axis. Sitting, standing, and twisting are some of the motions that turn around the axis. The **axial skeleton** is the part of the skeleton that forms the axis. It provides support and protection. In the diagram, parts of the axial skeleton are colored in red.

The axial skeleton includes the skull, or the cranium (KRAY-nee-uhm). The major function of the cranium is protection of the brain. Most of the bones in the cranium do not move. The skull connects to the spinal column in a way that allows the head to move up and down as well as right and left.

Your spinal column makes up the main portion of the axial skeleton. The spinal column is made up of many bones called vertebrae. The many bones allow flexibility. If you run your finger along your back you will feel the vertebrae. Another set of bones belonging to the axial skeleton are the rib bones. The ribs function to protect the soft internal organs, such as the heart and lungs.

The Appendicular Skeleton

The diagram shows the bones in the appendicular skeleton in yellow. Bones in the **appendicular skeleton** function mainly to allow movement. The shoulder belongs to the upper part of the appendicular skeleton. The upper arm bone that connects to the shoulder is the longest bone in the upper body. It connects with the two bones of the lower arm. The wristbone is the end of one of these bones in the lower arm.

The lower part of the body includes the legs and the hip bones. This part of the body bears all of the body's weight when you are standing. The leg bones are the strongest of all the bones in the skeleton. Just as the lower arm includes two bones, the lower leg has two bones. The larger of these two bones carries most of the weight of the body.

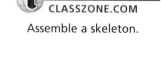

SIMULATION
CLASSZONE.COM
Assemble a skeleton.

 CHECK YOUR READING How are the axial and appendicular skeletons alike? How are they different?

The Skeletal System

The skeletal system interacts with other body systems to allow this soccer player to stand, run, and kick.

- ■ axial skeleton
- ■ appendicular skeleton

The **skull** protects the brain.

The lower jaw is the only bone in the skull that can move.

Twelve pairs of **ribs** protect the lungs and heart.

The shoulder blade is called the **scapula**.

The **vertebrae** of the spinal column protect the spinal cord and support the cranium and other bones.

The upper arm bone is called the **humerus**.

The lower arm bones are the **ulna** and **radius**.

The many bones in the wrist and the hand allow it to perform a great variety of activities.

The upper leg bone, called the **femur**, is the longest bone in the body.

The kneecap is called the **patella**.

The lower leg bones are called the **tibia** and the **fibula**.

There are 26 bones in the ankle and the foot.

READING VISUALS The word *appendicular* has the same root as the word *append,* which means to attach. How do you think this word applies to the appendicular skeleton?

The skeleton changes as the body develops and ages.

MAIN IDEA WEB Make a web of the important terms and details about the main idea: *The skeleton changes as the body develops and ages.*

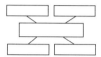

REMINDER

Density is the ratio of mass over volume. Bone density is a measure of the mass of a bone divided by the bone's volume.

You will remember that bones are living tissue. During infancy and childhood, bones grow as the rest of the body grows. Bones become harder as they stop growing. In adulthood, bones continue to change.

Infancy The skull of a newborn is made up of several bones that have spaces between them. As the brain grows, the skull also grows. During the growth of the skull, the spaces between the bones close.

Childhood Bone growth occurs at areas called growth plates. These growth plates are made of cartilage, a flexible bone tissue. The length and shape of bones is determined by growth plates. Long bones grow at the ends of the bone surrounding growth plates.

Adolescence At the end of adolescence (AD-uhl-EHS-uhns) bones stop growing. The growth plate is the last portion of the bone to become hard. Once growth plates become hard, arms and legs stop growing and the skull plates fuse.

Adulthood Even after bones stop growing, they go through cycles in which old bone is broken down and new bone is formed. As people age, more bone is broken down than is formed. This can lead to a decrease in bone mass, which causes a decrease in bone density. The strength of bones depends upon their density. As people age, their bone density may decrease. Bones that are less dense may break more easily. Many doctors recommend that adults over a certain age get regular bone density tests.

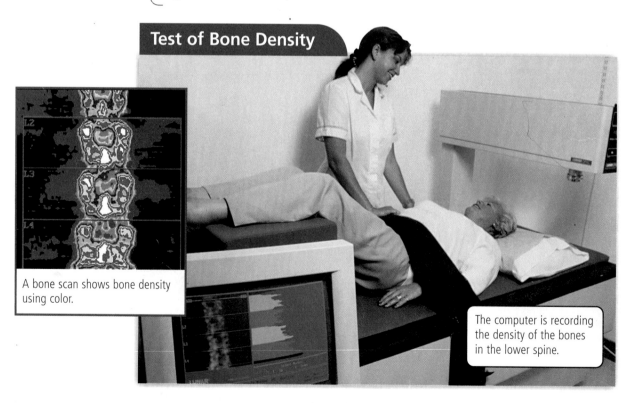

Test of Bone Density

A bone scan shows bone density using color.

The computer is recording the density of the bones in the lower spine.

Joints connect parts of the skeletal system.

A joint is a place at which two parts of the skeletal system meet. There are three types of joints: immovable, slightly movable, and freely movable.

Immovable and Slightly Movable Joints An immovable joint locks bones together like puzzle pieces. The bones of your skull are connected by immovable joints. Slightly movable joints are able to flex slightly. Your ribs are connected to your sternum by slightly movable joints.

Freely Movable Joints Freely movable joints allow your body to bend and to move. Tissues called ligaments hold the bones together at movable joints. Other structures inside the joint cushion the bones and keep them from rubbing together. The entire joint also is surrounded by connective tissue.

Movable joints can be classified by the type of movement they produce. Think about the movement of your arm when you eat an apple. Your arm moves up, then down, changing the angle between your upper and lower arms. This is angular movement. The joint that produces this movement is called a hinge joint.

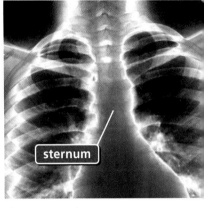

sternum

The sternum is an example of a slightly movable joint.

INVESTIGATE Movable Joints

How can you move at joints?

PROCEDURE

1. Perform several activities that involve your joints. Twist at the waist. Bend from your waist to one side. Reach into the air with one arm. Open and close your mouth. Push a book across your desk. Lift the book.

2. Record each activity and write a note describing the motion that you feel at each joint.

3. Try to see how many different ways you can move at joints.

WHAT DO YOU THINK?

- How was the motion you felt similar for each activity? How was it different?
- Based on your observations, identify two or more ways that joints move.

CHALLENGE Draw a diagram showing how you think each joint moves. How might you classify different types of joints based upon the way they move?

SKILL FOCUS
Observing

MATERIALS
book

TIME
20 minutes

Movable Joints

The joints in the elbow and hip allow different types of movement.

Angular movement (elbow)

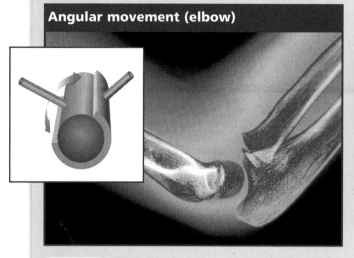

Rotational movement (hip)

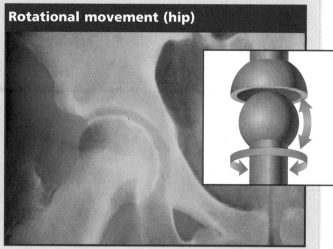

READING VISUALS **INFER** How do the structure and shape of each joint allow bones to move?

Your arm can also rotate from side to side, as it does when you turn a doorknob. Rotational movement like this is produced by a pivot joint in the elbow. You can also rotate your arm in a circle, like the motion of a softball pitcher winding up and releasing a ball. The joint in the shoulder that produces this type of rotational movement is called a ball-and-socket joint.

Joints also produce gliding movement. All joints glide, that is, one bone slides back and forth across another. In some cases, as with the joints in your backbone, a small gliding movement is the only movement the joint produces.

1.2 Review

KEY CONCEPTS

1. What are the functions of the two types of bone tissue?
2. What are the main divisions of the human skeleton?
3. Name three types of movement produced by movable joints and give an example of each.

CRITICAL THINKING

4. **Infer** What function do immovable joints in the skull perform? Think about the different stages of development in the human body.
5. **Analyze** Which type of movable joint allows the most movement? How does the joint's shape and structure contribute to this?

⬥ CHALLENGE

6. **Classify** The joints in your hand and wrist produce three different types of movement. Using your own wrist, classify the joint movement of the fingers, palm, and wrist. Support your answer.

 MATH TUTORIAL
CLASSZONE.COM

Click on Math Tutorial for more help with unit rates.

Rates of Production

Where do red blood cells come from? They are produced inside bone marrow at the center of long bones. An average of about 200 billion red blood cells per day are produced by a healthy adult. When a person produces too few red blood cells, a condition called anemia may occur. Doctors study rates of blood cell production to diagnose and treat anemia.

A rate is a ratio that compares two quantities of different units. The number of cells produced per 24 hours is an example of a rate.

Example

A healthy adult produces red blood cells at a rate greater than 166 billion cells per 24 hours. Suppose a man's body produces 8 billion red blood cells per 1 hour. Would he be considered anemic?

(1) Write the two rates as fractions.

$$\frac{8}{1} \qquad \frac{166}{24}$$

(2) Simplify the fractions, so that the denominators are both 1. To simplify, divide the numerator by the denominator.

$$\frac{8}{1} \qquad \frac{6.9}{1}$$

(3) Compare the two whole numbers.
Is the first number $<$, $>$, or $=$ to the second number?

$$8 \qquad > \qquad 6.9$$

ANSWER The rate is greater than 6.9. The patient is not anemic.

Compare the following rates to see if they indicate that a person is anemic or normal.

1. For women, a normal rate is about 178 billion red blood cells per day. A certain woman produces 6 billion red blood cells per hour. Is her rate low or healthy?

2. Suppose a different woman produces 150 million (not billion) red blood cells per minute. How does that rate compare to 178 billion cells per day? Is it $<$, $>$, or $=$ to it?

3. Suppose a certain man is producing 135 million red blood cells per minute. Is that rate low or healthy?

CHALLENGE In the example above of a man producing 166 billion cells per day, calculate the percentage by which the rate would need to increase to bring it up to the average count of 200 billion per day.

1.3 The muscular system makes movement possible.

◀ **BEFORE, you learned**

- There are different types of bone tissue
- The human skeleton has two separate divisions
- Joints function in several different ways

▶ **NOW, you will learn**

- About the functions of muscles
- About the different types of muscles and how they work
- How muscles grow and heal

VOCABULARY

muscular system p. 23
skeletal muscle p. 24
voluntary muscle p. 24
smooth muscle p. 24
involuntary muscle p. 24
cardiac muscle p. 24

EXPLORE Muscles

How do muscles change as you move?

PROCEDURE

① Sit on a chair with your feet on the floor.

② Place your hand around your leg. Straighten one leg as shown in the photograph.

③ Repeat step 2 several times.

WHAT DO YOU THINK?

- How did your muscles change during the activity?
- Record your observations.
- What questions do you have about the muscular system?

Muscles perform important functions.

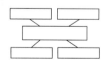

MAIN IDEA WEB
Make a web for the main idea: *Muscles perform important functions.*

Every movement of your body—from the beating of your heart, to the movement of food down your throat, to the blinking of your eyes—occurs because of muscles. Some movements are under your control, and other movements seem to happen automatically. However, muscles do more than produce movement. They perform other functions as well. Keeping body temperature stable and maintaining posture are two additional functions of muscles.

 CHECK YOUR READING What are three functions that muscles perform?

Movement

RESOURCE CENTER
CLASSZONE.COM

Discover more about muscles.

The **muscular system** works with the skeletal system to allow movement. Like all muscles, the muscles that produce movement are made up of individual cells called muscle fibers. These fibers contract and relax.

Most of the muscles involved in moving the body work in pairs. As they contract, muscles shorten, pulling against bones. It may surprise you to know that muscles do not push. Rather, a muscle on one side of a bone pulls in one direction, while another muscle relaxes. Muscles are attached to bones by stretchy connective tissue.

Maintaining Body Temperature

Earlier you read that processes within the body require certain conditions, such as temperature and the right amount of water and other materials. The balance of conditions is called homeostasis. One of the functions of the muscular system is related to homeostasis. Muscles function to maintain body temperature.

When muscles contract, they release heat. Without this heat from muscle contraction, the body could not maintain its normal temperature. You may have observed the way your muscles affect your body temperature when you shiver. The quick muscle contractions that occur when you shiver release heat and raise your body temperature.

 CHECK YOUR READING How do muscles help maintain homeostasis?

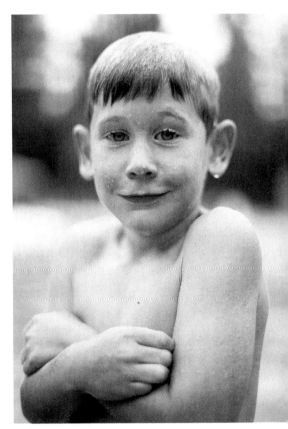

Muscles contract during shivering, raising body temperature.

Maintaining Posture

Have you ever noticed that you stand up straight without thinking about it, even though gravity is pulling your body down? Most muscles in your body are always a little bit contracted. This tension, or muscle tone, is present even when you are sleeping. The muscles that maintain posture relax completely only when you are unconscious.

Try standing on the balls of your feet for a few moments, or on one leg. When you are trying to balance or hold one position for any length of time, you can feel different muscles contracting and relaxing. Your muscles make constant adjustments to keep you sitting or standing upright. You don't have to think about these tiny adjustments; they happen automatically.

Your body has different types of muscle.

Your body has three types of muscle. All three types of muscle tissue share certain characteristics. For example, each type of muscle contracts and relaxes. Yet all three muscle types have different functions, and different types of muscle are found in different locations.

Skeletal Muscle

The muscles that are attached to your skeleton are called **skeletal muscles.** Skeletal muscle performs voluntary movement— that is, movement that you choose to make. Because they are involved in voluntary movement, skeletal muscles are also called **voluntary muscles.**

READING TiP

The root of the word *voluntary* comes from the Latin root *vol-*, meaning "wish." In the word *involuntary* the prefix *in-* suggests the meaning "unwished for." *Involuntary movement* means movement you can't control.

Skeletal muscle, like all muscle, is made of long fibers. The fibers are made up of many smaller bundles, as a piece of yarn is made up of strands of wool. One type of bundle allows your muscles to move slowly. Those muscles are called slow-twitch muscles. Another type of bundle allows your muscles to move quickly. These are called fast-twitch muscles. If you were a sprinter, you would want to develop your fast-twitch muscles. If you were a long distance runner, you would develop your slow-twitch muscles.

 CHECK YOUR READING What does it mean that skeletal muscles are voluntary muscles?

Smooth Muscle

Smooth muscle is found inside some organs, such as the intestines and the stomach. Smooth muscles perform automatic movement and are called **involuntary muscles.** In other words, smooth muscles work without your knowing it. You have no control over their movement. For example, smooth muscles line your stomach wall and push food through your digestive system. Smooth muscle fibers are not as long as skeletal muscle fibers. Also, unlike skeletal muscles, smooth muscles are not fast-twitch. Smooth muscles contract slowly.

VOCABULARY
Remember to add four squares for *involuntary muscles* and *voluntary muscles* to your notebook. Note differences in the two diagrams.

Cardiac Muscle

Your heart is made of **cardiac muscle.** Like smooth muscle, cardiac muscle moves without conscious control. Each cardiac muscle cell has a branched shape. The cells of the heart connect in a chain. These chains form webs of layered tissue that allow cardiac cells to contract together and make the heart beat. Just like the smooth muscle cells, the cardiac muscle cells contract slowly, except in emergencies.

 CHECK YOUR READING Compare and contrast the three types of muscle described: skeletal, smooth, and cardiac.

Muscle Tissue

The marchers in this band are using all three different types of muscle tissue.

250 ×

Cardiac muscle allows the hearts of the band members to pump blood as they march to the beat of the music.

150 ×

Smooth muscle in the air passages of the lungs allows the band members to breathe as they play their instruments.

360 ×

Skeletal muscle moves the legs of these marchers.

READING VISUALS Which movements of these band members are voluntary, and which are involuntary?

Skeletal muscles and tendons allow bones to move.

Skeletal muscles are attached to your bones by strong tissues called tendons. The tendons on the end of the muscle attach firmly to the bone. As the fibers in a muscle contract, they shorten and pull the tendon. The tendon, in turn, pulls the bone and makes it move.

You can feel your muscles moving your bones. Place your left arm, stretched out flat, in front of you on a table. Place the fingers of your right hand just above your left elbow. Bend your elbow and raise and lower your left arm. You are contracting your biceps. Can you feel the muscle pull on the tendon?

The dancers in the photograph are using many sets of muscles. The diagrams show how muscles and tendons work together to move bones. Muscles are shown in red. Notice how each muscle crosses a joint. Most skeletal muscles do. One end of the muscle attaches to one bone, crosses a joint, then attaches to a second bone. As the muscle contracts, it pulls on both bones. This pulling produces movement—in the case of these dancers, very exciting movement.

tendon

muscle relaxes

muscle contracts

bones

tendons

Skeletal muscles contract by shortening and pulling the tendon.

tendon

muscle contracts

muscle relaxes

bones

tendons

Muscle fibers can return to their original length after being shortened.

Muscles grow and heal.

Developing Muscles An infant's muscles cannot do very much. A baby cannot lift its head, because the neck muscles are not strong enough to support it. For the first few months of life, a baby needs extra support, until the neck muscles grow strong and can hold up the baby's head.

The rest of the skeletal muscles also have to develop and strengthen. During infancy and childhood and into adolescence, humans develop muscular coordination and become more graceful in their movements. Coordination reaches its natural peak in adolescence but can be further improved by additional training.

Exercise and Muscles When you exercise regularly, your muscles may get bigger. Muscles increase in size with some types of exercise, because their cells reproduce more rapidly in response to the increased activity. Exercise also stimulates growth of individual muscle cells, making them larger.

Stretching your muscles before exercise helps prevent injury.

You may have experienced sore muscles during or after exercising. During exercise, chemicals can build up in the muscles and make them cramp or ache. The muscle soreness you feel a day or so after exercise is caused by damage to the muscle fibers. The muscle fibers have been overstretched or torn. Such injuries take time to heal, because the body must remove injured cells, and new ones must form.

1.3 Review

KEY CONCEPTS

1. What are the three main functions of the muscular system?
2. Make a rough outline of a human body and label places where you could find each of the three types of muscles.
3. Explain why you may be sore after exercise.

CRITICAL THINKING

4. **Apply** You are exercising and you begin to feel hot. Explain what is happening in your muscles.
5. **Analyze** Describe what happens in your neck muscles when you nod your head.

⬥ CHALLENGE

6. **Infer** The digestive system breaks down food and transports materials. How are the short length and slow movement of smooth muscle tissues in the stomach and intestines related to the functions of these organs?

CHAPTER INVESTIGATION

A Closer Look at Muscles

OVERVIEW AND PURPOSE You use the muscles in your body to do a variety of things. Walking, talking, reading the words on this page, and scratching your head are all actions that require muscles. How do your muscles interact with your bones? In this investigation you will

- examine chicken wings to see how the muscles and the bones interact
- compare the movement of the chicken wing with the movement of your own bones and muscles

▶ Problem

What are some characteristics of muscles?

▶ Hypothesize

Write a hypothesis to propose how muscles interact with bones. Your hypothesis should take the form of an "If . . . , then . . . , because . . ." statement.

▶ Procedure

MATERIALS
- uncooked chicken wing and leg (soaked in bleach)
- paper towels
- dissection tray
- scissors

1. Make a data table like the one shown on the sample notebook page. Put on your protective gloves. Be sure you are wearing gloves whenever you touch the chicken.

2. Obtain a chicken wing from your teacher. Rinse it in water and pat dry with a paper towel. Place it in the tray.

3. Extend the wing. In your notebook, draw a diagram of the extended wing. Be sure to include any visible external structures. Label the following on your diagram: lower limb, upper joint, and the wing tip.

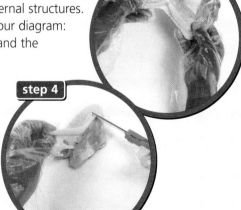

step 3

step 4

4. Use scissors to remove the skin. Use caution so that you cut only through the skin. Peel back the skin and any fat so you can examine the muscles.

5. The muscles are the pink tissues that extend from one end of the bone to the other. Locate these in the upper wing and observe the way they move when you move the wing. Record your observations in your notebook.

6. Repeat this procedure for the muscles in the lower wing. In your notebook, draw a diagram of the muscles in the chicken wing.

7. There are also tendons in the chicken wing. These are the shiny white tissues at the end of the muscles. Add the tendons to your diagram.

8. Dispose of the chicken wing and parts according to your teacher's instructions. **Be sure to wash your hands well.**

▶ Observe and Analyze
Write It Up

1. **RECORD** Write a brief description of how the bones and muscles work together to allow movement.

2. **EVALUATE** What difficulties, if any, did you encounter in carrying out this experiment?

▶ Conclude
Write It Up

1. **INTERPRET** How does the chicken wing move when you bend it at the joint?

2. **OBSERVE** What happens when you pull on one of the wing muscles?

3. **COMPARE** Using your diagram of the chicken wing as an example, locate the same muscle groups in your own arm. How do they react when you bend your elbow?

4. **APPLY** What role do the tendons play in the movement of the muscles or bones?

▶ INVESTIGATE Further

CHALLENGE Using scissors, carefully remove the muscles and the tendons from the bones. Next find the ligaments, which are located between the bones. Add these to your diagram. Describe how you think ligaments function.

A Closer Look at Muscles
Problem What are some characteristics of muscles?

Table 1. Observations

Draw your diagrams	Write your observations
Extended wing	Muscles in the upper wing
	Muscles in the lower wing
Muscles in the wing	

Chapter Review

the BIG idea

The human body is made up of systems that work together to perform necessary functions.

CONTENT REVIEW
CLASSZONE.COM

◀ KEY CONCEPTS SUMMARY

1.1 The human body is complex.

You can think of the body as having five levels of organization: cells, tissues, organs, organ systems, and the whole organism itself. The different systems of the human body work together to maintain homeostasis.

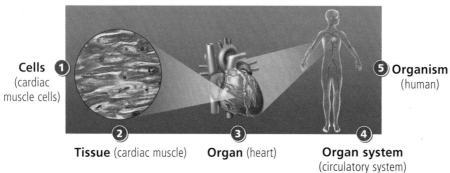

Cells ① (cardiac muscle cells)

⑤ Organism (human)

② Tissue (cardiac muscle)   **③ Organ** (heart)   **④ Organ system** (circulatory system)

VOCABULARY
tissue p. 10
organ p. 11
organ system p. 12
homeostasis p. 12

1.2 The skeletal system provides support and protection.

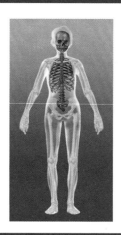

Bones are living tissue. The skeleton is the body's framework and has two main divisions, the **axial skeleton** and the **appendicular skeleton**. Bones come together at joints.

VOCABULARY
skeletal system p. 14
compact bone p. 15
spongy bone p. 15
axial skeleton p. 16
appendicular skeleton
  p. 16

1.3 The muscular system makes movement possible.

Types of muscle	Function
skeletal muscle, voluntary	moves bones, maintains posture, maintains body temperature
smooth muscle, involuntary	moves internal organs, such as the intestines
cardiac muscle, involuntary	pumps blood throughout the body

VOCABULARY
muscular system p. 23
skeletal muscle p. 24
voluntary muscle 24
smooth muscle p. 24
involuntary muscle
  p. 24
cardiac muscle p. 24

Reviewing Vocabulary

In one or two sentences describe how the vocabulary terms in each of the following pairs of words are related. Underline each vocabulary term in your answer.

1. cells, tissues

2. organs, organ systems

3. axial skeleton, appendicular skeleton

4. skeletal muscle, voluntary muscle

5. smooth muscle, involuntary muscle

6. compact bone, spongy bone

Reviewing Key Concepts

Multiple Choice *Choose the letter of the best answer.*

7. Which type of tissue carries electrical impulses from your brain?
   a. epithelial tissue
   b. muscle tissue
   c. nerve tissue
   d connective tissue

8. Connective tissue functions to provide
   a. support and strength
   b. messaging system
   c. movement
   d. heart muscle

9. Bone cells lie within a network made of
   a. tendons
   b. calcium
   c. marrow
   d. joints

10. The marrow produces
    a. spongy bone
    b. red blood cells
    c. compact bone
    d. calcium

11. Which bones are part of the axial skeleton?
    a. skull, shoulder blades, arm bones
    b. skull, spinal column, leg bones
    c. shoulder blades, spinal column, and hip bones
    d. skull, spinal column, ribs

12. Bones of the skeleton connect to each other at
    a. tendons
    b. ligaments
    c. joints
    d. muscles

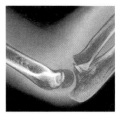

13. How do muscles contribute to homeostasis?
    a. They keep parts of the body together.
    b. They control the amount of water in the body.
    c. They help you move.
    d. They produce heat when they contract.

14. Cardiac muscle is found in the
    a. heart
    b. stomach
    c. intestines
    d. arms and legs

15. The stomach is made up of
    a. cardiac muscle
    b. skeletal muscle
    c. smooth muscle
    d. voluntary muscle

Short Answer *Write a short answer to each question.*

16. What is the difference between spongy bone and compact bone?

17. The root word *homeo* means "same," and the root word *stasis* means "to stay." How do these root words relate to the definition of *homeostasis*?

18. Hold the upper part of one arm between your elbow and shoulder with your opposite hand. Feel the muscles there. What happens to those muscles as you bend your arm?

Thinking Critically

19. **PROVIDE EXAMPLES** What are the levels of organization of the human body from simple to most complex? Give an example of each.

20. **CLASSIFY** There are four types of tissue in the human body: epithelial, nerve, muscles, and connective. How would you classify blood? Explain your reasoning.

21. **CONNECT** A clam shell is made of a calcium compound. The material is hard, providing protection to the soft body of a clam. It is also lightweight. Describe three ways in which the human skeleton is similar to a seashell. What is one important way in which it is different?

Use the diagram below to answer the next two questions

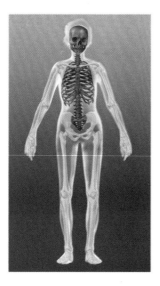

22. **SYNTHESIZE** Identify the type of joints that hold together the bones of the skull and sternum. How does this type of joint relate to the function of the skull and sternum?

23. **SYNTHESIZE** The human skeleton has two main divisions. Which skeleton do the arms and legs belong to? How do the joints that connect the arms to the shoulders and the legs to the hips relate to the function of this skeleton?

24. **COMPARE AND CONTRAST** How is the skeletal system of your body like the framework of a house or building? How is it different?

25. **SUMMARIZE** Describe three important functions of the skeleton.

26. **APPLY** The joints in the human body can be described as producing three types of movement. Relate these three types of movement to the action of brushing your teeth.

27. **COMPARE AND CONTRAST** When you stand, the muscles in your legs help to keep you balanced. Some of the muscles on both sides of your leg bones contract. How does this differ from how the muscles behave when you start to walk?

28. **INFER** Muscles are tissues that are made up of many muscle fibers. A muscle fiber can either be relaxed or contracted. Some movements you do require very little effort, like picking up a piece of paper. Others require a lot of effort, like picking up a book bag. How do you think a muscle produces the effort needed for a small task compared with a big task?

the **BIG** idea

29. **INFER** Look again at the picture on pages 6–7. Now that you have finished the chapter, how would you change or add details to your answer to the question on the photograph?

30. **SUMMARIZE** Write a paragraph explaining how skeletal muscles, bones, and joints work together to allow the body to move and be flexible. Underline the terms in your paragraph.

UNIT PROJECTS

If you are doing a unit project, make a folder for your project. Include in your folder a list of resources you will need, the date on which the project is due, and a schedule to track your progress. Begin gathering data.

Interpreting Diagrams

The action of a muscle pulling on a bone can be compared to a simple machine called a lever. A lever is a rod that moves about a fixed point called the fulcrum. Effort at one end of the rod can move a load at the other end. In the human body, a muscle supplies the effort needed to move a bone—the lever. The joint is the fulcrum, and the load is the weight of the body part being moved. There are three types of levers, which are classified according to the position of the fulcrum, the effort, and the load.

Read the text and study the diagrams, and then choose the best answer for the questions that follow.

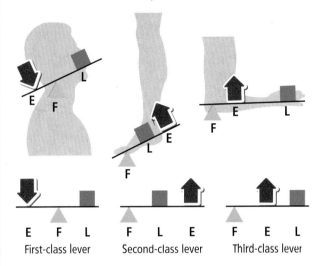

E F L	F L E	F E L
First-class lever	Second-class lever	Third-class lever

1. In a first-class lever

  a. the load is at end of the lever opposite the fulcrum

  b. the load is between the effort and the fulcrum

  c. the fulcrum is between the load and the effort

  d. the effort and load are on the same side

2. What is true of all levers?

  a. The fulcrum must be located at the center of a lever.

  b. The force of the load and effort point in the same direction.

  c. The load and effort are on the same side of the fulcrum.

  d. The fulcrum exerts a force in a direction opposite the weight of the load.

3. The fulcrum represents what structure in the human body?

  a. a joint   **c.** a muscle

  b. a bone   **d.** a part of the body

4. The main point of the diagram is to show

  a. how bones work

  b. that there are three types of levers and how they are classified

  c. where to apply a force

  d. the forces involved in moving parts of the body

Extended Response

Use the diagrams above and terms from the word box to answer the next question. Underline each term you use in your answer.

fulcrum	load	effort	rod
bone	muscle	joint	

5. Suppose you had a heavy box to lift. Your first thought might be to bend over, stretch out your arms, and grab the box. Your body would be acting as a simple machine. Identify the type of lever this is and the parts of this machine.

6. A doctor would advise you not to lift a heavy object, like a box, simply by bending over and picking it up. That action puts too much strain on your back. It is better to bend your knees, hold the box close to your body, and then lift. How does this way of lifting change how you are using your body?

CHAPTER

2 Absorption, Digestion, and Exchange

the **BIG** idea

Systems in the body obtain and process materials and remove waste.

Key Concepts

SECTION

2.1 The respiratory system gets oxygen and removes carbon dioxide.
Learn how the respiratory system functions.

SECTION

2.2 The digestive system breaks down food.
Learn how the digestive system provides cells with necessary materials.

SECTION

2.3 The urinary system removes waste materials.
Learn how the urinary system removes wastes.

 Internet Preview

CLASSZONE.COM
Chapter 2 online resources: Content Review, two Visualizations, two Resource Centers, Math Tutorial, Test Practice.

What materials does your body need to function properly?

EXPLORE (the BIG idea)

Mirror, Mirror

Hold a small hand mirror in front of your mouth. Slowly exhale onto the surface of the mirror. What do you see? Exhale a few more times onto the mirror, observing the interaction of your breath with the cool surface of the mirror.

Observe and Think What did you see on the surface of the mirror? What does this tell you about the content of the air that you exhale?

Water Everywhere

Keep track of how much liquid you drink in a 24-hour period of time. Do not include carbonated or caffeinated beverages. Water, juice, and milk can count. Add up the number of ounces of liquid you drink in that period of time.

Observe and Think How many ounces did you drink in one day? Do you drink fluids only when you feel thirsty?

Internet Activity: Lung Movement

Go to **ClassZone.com** to watch a visualization of lung and diaphragm movement during respiration. Observe how movements of the diaphragm and other muscles affect the lungs.

Observe and Think How do the diaphragm and lungs move during inhalation? during exhalation? Why do movements of the diaphragm cause the lungs to move?

Digestion **Code: MDL045**

Getting Ready to Learn

◀ CONCEPT REVIEW

- Cells make up tissues, and tissues make up organs.
- The body's systems interact.
- The body's systems work to maintain internal conditions.

◀ VOCABULARY REVIEW

homeostasis p. 12

smooth muscle p. 24

energy *See Glossary.*

CONTENT REVIEW
CLASSZONE.COM
Review concepts and vocabulary.

▶ TAKING NOTES

OUTLINE

As you read, copy the blue headings on your paper in the form of an outline. Then add notes in your own words that summarize what you read.

VOCABULARY STRATEGY

Think about a vocabulary term as a **magnet word** diagram. Write the other terms or ideas related to that term around it.

See the Note-Taking Handbook on pages R45–R51.

SCIENCE NOTEBOOK

THE RESPIRATORY SYSTEM GETS OXYGEN AND REMOVES CARBON DIOXIDE.

    A. Your body needs oxygen.

        1. Oxygen is used to release energy

        2. Oxygen is in air you breathe

    B. Structures in the respiratory system function together

        1. nose, throat, trachea

        2. lungs

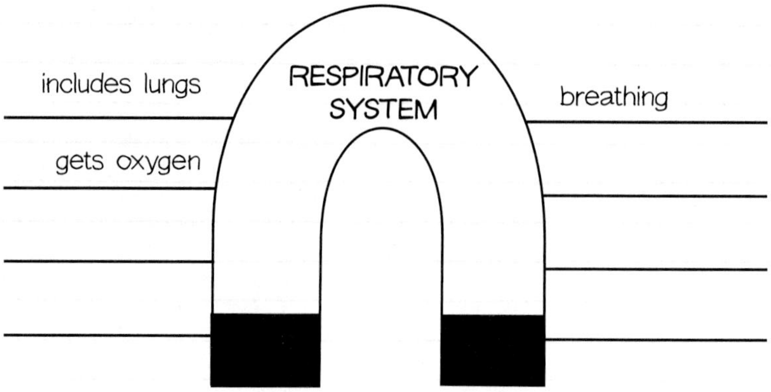

includes lungs   **RESPIRATORY SYSTEM**   breathing

gets oxygen

2.1

The respiratory system gets oxygen and removes carbon dioxide.

BEFORE, you learned

- Cells, tissues, organs, and organ systems work together
- Organ systems provide for the body's needs
- Organ systems are important to the body's survival

NOW, you will learn

- About the structures of the respiratory system that function to exchange gases
- About the process of cellular respiration
- About other functions of the respiratory system

VOCABULARY

respiratory system p. 37
cellular respiration p. 39

EXPLORE Breathing

How do your ribs move when you breathe?

PROCEDURE

1. Place your hands on your ribs.
2. Breathe in and out several times, focusing on what happens when you inhale and exhale.
3. Record your observations in your notebook.

WHAT DO YOU THINK?

- What movement did you observe?
- Think about your observations. What questions do you have as a result of your observations?

Your body needs oxygen.

VOCABULARY
Make a word magnet diagram for the term *respiratory system.*

During the day, you eat and drink only a few times, but you breathe thousands of times. In fact, breathing is a sign of life. The body is able to store food and liquid, but it is unable to store very much oxygen. The **respiratory system** is the body system that functions to get oxygen from the environment and remove carbon dioxide and other waste products from your body. The respiratory system interacts with the environment and with other body systems.

The continuous process of moving and using oxygen involves mechanical movement and chemical reactions. Air is transported into your lungs by mechanical movements, and oxygen is used during chemical reactions that release energy in your cells.

 What are the two main functions of your respiratory system?

Exchanging Oxygen and Carbon Dioxide

Like almost all living things, the human body needs oxygen to survive. Without oxygen, cells in the body die quickly. How does the oxygen you need get to your cells? Oxygen, along with other gases, enters the body when you inhale. Oxygen is then transported to cells throughout the body.

The air that you breathe contains only about 20 percent oxygen and less than 1 percent carbon dioxide. Almost 80 percent of air is nitrogen gas. The air that you exhale contains more carbon dioxide and less oxygen than the air that you inhale. It's important that you exhale carbon dioxide because high levels of it will damage, even destroy, cells.

In cells and tissues, proper levels of both oxygen and carbon dioxide are essential. Recall that systems in the body work together to maintain homeostasis. If levels of oxygen or carbon dioxide change, your brain or blood vessels signal the body to breathe faster or slower.

The photograph shows how someone underwater maintains proper levels of carbon dioxide and oxygen. The scuba diver needs to inhale oxygen from a tank. She removes carbon dioxide wastes with other gases when she exhales into the water. The bubbles you see in the water are formed when she exhales.

 CHECK YOUR READING What gases are in the air that you breathe?

Gas Exchange

This scuba diver breathes the same mixture of gases present in air.

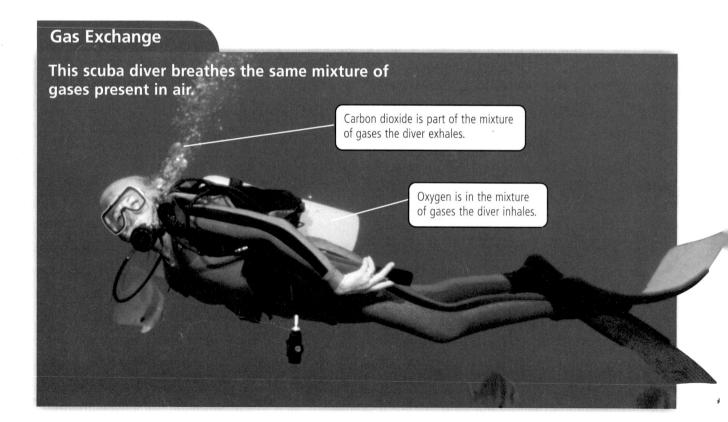

Carbon dioxide is part of the mixture of gases the diver exhales.

Oxygen is in the mixture of gases the diver inhales.

INVESTIGATE Lungs

How does air move in and out of lungs?

PROCEDURE

① Create a model of your lungs as shown. Insert an uninflated balloon into the top of the plastic bottle. While squeezing the bottle to force out some air, stretch the end of the balloon over the lip of the bottle. The balloon should still be open to the outside air. Tape the balloon in place with duct tape to make a tight seal

② Release the bottle so that it expands back to its normal shape. Observe what happens to the balloon. Squeeze and release the bottle several times while observing the balloon. Record your observations.

WHAT DO YOU THINK?

- Describe, in words, what happens when you squeeze and release the bottle.

- How do you think your lungs move when you inhale? when you exhale?

CHALLENGE Design an addition to your model that could represent a muscle called the diaphragm. What materials do you need? How would this work? Your teacher may be able to provide additional materials so you can test your model. Be sure to come up with a comprehensive list of materials as well as a specific diagram.

MATERIALS
- one medium balloon
- 1-L clear plastic bottle with labels removed
- duct tape

TIME
15 minutes

Cellular Respiration

Inside your cells, a process called **cellular respiration** uses oxygen in chemical reactions that release energy. The respiratory system works with the digestive and circulatory systems to make cellular respiration possible. Cellular respiration requires glucose, or sugars, which you get from food, in addition to oxygen, which you get from breathing. These materials are transported to every cell in your body through blood vessels. You will learn more about the digestive and circulatory systems later in this unit.

During cellular respiration, your cells use oxygen and glucose to release energy. Carbon dioxide is a waste product of the process. Carbon dioxide must be removed from cells.

VOCABULARY
Add a magnet diagram for *cellular respiration* to your notebook. Include the word *energy* in your diagram.

 CHECK YOUR READING What three body systems are involved in cellular respiration?

Structures in the respiratory system function together.

OUTLINE

Add *Structures in the respiratory system function together* to your outline. Be sure to include the six respiratory structures in your outline.

I. Main idea
   A. Supporting idea
      1. Detail
      2. Detail
   B. Supporting idea

The respiratory system is made up of many structures that allow you to move air in and out of your body, communicate, and keep out harmful materials.

Nose, Throat, and Trachea When you inhale, air enters your body through your nose or mouth. Inside your nose, tiny hairs called cilia filter dirt and other particles out of the air. Mucus, a sticky liquid in your nasal cavity, also helps filter air by trapping particles such as dirt and pollen as air passes by. The nasal cavity warms the air slightly before it moves down your throat toward a tubelike structure called the windpipe, or trachea (TRAY-kee-uh). A structure called the epiglottis (EHP-ih-GLAHT-ihs) keeps air from entering your stomach.

Lungs The lungs are two large organs located on either side of your heart. When you breathe, air enters the throat, passes through the trachea, and moves to the lungs through structures called bronchial tubes. Bronchial tubes branch throughout the lungs into smaller and smaller tubes. At the ends of the smallest tubes air enters tiny air sacs called alveoli. The walls of the alveoli are only one cell thick. In fact, one page in this book is much thicker than the walls of the alveoli. Oxygen passes from inside the alveoli through the thin walls and is dissolved into the blood. At the same time, carbon dioxide waste passes from the blood into the alveoli.

 Through which structures does oxygen move into the lungs?

Ribs and Diaphragm If you put your hands on your ribs and take a deep breath, you can feel your ribs expand. The rib cage encloses a space inside your body called the thoracic (thuh-RAS-ihk) cavity. Some ribs are connected by cartilage to the breastbone or to each other, which makes the rib cage flexible. This flexibility allows the rib cage to expand when you breathe and make room for the lungs to expand and fill with air.

A large muscle called the diaphragm (DY-uh-FRAM) stretches across the floor of the thoracic cavity. When you inhale, your diaphragm contracts and pulls downward, which makes the thoracic cavity expand. This movement causes the lungs to push downward, filling the extra space. At the same time, other muscles draw the ribs outward and expand the lungs. Air rushes into the lungs, and inhalation is complete. When the diaphragm and other muscles relax, the process reverses and you exhale.

 Describe how the diaphragm and the rib cage move.

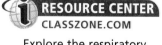

RESOURCE CENTER
CLASSZONE.COM

Explore the respiratory system.

Respiratory System

The structures in the respiratory system allow this flutist to play music.

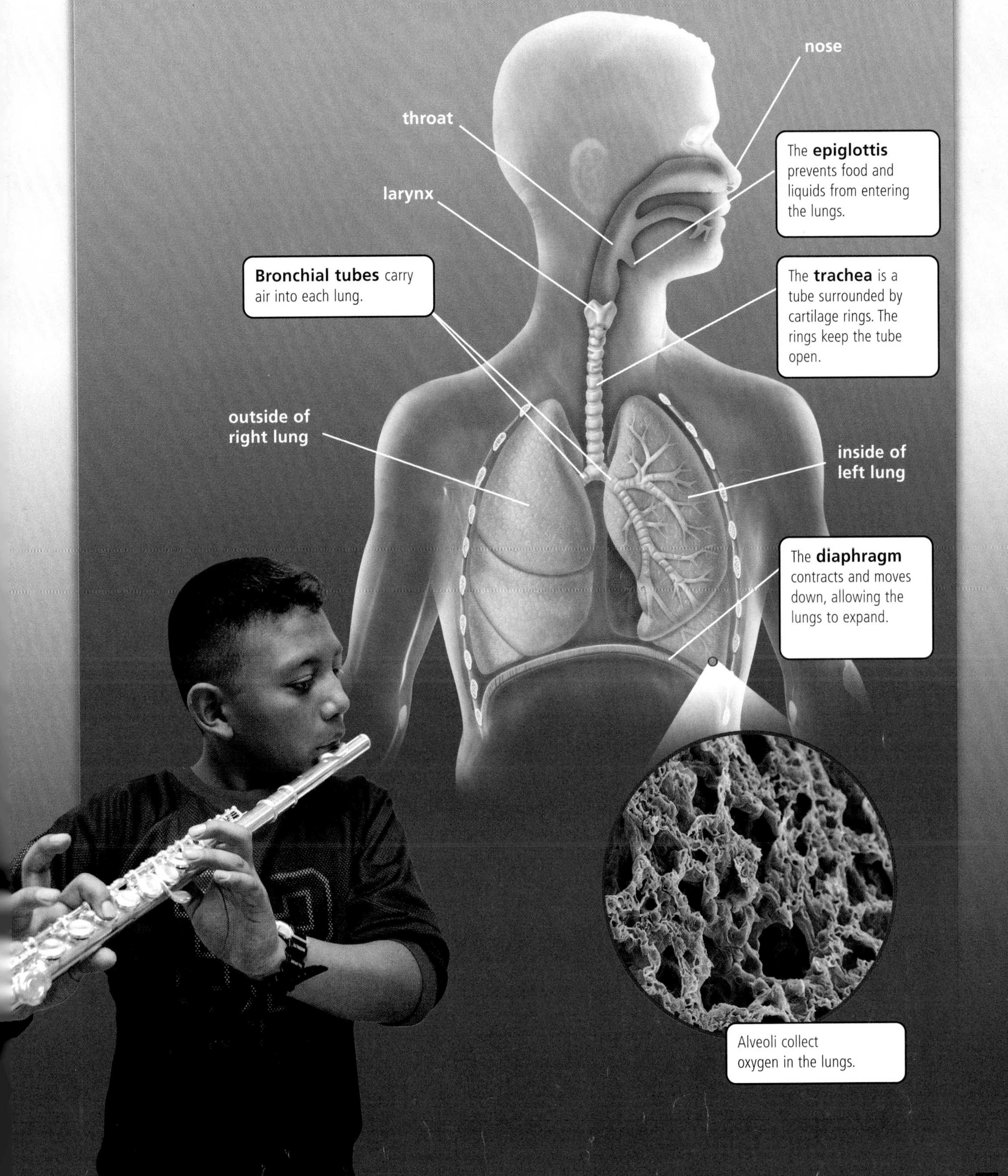

nose

throat

larynx

The **epiglottis** prevents food and liquids from entering the lungs.

Bronchial tubes carry air into each lung.

The **trachea** is a tube surrounded by cartilage rings. The rings keep the tube open.

outside of right lung

inside of left lung

The **diaphragm** contracts and moves down, allowing the lungs to expand.

Alveoli collect oxygen in the lungs.

The respiratory system is also involved in other activities.

In addition to providing oxygen and removing carbon dioxide, the respiratory system is involved in other activities of the body. Speaking and singing, along with actions such as sneezing, can be explained in terms of how the parts of the respiratory system work together.

Speech and Other Respiratory Movements

If you place your hand on your throat and hum softly, you can feel your vocal cords vibrating. Air moving over your vocal cords allows you to produce sound, and the muscles in your throat, mouth, cheeks, and lips allow you to form sound into words. The vocal cords are folds of tissue in the larynx. The larynx, sometimes called the voice box, is a two-inch, tube-shaped organ about the length of your thumb, located in the neck, at the top of the trachea. When you speak, the vocal cords become tight, squeeze together, and force air from the lungs to move between them. The air causes the vocal cords to vibrate and produce sound.

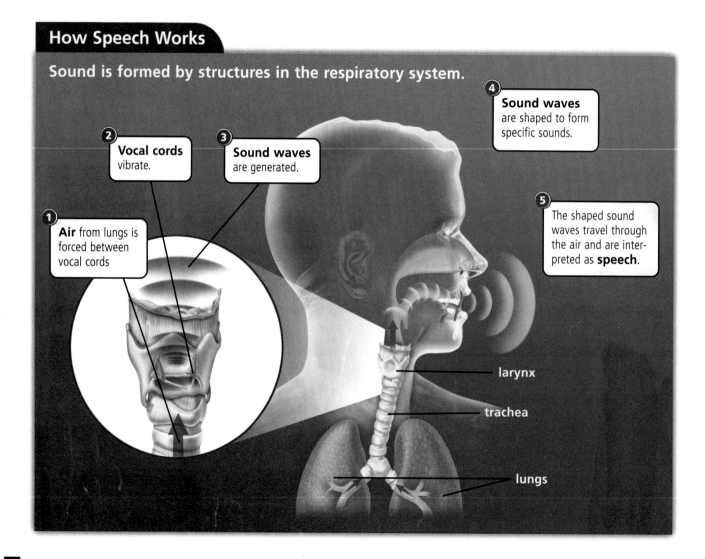

How Speech Works

Sound is formed by structures in the respiratory system.

1. **Air** from lungs is forced between vocal cords

2. **Vocal cords** vibrate.

3. **Sound waves** are generated.

4. **Sound waves** are shaped to form specific sounds.

5. The shaped sound waves travel through the air and are interpreted as **speech**.

larynx

trachea

lungs

Some movements of the respiratory system allow you to clear particles out of your nose and throat or to express emotion. The respiratory system is involved when you cough or sneeze. Sighing, yawning, laughing, and crying also involve the respiratory system.

Sighing and yawning both involve taking deep breaths. A sigh is a long breath followed by a shorter exhalation. A yawn is a long breath taken through a wide-open mouth. Laughing and crying are movements that are very similar to each other. In fact, sometimes it's difficult to see the difference between laughing and crying.

The respiratory system also allows you to hiccup. A hiccup is a sudden inhalation that makes the diaphragm contract. Several systems are involved when you hiccup. Air rushes into the throat, causing the diaphragm to contract. When the diaphragm contracts, the air passageway between the vocal cords closes. The closing of this passageway produces the sound of the hiccup. Hiccups can be caused by eating too fast, sudden temperature changes, and stress.

Water Removal

Hiccups, coughs, yawns, and all other respiratory movements, including speaking and breathing, release water from your body into the environment. Water is lost through sweat, urine, and exhalations of air. When it is cold enough outside, you can see your breath in the air. That is because the water vapor you exhale condenses into larger droplets when it moves from your warm body to the cold air.

Water leaves your body through your breath every time you exhale.

2.1 Review

KEY CONCEPTS

1. How is oxygen used by your body's cells?
2. What are the structures in the respiratory system and what do they do?
3. In addition to breathing, what functions does the respiratory system perform?

CRITICAL THINKING

4. **Sequence** List in order the steps that occur when you exhale.
5. **Compare and Contrast** How is the air you inhale different from the air you exhale?

⬥ CHALLENGE

6. **Hypothesize** Why do you think a person breathes more quickly when exercising?

Breathing and Yoga

If you're reading this, you must be breathing. Are you thinking about how you are breathing? Yoga instructors help their students learn deep, slow breathing. The practice of yoga uses an understanding of the respiratory system as a tool for healthy exercise.

nostrils

Abdominal Breathing

Yoga instructors tell students to slowly expand and release the diaphragm:
• The diaphragm is a muscle below the lungs.
• When the muscle contracts, air enters into the lungs.
• When it relaxes, air is pushed out of the lungs.

Nostril Breathing

An important aspect of breathing is removing wastes from the body:
• Yoga instructors teach students to inhale through the nostrils and exhale through the mouth.
• The nostrils filter dust and other particles, keeping dirt out of the lungs.
• The nostrils also warm the air as it enters the body.

lungs

diaphragm muscle

Full Lung Breathing

Yoga instructors help students breathe in slowly so that first the abdomen expands, then the rib cage area, and finally the upper chest by the shoulders. When students exhale, they collapse the diaphragm, then release the chest, and lastly relax the shoulders.

EXPLORE

1. **APPLY** Try one of the three breathing methods described. Start by taking a few slow deep breaths; then try the yoga breathing. Count to 4 as you inhale, and to 4 again breathing out. How do you feel after each breath?

2. **CHALLENGE** Choose one of the breathing methods above. Describe what happens to air each time you inhale and exhale. Draw or write your answer.

2.2 The digestive system breaks down food.

◀ **BEFORE, you learned**

- The respiratory system takes in oxygen and expels waste
- Oxygen is necessary for cellular respiration
- The respiratory system is involved in speech and water removal

▶ **NOW, you will learn**

- About the role of digestion in providing energy and materials
- About the chemical and mechanical process of digestion
- How materials change as they move through the digestive system

VOCABULARY

nutrient p. 45
digestion p. 46
digestive system p. 46
peristalsis p. 46

EXPLORE Digestion

How does the digestive system break down fat?

PROCEDURE

① Using a dropper, place 5 mL of water into a test tube. Add 5 mL of vegetable oil. Seal the test tube with a screw-on top. Shake the test tube for 10 seconds, then place it in a test tube stand. Record your observations.

② Drop 5 mL of dish detergent into the test tube. Seal the tube. Shake the test tube for 10 seconds, then place in the stand. Observe the mixture for 2 minutes. Record your observations.

WHAT DO YOU THINK?

- What effect does detergent have on the mixture of oil and water?
- How do you think your digestive system might break down fat?

MATERIALS

- water
- graduated cylinders
- test tube with cap
- vegetable oil
- test tube stand
- liquid dish detergent

OUTLINE

Remember to add *The body needs energy and materials* to your outline.

I. Main idea
  A. Supporting idea
    1. Detail
    2. Detail
  B. Supporting idea

The body needs energy and materials.

After not eating for a while, have you ever noticed how little energy you have to do the simplest things? You need food to provide energy for your body. You also need materials from food. Most of what you need comes from nutrients within food. **Nutrients** are important substances that enable the body to move, grow, and maintain homeostasis. Proteins, carbohydrates, fats, and water are some of the nutrients your body needs.

You might not think of water as a nutrient, but it is necessary for all living things. More than half of your body is made up of water.

Protein is another essential nutrient; it is the material that the body uses for growth and repair. Cells in your body—such as those composing muscles, bones, and skin—are built of proteins. Carbohydrates are nutrients that provide cells with energy. Carbohydrates make up cellulose, which helps move materials through the digestive system. Another nutrient, fat, stores energy.

Before your body can use these nutrients, they must be broken into smaller substances. **Digestion** is the process of breaking down food into usable materials. Your digestive system transforms the energy and materials in food into forms your body can use.

The digestive system moves and breaks down food.

VISUALIZATION
CLASSZONE.COM

Observe the process of peristalsis.

Your **digestive system** performs the complex jobs of moving and breaking down food. Material is moved through the digestive system by wavelike contractions of smooth muscles. This muscular action is called **peristalsis** (PEHR-ih-STAWL-sihs). Mucous glands throughout the system keep the material moist so it can be moved easily, and the muscles contract to push the material along. The muscles move food along in much the same way as you move toothpaste from the bottom of the tube with your thumbs. The body has complicated ways of moving food, and it also has complicated ways of breaking down food. The digestive system processes food in two ways: physically and chemically.

Peristalsis

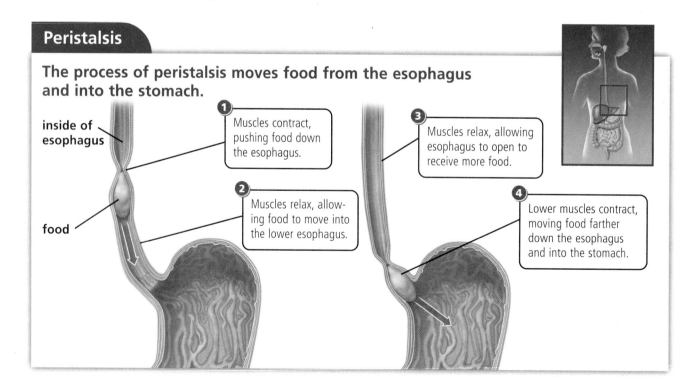

The process of peristalsis moves food from the esophagus and into the stomach.

inside of esophagus

food

1 Muscles contract, pushing food down the esophagus.

2 Muscles relax, allowing food to move into the lower esophagus.

3 Muscles relax, allowing esophagus to open to receive more food.

4 Lower muscles contract, moving food farther down the esophagus and into the stomach.

INVESTIGATE Chemical Digestion

How does saliva affect starch?

SKILL FOCUS
Making Models

PROCEDURE

1. Cut two slices of the same thickness from the center of a potato. Lay the slices on a plate or tray.

2. Using a dropper, add 15 drops of solution A to one potato slice. Add 15 drops of water to the other potato slice. Observe both potato slices for several minutes. Record your observations.

WHAT DO YOU THINK?

- What evidence did you see that starch is being broken down?
- How would you identify the substance left by the breakdown of starch?
- What is the purpose of the water in this activity?

CHALLENGE How could you change your experiment to model mechanical digestion? What structures in your mouth mechanically break down food?

MATERIALS
- cooked potato slices
- droppers
- solution A
- water

TIME
25 minutes

Mechanical Digestion

Physical changes, which are sometimes called mechanical changes, break food into smaller pieces. You chew your food with your teeth so you are able to swallow it. Infants without teeth need an adult to cut up or mash food for them. They need soft food that they can swallow without chewing. Your stomach also breaks down food mechanically by mashing and pounding it during peristalsis.

Chemical Digestion

Chemical changes actually change food into different substances. For example, chewing a cracker produces a physical change—the cracker is broken into small pieces. At the same time, liquid in the mouth called saliva produces a chemical change—starches in the cracker are changed to sugars. If you chew a cracker, you may notice that after you have chewed it for a few seconds, it begins to taste sweet. The change in taste is a sign of a chemical reaction.

VOCABULARY
Don't forget to add magnet word diagrams for *digestion, digestive system,* and *peristalsis* to your notebook.

 CHECK YOUR READING What are the two types of changes that take place during digestion?

Materials are broken down as they move through the digestive tract.

The digestive system contains several organs. Food travels through organs in the digestive tract: the mouth, esophagus, stomach, small intestine, and large intestine. Other organs, such as the pancreas, liver, and gall bladder, release chemicals that are necessary for chemical digestion. The diagram on page 49 shows the major parts of the entire digestive system.

Mouth and Esophagus Both mechanical and chemical digestion begin in the mouth. The teeth break food into small pieces. The lips and tongue position food so that you can chew. When food is in your mouth, salivary glands in your mouth release saliva, which softens the food and begins chemical reactions. The tongue pushes the food to the back of the mouth and down the throat while swallowing.

As you read about the digestive tract, look at the structures on page 49.

CHECK YOUR READING What part does the mouth play in digestion?

When you swallow, your tongue pushes food down into your throat. Food then travels down the esophagus to the stomach. The muscle contractions of peristalsis move solid food from the throat to the stomach in about eight seconds. Liquid foods take about two seconds.

Stomach Strong muscles in the stomach further mix and mash food particles. The stomach also uses chemicals to break down food. Some of the chemicals made by the stomach are acids. These acids are so strong that they could eat through the stomach itself. To prevent this, the stomach's lining is replaced about every three days.

Small Intestine Partially digested food moves from the stomach to the small intestine. There, chemicals released by the pancreas, liver, and gallbladder break down nutrients. Most of the nutrients broken down in digestion are absorbed in the small intestine. Structures called villi are found throughout the small intestine. These structures contain folds that absorb nutrients from proteins, carbohydrates, and fats. Once absorbed by the villi, nutrients are transported by the circulatory system around the body. You will read more about the circulatory system in Chapter 3.

Large Intestine In the large intestine, water and some other nutrients are absorbed from the digested material. Most of the solid material then remaining is waste material, which is compacted and stored. Eventually it is eliminated through the rectum.

Villi allow broken-down nutrients to be absorbed into your bloodstream.

CHECK YOUR READING Where in your digestive system does mechanical digestion occur?

As food moves through the digestive tract, structures of the digestive system break it down and absorb necessary materials.

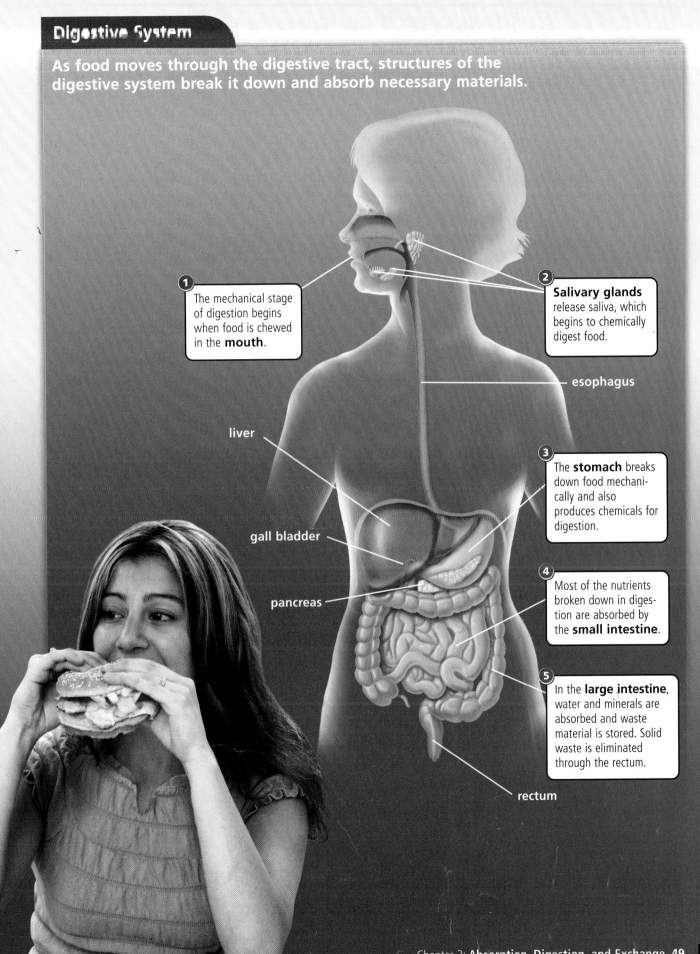

1 The mechanical stage of digestion begins when food is chewed in the **mouth**.

2 **Salivary glands** release saliva, which begins to chemically digest food.

esophagus

liver

3 The **stomach** breaks down food mechanically and also produces chemicals for digestion.

gall bladder

pancreas

4 Most of the nutrients broken down in digestion are absorbed by the **small intestine**.

5 In the **large intestine**, water and minerals are absorbed and waste material is stored. Solid waste is eliminated through the rectum.

rectum

Other organs aid digestion and absorption.

The digestive organs not in the digestive tract—the liver, gallbladder, and pancreas—also play crucial roles in your body. Although food does not move through them, all three of these organs aid in chemical digestion by producing or concentrating important chemicals.

Liver The liver—the largest internal organ of the body—is located in your abdomen, just above your stomach. Although you can survive losing a portion of your liver, it is an important organ. The liver filters blood, cleansing it of harmful substances, and stores unneeded nutrients for later use in the body. It produces a golden yellow substance called bile, which is able to break down fats, much like the way soap breaks down oils. The liver also breaks down medicines and produces important proteins, such as those that help clot blood if you get a cut.

Gallbladder The gallbladder is a tiny pear-shaped sac connected to the liver. Bile produced in the liver is stored and concentrated in the gallbladder. The bile is then secreted into the small intestine.

Pancreas Located between the stomach and the small intestine, the pancreas produces chemicals that are needed as materials move between the two. The pancreas quickly lowers the acidity in the small intestine and breaks down proteins, fats, and starch. The chemicals produced by the pancreas are extremely important for digesting and absorbing food substances. Without these chemicals, you could die of starvation, even with plenty of food in your system. Your body would not be able to process and use the food for energy without the pancreas.

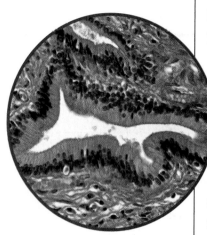

Bile is transferred from the liver to the gallbladder and small intestines through the bile duct.

 CHECK YOUR READING How does the pancreas aid in digestion?

2.2 Review

KEY CONCEPTS

1. List three of the functions of the digestive system.
2. Give one example each of mechanical digestion and chemical digestion.
3. How does your stomach process food?

CRITICAL THINKING

4. **Apply** Does an antacid deal with mechanical or chemical digestion?
5. **Apply** You have just swallowed a bite of apple. Describe what happens as the apple moves through your digestive system. Include information about what happens to the material in the apple.

CHALLENGE

6. **Compare and Contrast** Describe the roles of the large and the small intestines. How are they similar? How are they different?

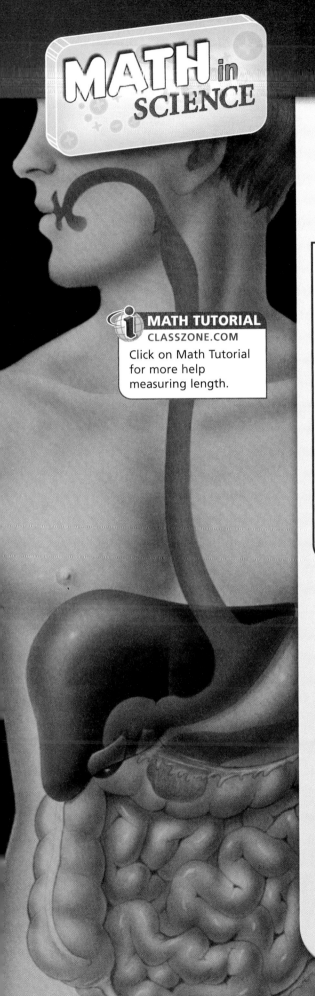

Internal Measurement

It wouldn't be useful if someone told you the length of your tongue in meters, or the length of a tooth in centimeters. To be meaningful, these measurements must be given in appropriate units.

Example

Your esophagus is about the length of your forearm. Choose the appropriate units to measure its length. Would meters, centimeters, or millimeters be most appropriate?

(1) Look at your arm from your wrist to your elbow. It is about the same as a rolling pin. You don't need to measure your stomach to see that a meter would be too large a unit. One meter is about the height of a lab table.

(2) Look at the ruler in the picture. Compare your arm to the centimeters shown and the millimeters.

(3) You can measure your arm with either unit, but if you wiggle a bit, the count of millimeters is thrown off.

ANSWER Centimeters are the most appropriate units.

Answer the following questions.

1. If you uncoiled a human intestine, its length would be about equal to that of 2 cars parked end to end. What would be appropriate units to use to measure that?

2. What units would you use to measure the length of your tongue? The length of a tooth?

3. The large intestine is actually shorter than the small intestine. The small intestine is about the length of a small bus, and the large is about as long as a car's back seat. Tell the units you would choose for each. Explain why.

CHALLENGE Your stomach when empty is about the size of your clenched fist. To measure its volume (the space it takes up), what units would you use?

The ruler shows 20 centimeters (cm). There are 10 millimeters (mm) in each centimeter.

1 cm

MATH TUTORIAL
CLASSZONE.COM
Click on Math Tutorial for more help measuring length.

KEY CONCEPT

2.3 The urinary system removes waste materials.

BEFORE, you learned	NOW, you will learn
• The digestive system breaks down food • Organs in the digestive system have different roles	• How different body systems remove different types of waste • Why the kidneys are important organs • About the role of the kidneys in homeostasis

VOCABULARY

urinary system p. 53
urine p. 53

EXPLORE Waste Removal

How does the skin get rid of body waste?

PROCEDURE

1. Place a plastic bag over the hand you do not use for writing and tape it loosely around your wrist.

2. Leave the bag on for five minutes. Write down the changes you see in conditions within the bag.

WHAT DO YOU THINK?

• What do you see happen to the bag?
• How does what you observe help explain the body's method of waste removal?

MATERIALS
• plastic bag
• tape
• stopwatch

OUTLINE

Add *Life processes produce wastes* to your outline. Include four ways the body disposes of waste products.

I. Main idea
  A. Supporting idea
    1. Detail
    2. Detail
  B. Supporting idea

Life processes produce wastes.

You have read that the respiratory system and the digestive system provide the body with energy and materials necessary for important processes. During these processes, waste materials are produced. The removal of these wastes is essential for the continuing function of body systems. Several systems in your body remove wastes.

• The urinary system disposes of liquid waste products removed from the blood.

• The respiratory system disposes of water vapor and waste gases from the blood.

• The digestive system disposes of solid waste products from food.

• The skin releases wastes through sweat glands.

 CHECK YOUR READING What are four ways the body disposes of waste products?

The urinary system removes waste from the blood.

If you have observed an aquarium, you have seen a filter at work. Water moves through the filter, which removes waste materials from the water. Just as the filter in a fish tank removes wastes from the water, structures in your urinary system filter wastes from your blood.

As shown in the diagram, the **urinary system** contains several structures. The kidneys are two organs located high up and toward the rear of the abdomen, one on each side of the spine. Kidneys function much as the filter in the fish tank does. In fact, the kidneys are often called the body's filters. Materials travel in your blood to the kidneys. There, some substances are removed, and others are returned to the blood.

After the kidneys filter chemical waste from the blood, the liquid travels down two tubes called ureters (yu-REE-tuhrz). The ureters bring the waste to the bladder, a storage sac with a wall of smooth muscle. The lower neck of the bladder leads into the urethra, a tube that carries the liquid waste outside the body. Voluntary muscles at one end of the bladder allow a person to hold the urethra closed until he or she is ready to release the muscles. At that time, the bladder contracts and sends the liquid waste, or **urine,** out of the body.

VOCABULARY
Add a magnet diagram for *urinary system* to your notebook. Include in your diagram information about how kidneys function.

Urinary System

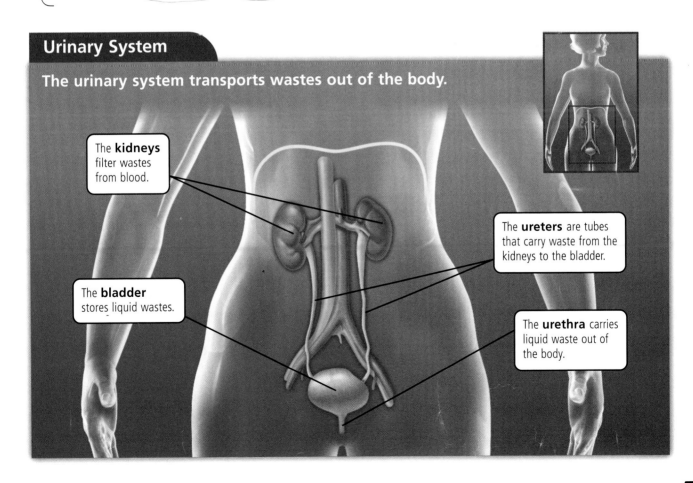

The urinary system transports wastes out of the body.

The **kidneys** filter wastes from blood.

The **ureters** are tubes that carry waste from the kidneys to the bladder.

The **bladder** stores liquid wastes.

The **urethra** carries liquid waste out of the body.

The kidneys act as filters.

RESOURCE CENTER
CLASSZONE.COM

Find out more about the
urinary system.

At any moment, about one quarter of the blood leaving your heart is
headed toward your kidneys to be filtered. The kidneys, which are
about as long as your index finger—only 10 centimeters (3.9 in.)
long—filter all the blood in your body many times a day.

The Nephron

Inside each kidney are approximately one million looping tubes called
nephrons. The nephron regulates the makeup of the blood.

1 Fluid is filtered from the blood into the nephron through a structure called the glomerulus (gloh-MEHR-yuh-luhs). Filtered blood
leaves the glomerulus and circulates around the tubes that make
up the nephron.

2 As the filtered fluid passes through the nephron, some nutrients
are absorbed back into the blood surrounding the tubes. Some
water is also filtered out in the glomerulus, but most water is
returned to the blood.

3 Waste products travel to the end of the nephron into the collecting duct. The remaining liquid, now called urine, passes out of the
kidney and into the ureters.

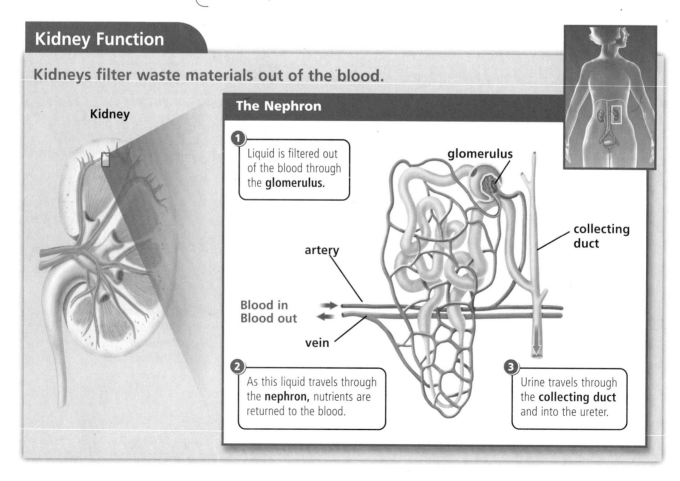

Kidney Function

Kidneys filter waste materials out of the blood.

Kidney

The Nephron

1 Liquid is filtered out of the blood through the **glomerulus**.

glomerulus

collecting duct

artery

Blood in
Blood out

vein

2 As this liquid travels through the **nephron**, nutrients are returned to the blood.

3 Urine travels through the **collecting duct** and into the ureter.

The amount of water in your body affects your blood pressure. Excess water increases blood pressure.

Water Balance

The kidneys not only remove wastes from blood, they also regulate the amount of water in the body. You read in Chapter 1 about the importance of homeostasis—a stable environment within your body. The amount of water in your cells affects homeostasis. If your body contains too much water, parts of your body may swell. Having too little water interferes with cell processes.

About one liter of water leaves the body every day. The kidneys control the amount of water that leaves the body in urine. Depending on how much water your body uses, the kidneys produce urine with more or less water.

  How do your kidneys regulate the amount of water in your body?

2.3 Review

KEY CONCEPTS

1. Describe the four organ systems that remove waste and explain how each removes waste.

2. Describe the function of four organs in the urinary system.

3. Describe homeostasis and explain why the kidneys are important to homeostasis.

CRITICAL THINKING

4. **Connect** Make a word web with the term *kidney* in the center. Add details about kidney function to the web.

⬤ CHALLENGE

5. **Synthesize** Explain why you may become thirsty on a hot day. Include the term *homeostasis* in your explanation.

CHAPTER INVESTIGATION

Modeling a Kidney

OVERVIEW AND PURPOSE Your kidneys are your body's filters. Every 20 to 30 minutes, every drop of your blood passes through the kidneys and is filtered. What types of materials are filtered by the kidneys? In this investigation you will
- model the filtering process of the kidneys
- determine what types of materials are filtered by your kidneys

▶ Problem

Write It Up

What types of materials can be removed from the blood by the kidneys?

▶ Hypothesize

Write It Up

Write a hypothesis to explain how substances are filtered out of the blood by the kidneys. Your hypothesis should take the form of an "If . . . , then . . . , because . . ." statement.

▶ Procedure

1 Make a data table like the one shown on the sample notebook page. Fold the filter paper as shown. Place the filter paper in the funnel, and place the funnel in the graduated cylinder.

2 Pour 20 mL of solution A into a beaker. Test the solution for salt concentration using a test strip for salinity. Record the results in your notebook. Slowly pour the solution into the funnel. Wait for it all to drip through the filter paper.

step 2

MATERIALS
- fine filter paper
- small funnel
- graduated cylinder
- 100 mL beaker
- solution A
- solution B
- solution C
- salinity test strips
- glucose test strips
- protein test strips

3 Test the filtered liquid for salt concentration again. Record the results.

4 Repeat steps 1, 2, and 3 for solution B using glucose test strips. Record the results in your notebook.

5 Repeat steps 1, 2, and 3 for solution C using protein test strips. Record the results in your notebook.

step 5

▶ Observe and Analyze

Write It Up

1. **RECORD** Be sure your data table is complete.

2. **OBSERVE** What substances were present in solutions A, B, and C?

3. **IDENTIFY VARIABLES** Identify the variables and constants in the experiment. List them in your notebook.

▶ Conclude

Write It Up

1. **COMPARE AND CONTRAST** In what ways does your model function like a kidney? How is your model not like a kidney?

2. **INTERPRET** Which materials were able to pass through the filter and which could not?

3. **INFER** What materials end up in the urine? How might materials be filtered out of the blood but not appear in the urine?

4. **APPLY** How could a filtering device be useful in your body?

▶ INVESTIGATE Further

CHALLENGE Your blood contains many chemicals. Some of these chemicals are waste products, but some are in the blood to be transported to different parts of the body. What other substances are filtered out of the blood by the kidneys? Which of the filtered substances are normally present in the urine? Use a variety of reference materials to research the chemicals found in urine. Revise your experiment to test the ability of your model kidney to filter other substances.

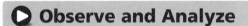

Modeling a Kidney

Table 1. Test-strip results

	Before filtering	After filtering
Solution A		
Solution B		
Solution C		

Chapter Review

the BIG idea

Systems in the body obtain and process materials and remove waste.

CONTENT REVIEW
CLASSZONE.COM

KEY CONCEPTS SUMMARY

2.1

The respiratory system gets oxygen and removes carbon dioxide.

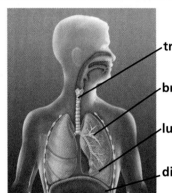

- trachea
- bronchial tube
- lung
- diaphragm

- Your body needs oxygen
- Structures in the respiratory system function together
- Your respiratory system is involved in other functions

VOCABULARY
respiratory system p. 37
cellular respiration p. 39

2.2

The digestive system breaks down food.

Structure	Function
Mouth	chemical and mechanical digestion
Esophagus	movement of food by peristalsis from mouth to stomach
Stomach	chemical and mechanical digestion; absorption of broken-down nutrients
Small intestine	chemical digestion; absorption of broken-down nutrients
Large intestine	absorption of water and broken-down nutrients, elimination of wastes

VOCABULARY
nutrient p. 45
digestion p. 46
digestive system p. 46
peristalsis p. 46

2.3

The urinary system removes waste materials.

Waste Removal

Respiratory System removes carbon dioxide	Urinary System removes wastes from body	Digestive system removes wastes from food	Skin removes water

Kidneys — Urine

VOCABULARY
urinary system p. 53
urine p. 53

Reviewing Vocabulary

Copy the chart below and write the definition for each word. Use the meaning of the word's root to help you.

Word	Root meaning	Definition
EXAMPLE: rib cage	to arch over	bones enclosing the internal organs of the body
1. respiration	to breathe	
2. nutrient	to nourish	
3. digestion	to separate	
4. urine	to moisten, to flow	

Reviewing Key Concepts

Multiple Choice *Choose the letter of the best answer.*

5. Which system brings oxygen to your body and removes carbon dioxide?
   a. digestive system
   b. urinary system
   c. respiratory system
   d. muscular system

6. Which body structure in the throat keeps air from entering the stomach?
   a. trachea
   b. epiglottis
   c. lungs
   d. alveoli

7. Oxygen and carbon dioxide are exchanged through structures in the lungs called
   a. bronchial tubes
   b. alveoli
   c. cartilage
   d. villi

8. Carbon dioxide is a waste product that is formed during which process?
   a. cellular respiration
   b. peristalsis
   c. urination
   d. circulation

9. Carbohydrates are nutrients that
   a. make up most of the human body
   b. make up cell membranes
   c. enable cells to grow and repair themselves
   d. provide cells with energy

10. Which is *not* a function of the digestive system?
    a. absorb water from food
    b. absorb nutrients from food
    c. filter wastes from blood
    d. break down food

11. Which is an example of a physical change?
    a. teeth grind cracker into smaller pieces
    b. liquids in mouth change starches to sugars
    c. bile breaks down fats
    d. stomach breaks down proteins

12. Where in the digestive system is water absorbed?
    a. small intestine
    b. stomach
    c. large intestine
    d. esophagus

13. Chemical waste is filtered from the body in which structure?
    a. alveoli
    b. kidney
    c. stomach
    d. villi

14. The kidneys control the amount of
    a. oxygen that enters the blood
    b. water that is absorbed by the body
    c. urine that leaves the body
    d. water that leaves the body

Short Answer *Write a short answer to each question.*

15. Draw a sketch that shows how the thoracic cavity changes as the diaphragm contracts and pulls downward.

16. What are two products that are released into the body as a result of cellular respiration?

17. Through which organs does food pass as it travels through the digestive system?

18. What is the function of the urinary system?

Thinking Critically

19. SUMMARIZE Describe how gas exchange takes place inside the lungs.

20. SYNTHESIZE Summarize what happens during cellular respiration. Explain how the digestive system and the respiratory system are involved.

21. ANALYZE When there is a lot of dust or pollen in the air, people may cough and sneeze. What function of the respiratory system is involved?

22. INFER When you exhale onto a glass surface, the surface becomes cloudy with a thin film of moisture. Explain why this happens.

23. COMPARE AND CONTRAST Where does mechanical digestion take place? How is it different from chemical digestion?

24. PREDICT People with stomach disease often have their entire stomachs removed and are able to live normally. Explain how this is possible. Would a person be able to live normally without the small intestine? Explain your answer.

25. APPLY An athlete drinks a liter of water before a basketball game and continues to drink water during the game. Describe how the athlete's body is able to maintain homeostasis during the course of the game.

26. INTERPRET Use the diagram of the nephron shown below to describe what happens to the blood as it travels through the vessels surrounding the nephron.

nephron

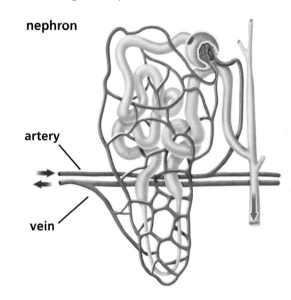

artery

vein

the **BIG** idea

27. INFER Look again at the picture on pages 34–35. Now that you have finished the chapter, how would you change or add details to your answer to the question on the photograph?

28. SYNTHESIZE Write a paragraph explaining how the respiratory system, the digestive system, and the urinary system work together with the circulatory system to eliminate waste materials from the body. Underline these terms in your paragraph.

UNIT PROJECTS

Check your schedule for your unit project. How are you doing? Be sure that you've placed data or notes from your research in your project folder.

Analyzing Data

The bar graph below shows respiration rates.

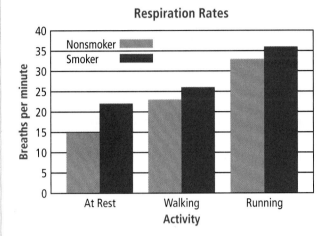

Respiration Rates

Nonsmoker
Smoker

Use the graph to answer the questions below.

1. What is the best title for this graph?
   a. Respiration Rates of Smokers and Nonsmokers
   b. Cigarettes Smoked During Exercise
   c. Activities Performed by Smokers and Nonsmokers
   d. Blood Pressure Levels of Smokers and Nonsmokers.

2. How many breaths per minute were taken by a nonsmoker at rest?
   a. 15 breaths per minute
   b. 22 breaths per minute
   c. 23 breaths per minute
   d. 33 breaths per minute

3. For the nonsmokers, by how much did the respiration rate increase between resting and running?
   a. 15 breaths per minute
   b. 18 breaths per minute
   c. 23 breaths per minute
   d. 33 breaths per minute

4. Which statement is *not* true?
   a. The nonsmoker at rest took more breaths per minute than the smoker at rest.
   b. The nonsmoker took more breaths per minute running than walking.
   c. The smoker took more breaths per minute than the nonsmoker while walking.
   d. The nonsmoker took fewer breaths per minute than the smoker while running.

5. Which statement is the most logical conclusion to draw from the data in the chart?
   a. Smoking has no effect on respiration rate.
   b. Increased activity has no effect on respiration rate.
   c. There is no difference in the respiration rates between the smoker and the nonsmoker.
   d. Smoking and activity cause an increase in respiration rate.

Extended Response

6. Tar, which is a harmful substance found in tobacco smoke, coats the lining of the lungs over time. Based on the information in the graph and what you know about the respiratory system, write a paragraph describing how smoking cigarettes affects the functioning of the respiratory system.

7. Ads for cigarettes and other tobacco products have been banned from television. However, they still appear in newspapers and magazines. These ads make tobacco use look glamorous and exciting. Using your knowledge of the respiratory system, design an ad that discourages the use of tobacco products. Create a slogan that will help people remember how tobacco affects the health of the respiratory system.

3 Transport and Protection

the **BIG** idea

Systems function to transport materials and to defend and protect the body.

Key Concepts

SECTION 3.1
The circulatory system transports materials.
Learn how materials move through blood vessels.

SECTION 3.2
The immune system defends the body.
Learn about the body's defenses and responses to foreign materials.

SECTION 3.3
The integumentary system shields the body.
Learn about the structure of skin and how it protects the body.

Internet Preview

CLASSZONE.COM

Chapter 3 online resources: Content Review, two Visualizations, four Resource Centers, Math Tutorial, Test Practice

Red blood cells travel through a blood vessel. How do you think blood carries materials around your body?

Blood Pressure

Fill a small, round balloon halfway full with air. Tie off the end. Gently squeeze the balloon in your hand. Release the pressure. Squeeze again.

Observe and Think As you squeeze your hand, what happens to the air in the balloon? What happens as you release the pressure?

Wet Fingers

Dip your finger into a cup of room-temperature water. Then hold the finger up in the air and note how it feels.

Observe and Think How does your finger feel now compared with the way it felt before you dipped it?

Internet Activity: Heart Pumping

Go to **ClassZone.com** to learn about how the heart pumps blood. See how the circulatory system interacts with the respiratory system.

Observe and Think Where does the blood go after it leaves the right side of the heart? the left side of the heart?

NSTA
scilinks.org

SCI
LINKS

Immune System **Code: MDL046**

Getting Ready to Learn

◀ CONCEPT REVIEW

- The body's systems interact.
- The body's systems work to maintain internal conditions.
- The digestive system breaks down food.
- The respiratory system gets oxygen and removes carbon dioxide.

◀ VOCABULARY REVIEW

organ p. 11

organ system p. 12

homeostasis p. 12

nutrient p. 45

 **CONTENT REVIEW**
CLASSZONE.COM
Review concepts and vocabulary.

▶ TAKING NOTES

MAIN IDEA AND DETAIL NOTES

Make a two-column chart. Write the main ideas, such as those in the blue headings, in the column on the left. Write details about each of those main heads in the column on the right.

VOCABULARY STRATEGY

Write each new vocabulary term in the center of a **frame game** diagram. Decide what information to frame it with. Use examples, descriptions, parts, sentences that use the term in context, or pictures. You can change the frame to fit each term.

See the Note-Taking Handbook on pages R45–R51.

SCIENCE NOTEBOOK

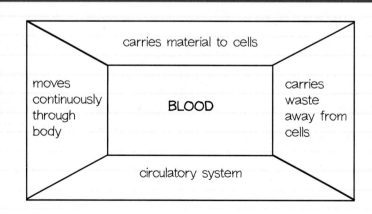

MAIN IDEAS	DETAIL NOTES
1. The circulatory system works with other body systems.	1. Transports materials from digestive and respiratory systems to cells
	2. Blood is fluid that carries materials and wastes
	3. Blood is always moving through the body
	4. Blood delivers oxygen and takes away carbon dioxide

carries material to cells

moves continuously through body

BLOOD

carries waste away from cells

circulatory system

The circulatory system transports materials.

◀ **BEFORE, you learned**

- The urinary system removes waste
- The kidneys play a role in homeostasis

▶ **NOW, you will learn**

- How different structures of the circulatory system work together
- About the structure and function of blood
- What blood pressure is and why it is important

VOCABULARY

circulatory system p. 65
blood p. 65
red blood cell p. 67
artery p. 69
vein p. 69
capillary p. 69

EXPLORE The Circulatory System

How fast does your heart beat?

PROCEDURE

 Hold out your left hand with your palm facing up.

 Place the first two fingers of your right hand on your left wrist below your thumb. Move your fingertips slightly until you can feel your pulse.

③ Use the stopwatch to determine how many times your heart beats in one minute.

WHAT DO YOU THINK?

- How many times did your heart beat?
- What do you think you would find if you took your pulse after exercising?

MATERIALS
stopwatch

The circulatory system works with other body systems.

VOCABULARY
Add a frame game diagram for the term *circulatory system* to your notebook.

You have read that the systems in your body provide materials and energy. The digestive system breaks down food and nutrients, and the respiratory system provides the oxygen that cells need to release energy. Another system, called the **circulatory system,** transports materials from the digestive and the respiratory systems to the cells.

Materials and wastes are carried in a fluid called **blood**. Blood moves continuously through the body, delivering oxygen and other materials to cells and removing carbon dioxide and other wastes from cells.

Structures in the circulatory system function together.

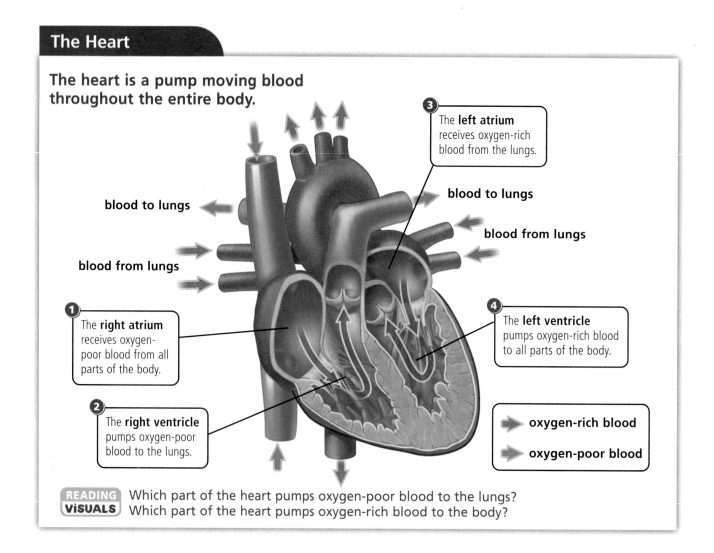

In order to provide the essential nutrients and other materials that your cells need, your blood must keep moving through your body. The circulatory system, which is made up of the heart and blood vessels, allows blood to flow to all parts of the body. The circulatory system works with other systems to provide the body with this continuous flow of life-giving blood.

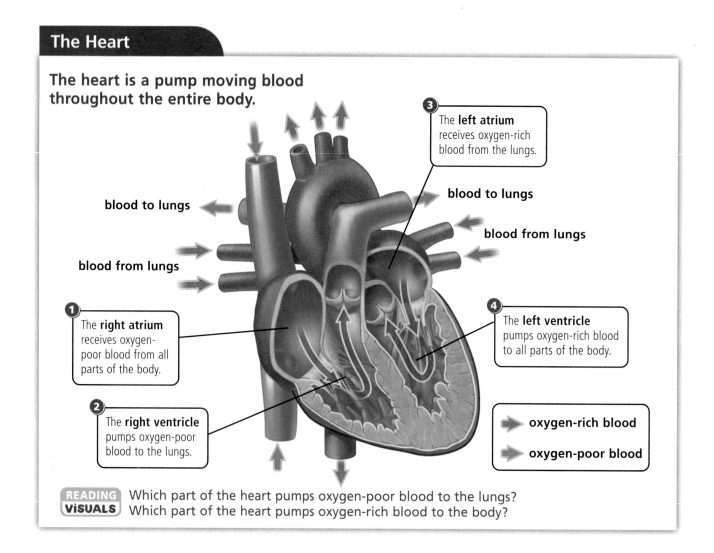
RESOURCE CENTER
CLASSZONE.COM
Find out more about the circulatory system.

The Heart

The heart is the organ that pushes blood throughout the circulatory system. The human heart actually functions as two pumps—one pump on the right side and one on the left side. The right side of the heart pumps blood to the lungs, and the left side pumps blood to the rest of the body. The lungs receive oxygen when you inhale and remove carbon dioxide when you exhale. Inside the lungs, the respiratory system interacts with the circulatory system.

The Heart

The heart is a pump moving blood throughout the entire body.

❸ The **left atrium** receives oxygen-rich blood from the lungs.

blood to lungs

blood from lungs

blood to lungs

blood from lungs

❶ The **right atrium** receives oxygen-poor blood from all parts of the body.

❹ The **left ventricle** pumps oxygen-rich blood to all parts of the body.

❷ The **right ventricle** pumps oxygen-poor blood to the lungs.

➤ oxygen-rich blood

➤ oxygen-poor blood

READING VISUALS Which part of the heart pumps oxygen-poor blood to the lungs? Which part of the heart pumps oxygen-rich blood to the body?

Each side of the heart is divided into two areas called chambers. Oxygen-poor blood, which is blood from the body with less oxygen, flows to the right side of your heart, into a filling chamber called the right atrium. With each heartbeat, blood flows into a pumping chamber, the right ventricle, and then into the lungs, where it releases carbon dioxide waste and absorbs oxygen.

After picking up oxygen, blood is pushed back to the heart, filling another chamber, which is called the left atrium. Blood moves from the left atrium to the left ventricle, a pumping chamber, and again begins its trip out to the rest of the body. Both oxygen-poor blood and oxygen-rich blood are red. However, oxygen-rich blood is a much brighter and lighter shade of red than is oxygen-poor blood. The diagram on page 66 shows oxygen-poor blood in blue, so that you can tell where in the circulatory system oxygen-poor and oxygen-rich blood are found.

 CHECK YOUR READING Summarize the way blood moves through the heart. Remember, a summary contains only the most important information.

Blood

The oxygen that your cells need in order to release energy must be present in blood to travel through your body. Blood is a tissue made up of plasma, red blood cells, white blood cells, and platelets. About 60 percent of blood is plasma, a fluid that contains proteins, glucose, hormones, gases, and other substances dissolved in water.

White blood cells help your body fight infection by attacking disease-causing organisms. **Red blood cells** are more numerous than white blood cells and have a different function. They pick up oxygen in the lungs and transport it throughout the body. As red blood cells travel through the circulatory system, they deliver oxygen to other cells.

Platelets are large cell fragments that help form blood clots when a blood vessel is injured. You know what a blood clot is if you've observed a cut or a scrape. The scab that forms around a cut or scrape is made of clotted blood. After an injury such as a cut, platelets nearby begin to enlarge and become sticky. They stick to the injured area of the blood vessels and release chemicals that result in blood clotting. Blood clotting keeps blood vessels from losing too much blood.

 CHECK YOUR READING What are the four components that make up blood?

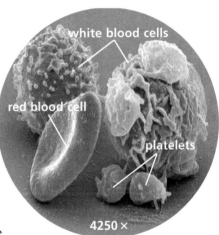

white blood cells

red blood cell

platelets

4250×

Blood is made mostly of red blood cells, white blood cells, and platelets surrounded by plasma.

Circulatory System

The circulatory system allows blood to flow continuously throughout the body. The runner depends on a constant flow of oxygen-rich blood to fuel his cells.

■ oxygen-rich blood
■ oxygen-poor blood

The **heart** pumps oxygen-poor blood to the lungs and oxygen-rich blood to all parts of the body.

In the vessels of the **lungs**, oxygen-poor blood becomes oxygen-rich blood.

This major **vein** carries oxygen-poor blood from all parts of the body to the heart.

This major **artery** and its branches deliver oxygen-rich blood to all parts of the body.

As blood travels through blood vessels, some fluid is lost. This fluid, called lymph, is collected in lymph vessels and returned to veins and arteries. As you will read in the next section, lymph and lymph vessels are associated with your immune system. Sometimes scientists refer to the lymph and lymph vessels as the lymphatic system. The lymphatic system helps you fight disease.

Blood Vessels

Blood moves through a network of structures called blood vessels. Blood vessels are tube-shaped structures that are similar to flexible drinking straws. The structure of blood vessels suits them for particular functions. **Arteries**, which are the vessels that take blood away from the heart, have strong walls. An artery wall is thick and elastic and can handle the tremendous force produced when the heart pumps. **Veins** are blood vessels that carry blood back to the heart. The walls of veins are thinner than those of arteries. However, veins are generally of greater diameter than are arteries.

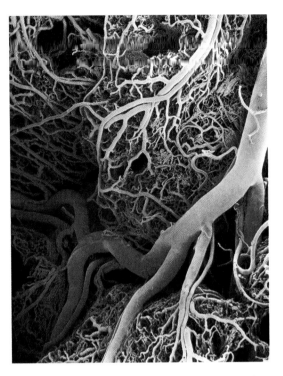

Arteries, capillaries, and veins form a complex web to carry blood to all the cells in the body (30×).

Most arteries carry oxygen-rich blood away from the heart, and most veins carry oxygen-poor blood back to the heart. However, the pulmonary blood vessels are exceptions. Oxygen-poor blood travels through the two pulmonary arteries, one of which goes to each lung. The two pulmonary veins carry oxygen-rich blood from the lungs to the heart.

Veins and arteries branch off into very narrow blood vessels called capillaries. **Capillaries** connect arteries with veins. Through capillaries materials are exchanged between blood and tissues. Oxygen and materials from nutrients move from the blood in the arteries to the body's tissues through tiny openings in the capillary walls. Waste materials and carbon dioxide move from the tissues' cells through the capillary walls and into the blood in the veins.

 Compare and contrast arteries, veins, and capillaries.

Blood exerts pressure on blood vessels.

As you have read, the contractions of the heart push blood through blood vessels. The force produced when the heart contracts travels through the blood, putting pressure on the blood vessels. This force is called blood pressure. Compare a vessel to a plastic bag filled with water.

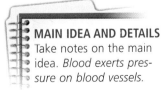

MAIN IDEA AND DETAILS
Take notes on the main idea. *Blood exerts pressure on blood vessels.*

If you push down at the center of the bag, you can see the water push out against the sides of the bag.

The heart pushes blood in a similar way, exerting pressure on the arteries, veins, and capillaries in the circulatory system. It is important to maintain healthy blood pressure so that materials in blood get to all parts of your body. If blood pressure is too low, some of the cells will not get oxygen and other materials. On the other hand, if blood pressure is too high, the force may weaken the blood vessels and require the heart to work harder to push blood through the blood vessels. High blood pressure is a serious medical condition, but it can be treated.

The circulatory system can be considered as two smaller systems: one, the pulmonary system, moves blood to the lungs; the other, the systemic system, moves blood to the rest of the body. Blood pressure is measured in the systemic part of the circulatory system.

You can think of blood pressure as the pressure that blood exerts on the walls of your arteries at all times. Health professionals measure blood pressure indirectly with a device called a sphygmomanometer (SFIHG-moh-muh-NAHM-ih-tuhr).

Blood pressure is expressed with two numbers—one number over another number. The first number refers to the pressure in the arteries when the heart contracts. The second number refers to the pressure in the arteries when the heart relaxes and receives blood from the veins.

Blood Pressure

Blood pressure allows materials to travel to all parts of your body.

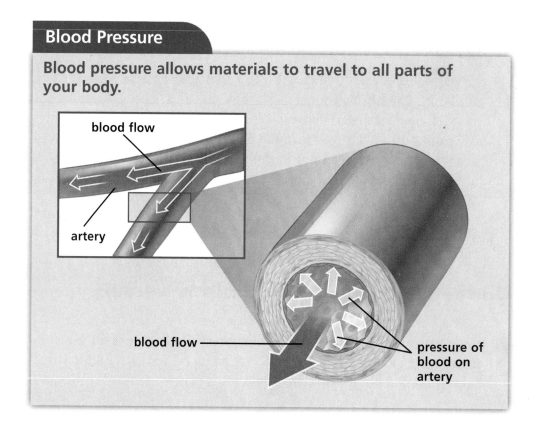

blood flow

artery

blood flow

pressure of blood on artery

There are four different blood types.

Each red blood cell has special proteins on its surface. One group of surface proteins determines blood type. There are two blood-type proteins, A and B. A person whose blood cells have the A proteins has type A blood. One with cells having B proteins has type B blood. Some people have both proteins—type AB blood. Other people have neither protein, a type of blood referred to as type O.

Maybe you, or someone you know, has had a blood transfusion, a procedure in which one person receives blood donated by another. Knowing blood type is important for transfusions. As you will learn in the next section, the body has structures that protect it from unknown substances. They are part of an immune system that recognizes and protects cells and molecules that are "self" from those that are unrecognized, or "nonself." The body attacks unrecognized substances, including those in donated blood.

The blood used for transfusions is usually the same type as the blood type of the receiver, but sometimes other blood types are used. The diagram shows which blood types are compatible. Because the cells in type O blood have neither protein, the immune system of someone with A, B, or AB blood will not attack O blood cells. A person with type O blood, however, cannot receive any other blood type because that person's immune system would attack A or B surface proteins.

Blood Type Compatibility		
Blood Type	Can Donate Blood To	Can Receive Blood From
A	A, AB	A, O
B	B, AB	B, O
AB	AB	A, B, AB, O
O	A, B, AB, O	O

People can donate blood to others.

 CHECK YOUR READING Why is it important to know your blood type?

RESOURCE CENTER
CLASSZONE.COM

Learn more about blood types.

 **Review**

KEY CONCEPTS

1. What are the functions of the two sides of the heart?

2. What is the primary function of red blood cells?

3. Why can both high and low blood pressure be a problem?

CRITICAL THINKING

4. **Apply** List three examples of the circulatory system working with another system in your body.

5. **Compare and Contrast** Explain why blood pressure is expressed with two numbers.

⬥ CHALLENGE

6. **Identify Cause and Effect** You can feel the speed at which your heart is pumping by pressing two fingers to the inside of your wrist. This is your pulse. If you run for a few minutes, your pulse rate is faster for a little while, then it slows down again. Why did your pulse rate speed up and slow down?

CHAPTER INVESTIGATION

Heart Rate and Exercise

OVERVIEW AND PURPOSE In this activity, you will calculate your resting, maximum, and target heart rates. Then you will examine the effect of exercise on heart rate. Before you begin, read through the entire investigation.

▶ Procedure

1. Make a data table like the one shown on the sample notebook page.

2. Measure your resting heart rate. Find the pulse in the artery of your neck, just below and in front of the bottom of your ear, with the first two fingers of one hand. Do not use your thumb to measure pulse since the thumb has a pulse of its own. Once you have found the pulse, count the beats for 30 seconds and multiply the result by 2. The number you get is your resting heart rate in beats per minute. Record this number in your notebook.

step 2

3. Calculate your maximum heart rate by subtracting your age from 220. Record this number in your notebook. Your target heart rate should be 60 to 75 percent of your maximum heart rate. Calculate and record this range in your notebook.

4. Someone who is very athletic or has been exercising regularly for 6 months or more can safely exercise up to 85 percent of his or her maximum heart rate. Calculate and record this rate in your notebook.

5. Observe how quickly you reach your target heart rate during exercise. Begin by running in place at an intensity that makes you breathe harder but does not make you breathless. As with any exercise, remember that if you experience difficulty breathing, dizziness, or chest discomfort, stop exercising immediately.

step 5

MATERIALS
- notebook
- stopwatch
- calculator
- graph paper

Every 2 minutes, measure your heart rate for 10 seconds. Multiply this number by 6 to find your heart rate in beats per minute and record it in your notebook. Try to exercise for a total of 10 minutes. After you stop exercising, continue recording your heart rate every 2 minutes until it returns to the resting rate you measured in step 2.

▶ Observe and Analyze

Write It Up

1. **GRAPH DATA** Make a line graph of your heart rate during and after the exercise. Graph the values in beats per minute versus time in minutes. Your graph should start at your resting heart rate and continue until your heart rate has returned to its resting rate. Using a colored pencil, shade in the area that represents your target heart-rate range.

2. **ANALYZE DATA** How many minutes of exercising were needed for you to reach your target heart rate of 60 to 75 percent of maximum? Did your heart rate go over your target range?

3. **INTERPRET DATA** How many minutes after you stopped exercising did it take for your heart rate to return to its resting rate? Why do you think your heart rate did not return to its resting rate immediately after you stopped exercising?

▶ Conclude

Write It Up

1. **INFER** Why do you think that heart rate increases during exercise?

2. **IDENTIFY** What other body systems are affected when the heart rate increases?

3. **PREDICT** Why do you think that target heart rate changes with age?

4. **CLASSIFY** Create a table comparing the intensity of different types of exercise, such as walking, skating, bicycling, weight lifting, and any others you might enjoy.

▶ INVESTIGATE Further

CHALLENGE Determine how other exercises affect your heart rate. Repeat this investigation by performing one or two of the other exercises from your table. Present your data, with a graph, to the class.

Heart Rate and Exercise

Resting heart rate:
Maximum heart rate:
Target heart rate (60-75% of maximum):
Target heart rate (85% of maximum):

Table 1. Heart Rate During and After Exercise

Time (minutes)	0	2	4	6	8	10	12	14	16	18	20
Heart rate (beats per minute)											

The immune system defends the body.

◀ BEFORE, you learned	▶ NOW, you will learn
• The circulatory system works with other systems to fuel the body cells • Structures in the circulatory system work together • Blood pressure allows materials to reach all parts of the body	• How foreign material enters the body • How the immune system responds to foreign material • Ways that the body can become immune to a disease

VOCABULARY

pathogen p. 74
immune system p. 75
antibody p. 75
antigen p. 78
immunity p. 80
vaccine p. 80
antibiotic p. 81

EXPLORE Membranes

How does the body keep foreign particles out?

PROCEDURE

1. Place a white cloth into a sandwich bag and seal it. Fill a bowl with water and stir in several drops of food coloring.

2. Submerge the sandwich bag in the water. After five minutes, remove the bag and note the condition of the cloth.

3. Puncture the bag with a pin. Put the bag back in the water for five minutes. Remove the bag and note the condition of the cloth.

WHAT DO YOU THINK?
• How does a puncture in the bag affect its ability to protect the cloth?

MATERIALS
• white cloth
• zippered sandwich bag
• large bowl
• water
• food coloring
• small pin

Many systems defend the body from harmful materials.

MAIN IDEA AND DETAILS
Add the main idea *Many systems defend the body from harmful materials* to your chart along with detail notes.

You might not realize it, but you come into contact with harmful substances constantly. Because your body has ways to defend itself, you don't even notice. One of the body's best defenses is to keep foreign materials from entering in the first place. The integumentary (ihn-TEHG-yu-MEHN-tuh-ree), respiratory, and digestive systems are the first line of defense against **pathogens,** or disease-causing agents. Pathogens can enter through your skin, the air you breathe, and even the food you eat or liquids you drink.

🔺 **CHECK YOUR READING** Which systems are your first line of defense against pathogens?

Integumentary System Defenses Most of the time, your skin functions as a barrier between you and the outside world. The physical barrier the skin forms is just one obstacle for pathogens and other foreign materials. The growth of pathogens on your eyes can be slowed by substances contained in tears. The millions of bacteria cells that live on the skin can also kill pathogens. A common way pathogens can enter the body is through a cut. The circulatory system is then able to help defend the body because blood contains cells that respond to foreign materials.

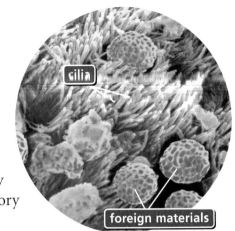

Cilia are hairlike protrusions that trap materials entering your respiratory system (600×).

Respiratory System Defenses Sneezing and coughing are two ways the respiratory system defends the body from harmful substances. Cilia and mucus also protect the body. Cilia are tiny, hairlike protrusions in the nose and the lungs that trap dust particles present in the air. Mucus is a thick and slippery substance found in the nose, throat, and lungs. Like the cilia, mucus traps dirt and other particles. Mucus contains substances similar to those in tears that can slow the growth of pathogens.

Digestive System Defenses Some foreign materials manage to enter your digestive system, but many are destroyed by saliva, mucus, enzymes, and stomach acids. Saliva in your mouth helps kill bacteria. Mucus protects the digestive organs by coating them. Pathogens can also be destroyed by enzymes produced in the liver and pancreas or by the acids in the stomach.

The immune system has response structures.

Sometimes foreign materials manage to get past the first line of defense. When this happens, the body relies on the **immune system** to respond. This system functions in several ways:

- Tissues in the bone marrow, the thymus gland, the spleen, and the lymph nodes produce white blood cells, which are specialized cells that function to destroy foreign organisms.
- Some white blood cells produce a nonspecific response to injury or infection.
- Some white blood cells produce proteins called **antibodies,** which are part of a specific immune response to foreign materials.

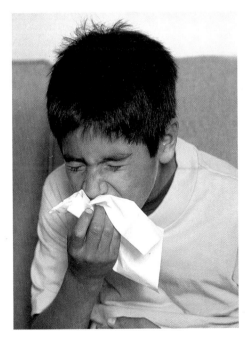

Sneezing helps to expel foreign substances from the body.

White Blood Cells

The immune system has specialized cells called white blood cells that recognize foreign materials in the body and respond. The number of white blood cells in the blood can increase during an immune response. These cells travel through the circulatory system and the lymphatic system to an injured or infected area of the body. White blood cells leave the blood vessels and travel into the damaged tissue, where the immune response takes place.

The Lymphatic System

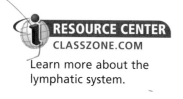
The lymphatic system transports pathogen-fighting white blood cells throughout the body, much as the circulatory system does. The lymphatic system carries lymph, and the circulatory system carries blood. Both fluids transport similar materials, such as white blood cells.

Lymph is the fluid left in the tissues by the circulatory system. It moves through lymph vessels, which are similar to veins. However, the lymphatic system has no pump like the heart to move fluid. Lymph drifts through the lymph vessels when your skeletal muscles contract or when your body changes position. As it moves, it passes through lymph nodes, which filter out pathogens and store white blood cells and antibodies. Because lymph nodes filter out pathogens, infections are often fought in your lymph nodes, causing them to swell when you get sick.

 CHECK YOUR READING   How does the lymphatic system help the immune system?

The immune system responds to attack.

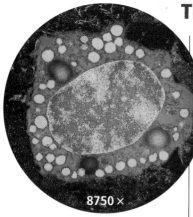

8750 ×

The mast cell above is an important part of the immune system.

Certain illnesses can cause symptoms such as coughing, sneezing, and fever. These symptoms make you uncomfortable when you are sick. But in fact, most symptoms are the result of the immune system's response to foreign materials in the body.

The immune system responds in two ways. The white blood cells that first respond to the site of injury or infection attack foreign materials in a nonspecific response. Some of these cells attack foreign materials and produce chemicals that help other white blood cells work better. The second part of the response is very specific to the types of pathogens invading the body. These white blood cells produce antibodies specific to each pathogen and provide your body with immunity.

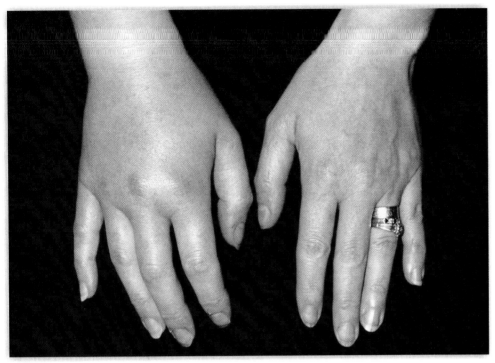

Wasp stings cause an immediate immune response. The area of the sting swells up and increases in temperature while your body battles the injury.

Nonspecific Response

Swelling, redness, and heat are some of the symptoms that tell you that a cut or scrape has become infected by foreign materials. They are all signs of inflammation, your body's first defense reaction against injuries and infections.

When tissue becomes irritated or damaged, it releases large amounts of histamine (HIHS-tuh-meen). Histamine raises the temperature of the tissues and increases blood flow to the area. Increased blood flow, which makes the injured area appear red, allows antibodies and white blood cells to arrive more quickly for battle. Higher temperatures improve the speed and power of white blood cells. Some pathogens cannot tolerate heat, so they grow weaker. The swelling caused by the production of histamine can be a small price to pay for this chemical's important work.

When a foreign material affects more than one area of your body, many tissues produce histamine. As a result, the temperature of your whole body rises. Any temperature above 37 degrees Celsius (98.6°F) is considered a fever, but only temperatures hot enough to damage tissues are dangerous. Trying to lower a high fever with medication is advisable in order to avoid tissue damage. When you have a small fever, lowering your body temperature might make you more comfortable, but it will not affect how long you stay sick.

 CHECK YOUR READING What causes a fever when you are sick?

Specific Response

Specific response differs from nonspecific response in two ways. First, specific responses are triggered by antigens. An **antigen** is a particular substance that the body recognizes as foreign and that stimulates a reaction. Second, specific response provides protection from future attacks by the same antigen. Three major types of white blood cells—phagocytes, T cells, and B cells—function together in specific response.

Phagocytes and T Cells Phagocytes process foreign materials into particles, which are presented to T cells. Antigens on the particles signal T cells to reproduce rapidly. Some of these T cells attack antigens, while others perform different functions. Because many of the antigens that provoke the immune response are on pathogens, the immune response allows humans to survive in a germ-filled world.

Immune Response

When antigens invade the body, several types of white blood cells function together to identify and attack pathogens.

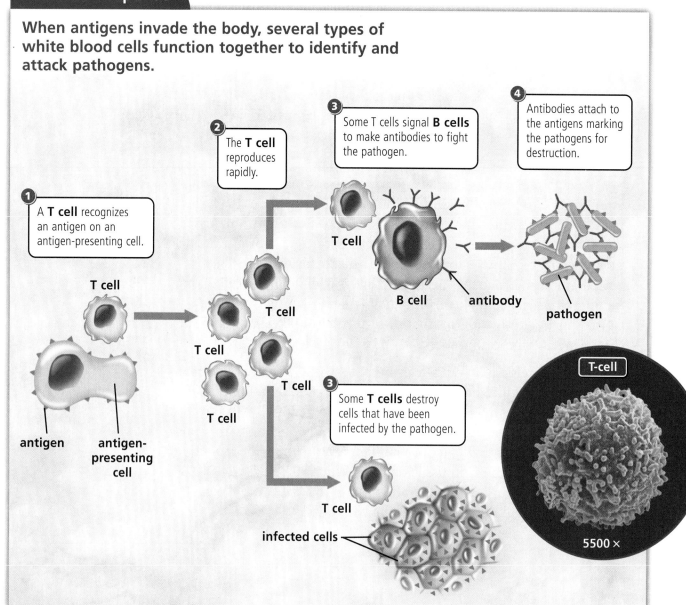

1 A **T cell** recognizes an antigen on an antigen-presenting cell.

2 The **T cell** reproduces rapidly.

3 Some T cells signal **B cells** to make antibodies to fight the pathogen.

4 Antibodies attach to the antigens marking the pathogens for destruction.

3 Some **T cells** destroy cells that have been infected by the pathogen.

T cell

T cell

T cell

T cell

T cell

T cell

T cell

T cell

B cell

antibody

pathogen

antigen

antigen-presenting cell

infected cells

T-cell

5500×

INVESTIGATE Antibodies

How do antibodies stop pathogens from spreading?

PROCEDURE

(1) Your teacher will hand out plastic lids, each labeled with the name of a different pathogen. You will see plastic containers spread throughout the room. There is one container in the room with the same label as your lid.

(2) At the signal, find the plastic container with the pathogen that has the same label as your lid and wait in place for the teacher to tell you to stop. If you still haven't found the matching container when time is called, your model pathogen has spread.

(3) If your pathogen has spread, write its name on the board.

WHAT DO YOU THINK?

Which pathogens spread?

- What do you think the lid and container represent? Why?
- How do antibodies identify pathogens?

CHALLENGE Why do you think it is important for your body to identify pathogens?

B Cells After T cells reproduce, B cells that also recognize a specific antigen are activated and reproduce. After several days, many of these B cells begin to produce antibodies that help destroy pathogens. Antibodies attach to the antigens, marking pathogens for attack by killer T cells or other cells and chemicals that destroy pathogens.

Some of the activated B cells do not make antibodies but remain in the body as a form of immune system memory. If the same type of foreign material enters the system at another time, the system can respond much more quickly, because the B cells are primed to multiply quickly and produce the antibody.

> **READING TIP**
>
> *Antigen* and *antibody* are words that look very similar. Antigens are markers on pathogens. Antibodies fight pathogens.

 Why is it important for the body to store activated B cells?

Development of Immunity

After your body has won out against a specific pathogen, B cells designed to fight that pathogen remain in your system. If the same pathogen were to attack again, your immune system would almost certainly destroy it before you became ill. This resistance to a sickness is called **immunity.**

Immunity takes two forms: passive and active. When babies are first born, they have only the immune defenses given to them by their mothers. They have not had the chance to develop antibodies of their own. This type of immunity is called passive immunity. Antibodies are not produced by the person's own body but given to the body from another source. Babies must develop their own antibodies after a few months.

COMPARE A doctor gives a girl a vaccination. Is getting a vaccination an example of passive or active immunity?

You have active immunity whenever your body makes its own antibodies. Your body will again fight against any specific pathogen you have developed antibodies against. For example, it is most unlikely that you will get chicken pox twice.

 CHECK YOUR READING What is the difference between active and passive immunity?

Most diseases can be prevented or treated.

Given enough time, your body will fight off most diseases. However, some infections can cause significant and lasting damage before they are defeated by the body's defenses. Other infections are so strong that the immune system cannot fight them. Medical advances in the prevention and treatment of diseases have reduced the risks of many serious illnesses.

Vaccination

Another way to develop an immunity is to receive a **vaccine.** Vaccines contain small amounts of weakened pathogens that stimulate your immune response. Your B cells are called into action to create antibodies as if you were fighting the real illness. The pathogens are usually weakened, so that you will not get sick, yet they still enable your body to develop an active immunity.

Today we have vaccines for many common pathogens. Most children who are vaccinated will not get many diseases that their great grandparents, grandparents, and even parents had. Vaccinations can be administered by injection or by mouth. Babies are not the only ones who get them, either. You can be vaccinated at any age.

 Why don't vaccinations usually make you sick?

Treatment

Not all diseases can be prevented, but many of them can be treated. In some cases, treatments can only reduce the symptoms of the disease while the immune system fights the disease-causing pathogens. Other treatments attack the pathogens directly.

In some cases, treatment can only prevent further damage to body tissues by a pathogen that cannot be cured or defeated by the immune system. The way in which a disease is treated depends on what pathogen causes it. Many bacterial infections can be treated with antibiotics. **Antibiotics** are medicines that block the growth and reproduction of bacteria. You may have taken antibiotics when you have had a disease such as strep throat or an ear infection. Other types of medicine can help fight infections caused by viruses, fungi, and parasites.

Types of Pathogens

Disease	Pathogen
Colds, chicken pox, hepatitis, AIDS, influenza, mumps, measles, rabies	virus
Food poisoning, strep throat, tetanus, tuberculosis, acne, ulcers, Lyme disease	bacteria
Athlete's foot, thrush, ringworm	fungus
Malaria, parasitic pneumonia, pinworm, lice, scabies	parasites

3.2 Review

KEY CONCEPTS

1. Make a chart showing three ways that foreign material enters the body and how the immune system defends against each type of attack.

2. What are white blood cells and what is their function in the body?

3. What are two ways to develop immunity?

CRITICAL THINKING

4. **Compare and Contrast** Make a chart comparing B cells and T cells. Include an explanation of the function of antibodies.

5. **Apply** Describe how your immune system responds when you scrape your knee.

CHALLENGE

6. **Hypothesize** Explain why, even if a person recovers from a cold, that person could get a cold again.

Pollen Counts

Every year, sometime between July and October, in nearly every state in the United States, the air will fill with ragweed pollen. For a person who has a pollen allergy, these months blur with tears. Linn County, Iowa, takes weekly counts of ragweed and non-ragweed pollen.

MATH TUTORIAL
CLASSZONE.COM
Click on Math Tutorial for more help making line graphs.

Weekly Pollen Counts, Linn County, Iowa											
	Jul. 29	Aug. 5	Aug. 12	Aug. 19	Aug. 26	Sept. 2	Sept. 9	Sept. 16	Sept. 23	Sept. 30	Oct. 7
Ragweed (Grain/m³)	0	9	10	250	130	240	140	25	20	75	0
Non-Ragweed (Grain/m³)	10	45	15	50	100	50	40	10	20	25	0

Example

A line graph of the data will show the pattern of increase and decrease of ragweed pollen in the air.

(1) Begin with a quadrant with horizontal and vertical axes.

(2) Mark the weekly dates at even intervals on the horizontal axis.

(3) Starting at 0 on the vertical axis, mark even intervals of 50 units.

(4) Graph each point. Connect the points with line segments.

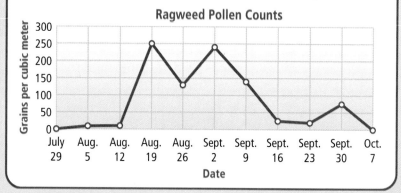

Complete and present your graph as directed below.

1. Use graph paper to make your own line graph of the non-ragweed pollen in Linn County.

2. Write some questions that can be answered by comparing the two graphs. Trade questions with a partner.

3. Which weeks have the highest pollen counts in Linn County?

CHALLENGE Try making a double line graph combining both sets of data in one graph.

The pollen of *Ambrosia artemisiifolia* (common ragweed) sets off a sneeze.

The integumentary system shields the body.

◀ BEFORE, you learned	▶ NOW, you will learn
• The body is defended from harmful materials • Response structures fight disease • The immune system responds in many ways to illness	• About the functions of the skin • How the skin helps protect the body • How the skin grows and heals

VOCABULARY

integumentary system p. 83

epidermis p. 84

dermis p. 84

EXPLORE The Skin

What are the functions of skin?

PROCEDURE

① Using a vegetable peeler, remove the skin from an apple. Take notes on the characteristics of the apple's peeled surface. Include observations on its color, moisture level, and texture.

② Place the apple on a dry surface. After fifteen minutes, note any changes in its characteristics.

WHAT DO YOU THINK?

• What is the function of an apple's skin? What does it prevent?

• What does this experiment suggest about how skin might function in the human body?

MATERIALS

• vegetable peeler

• apple

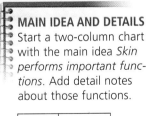

MAIN IDEA AND DETAILS Start a two-column chart with the main idea *Skin performs important functions*. Add detail notes about those functions.

Skin performs important functions.

Just as an apple's skin protects the fruit inside, your skin protects the rest of your body. Made up of flat sheets of cells, your skin protects the inside of your body from harmful materials outside. The skin is part of your body's **integumentary system** (ihn-TEHG-yu-MEHN-tuh-ree), which also includes your hair and nails.

Your skin fulfills several vital functions:

• Skin repels water.

• Skin guards against infection.

• Skin helps maintain homeostasis.

• Skin senses the environment.

When you look at your hand, you only see the outer layer of skin. The skin has many structures to protect your body.

sensory receptor

nerve

oil gland

pores

Epidermis: tough, protective outer layer

Dermis: strong, elastic inner layer

Fatty tissue: temperature protection and energy storage

hair

blood vessels

muscle

sweat gland

The structure of skin is complex.

Have you ever looked closely at your skin? Your skin is more complex than it might at first seem. It does more than just cover your body. The skin is made up of many structures, which perform many different jobs.

Dermis and Epidermis

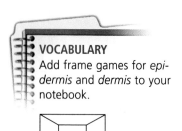

VOCABULARY
Add frame games for *epidermis* and *dermis* to your notebook.

As you can see in the diagram above, human skin is composed of two layers: an outer layer, called the **epidermis,** and an inner layer, called the **dermis.** The cells of the epidermis contain many protein fibers that give the skin tough, protective qualities. These cells are formed in the deepest part of the epidermis. Skin cells move upward slowly as new cells form below them. Above new cells, older cells rub off. The surface cells in the epidermis are dead but form a thick, waterproof layer about 30 cells deep.

The dermis, the inner layer of skin, is made of tissue that is strong and elastic. The structure of the dermis allows it to change shape instead of tear when it moves against surfaces. The dermis is rich in blood vessels, which supply oxygen and nutrients to the skin's living cells. Just beneath the dermis lies a layer of fatty tissue. This layer protects the body from extremes in temperature, and it stores energy for future use. Also in the dermis are structures that have special functions, including sweat and oil glands, hair, nails, and sensory receptors.

Sweat and Oil Glands

Deep within the dermis are structures that help maintain your body's internal environment. Sweat glands help control body temperature, and oil glands protect the skin by keeping it moist. Both types of glands open to the surface through tiny openings in the skin called pores. Pores allow important substances to pass to the skin's surface. Pores can become clogged with dirt and oil. Keeping the skin clean can prevent blockages.

Sweat glands, which are present almost everywhere on the body's surface, help maintain homeostasis. When you become too warm, the sweat glands secrete sweat, a fluid that is 99% water. This fluid travels from the sweat glands, through the pores, and onto the skin's surface. You probably know already about evaporation. Evaporation is the process by which a liquid becomes a gas. During evaporation, heat is released. Thus, sweating cools the skin's surface and the body.

Like sweat glands, oil glands are present almost everywhere on the body. They secrete an oil that moistens skin and hair and keeps them from becoming dry. Skin oils add flexibility and provide part, but not all, of the skin's waterproofing.

RESOURCE CENTER
CLASSZONE.COM

Explore the structure of skin.

 CHECK YOUR READING What are the functions of oil glands?

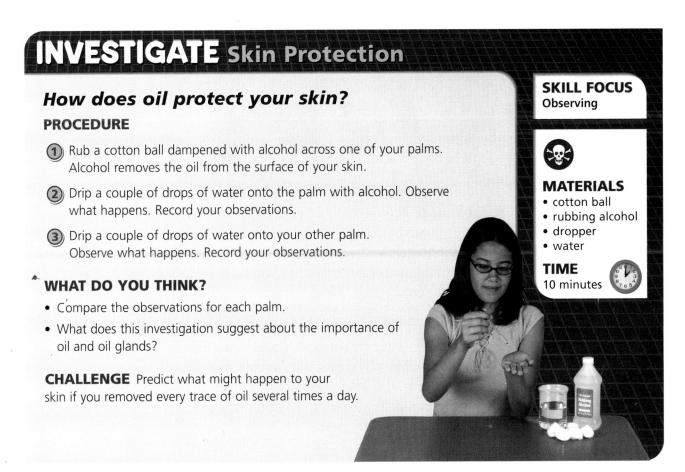

INVESTIGATE Skin Protection

How does oil protect your skin?

PROCEDURE

1. Rub a cotton ball dampened with alcohol across one of your palms. Alcohol removes the oil from the surface of your skin.

2. Drip a couple of drops of water onto the palm with alcohol. Observe what happens. Record your observations.

3. Drip a couple of drops of water onto your other palm. Observe what happens. Record your observations.

WHAT DO YOU THINK?

- Compare the observations for each palm.
- What does this investigation suggest about the importance of oil and oil glands?

CHALLENGE Predict what might happen to your skin if you removed every trace of oil several times a day.

SKILL FOCUS
Observing

MATERIALS
- cotton ball
- rubbing alcohol
- dropper
- water

TIME
10 minutes

Hair and Nails

In addition to your skin, your integumentary system includes your hair and nails. Many cells in your hair and nails are actually dead but continue to perform important functions.

The hair on your head helps your body in many ways. When you are outside, it shields your head from the Sun. In cold weather, it traps heat close to your head to keep you warmer. Your body hair works the same way, but it is much less effective at protecting your skin and keeping you warm.

Fingernails and toenails protect the tips of the fingers and toes from injury. Both are made of epidermal cells that are thick and tough. They grow from the nail bed, which continues to manufacture cells as the cells that form the nail bed bond together and grow.

○ **CHECK YOUR READING** What are the functions of hair and nails?

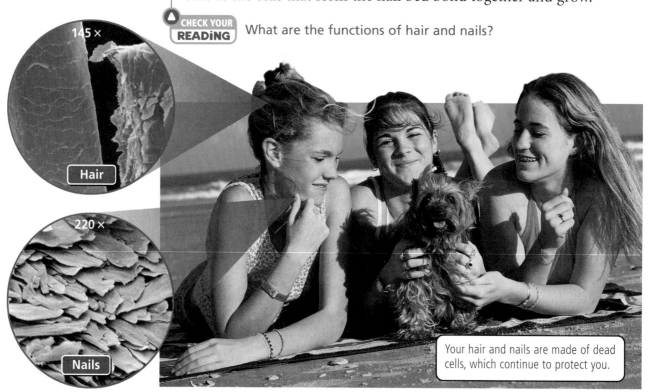

145 ×

Hair

220 ×

Nails

Your hair and nails are made of dead cells, which continue to protect you.

Sensory Receptors

How does your body know when you are touching something too hot or too cold? You get that information from sensory receptors attached to the nerves. These receptors are actually part of the nervous system, but they are located in your skin. Your skin contains receptors that sense temperature, pain, touch, and vibration. These sensors help protect the body. For example, temperature receptors sense when an object is hot. If it is too hot and you touch it, pain receptors send signals to your brain telling you that you have been burned.

○ **CHECK YOUR READING** What are the five types of sensory receptors in skin?

The skin grows and heals.

As a person grows, skin also grows. As you have noticed if you have ever had a bruise or a cut, your skin is capable of healing. Skin can often repair itself after injury or illness.

Growth

As your bones grow, you get taller. As your muscles develop, your arms and legs become thicker. Through all your body's growth and change, your skin has to grow, too.

Most of the growth of your skin occurs at the base of the epidermis, just above the dermis. The cells there grow and divide to form new cells, constantly replacing older epidermal cells as they die and are brushed off during daily activity. Cells are lost from the skin's surface all the time: every 2 to 4 weeks, your skin surface is entirely new. In fact, a percentage of household dust is actually dead skin cells.

Healing Skin

Small injuries to the skin heal by themselves over time.

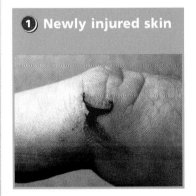

1 Newly injured skin

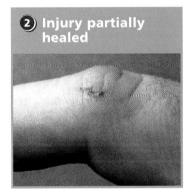

2 Injury partially healed

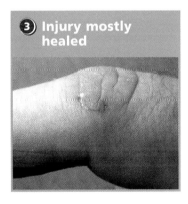

3 Injury mostly healed

READING VISUALS How do you think small injuries to the skin heal?

Injuries and Healing

You have probably experienced some injuries to your skin, such as blisters, burns, cuts, and bruises. Most such injuries result from the skin's contact with the outside world, such as a concrete sidewalk. In simple injuries, the skin can usually repair itself.

Burns can be serious injuries. They can be caused by heat, electricity, radiation, or certain chemicals. In mild cases—those of first-degree burns—skin merely becomes red, and the burn heals in a day or two. In severe cases—those of second-degree and third-degree burns—the body loses fluids, and death can result from fluid loss, infection, and other complications.

VISUALIZATION
CLASSZONE.COM

Explore how the skin heals.

Sunburns are usually minor first-degree burns, but that does not mean they cannot be serious. Rays from the Sun can burn and blister the skin much as a hot object can. Repeated burning can increase the chance of skin cancer. Specialized cells in the skin make a pigment that absorbs the Sun's ultraviolet rays and helps prevent tissue damage. These cells produce more of the skin pigment melanin when exposed to the Sun. The amount of melanin in your skin determines how dark your skin is.

Severe cold can damage skin as well. Skin exposed to cold weather can get frostbite, a condition in which the cells are damaged by freezing. Mild frostbite often heals just as well as a minor cut. In extreme cases, frostbitten limbs become diseased and have to be amputated.

 CHECK YOUR READING What types of weather can damage your skin?

Protection

Your skin is constantly losing old cells and gaining new cells. Although your skin is always changing, it is still important to take care of it.

- Good nutrition supplies materials the skin uses to maintain and repair itself. By drinking water, you help your body, and thus your skin, to remain moist and able to replace lost cells.

- Appropriate coverings, such as sunblock in summer and warm clothes in winter, can protect the skin from weather damage.

- Skin also needs to be kept clean. Many harmful bacteria cannot enter the body through healthy skin, but they should be washed off regularly. This prevents them from multiplying and then entering the body through small cuts or scrapes.

Wearing sunblock when you are outside protects your skin from harmful rays from the Sun.

3.3 Review

KEY CONCEPTS

1. List four functions of the skin.
2. How do the epidermis and dermis protect the body?
3. Make your own diagram with *How skin grows and repairs itself* at the center. Around the center, write at least five facts about skin growth and healing.

CRITICAL THINKING

4. **Apply** Give three examples from everyday life of sensory receptors in your skin reacting to changes in your environment.
5. **Connect** Describe a situation in which sensory receptors could be critical to survival.

CHALLENGE

6. **Infer** Exposure to sunlight may increase the number of freckles on a person's skin. Explain the connection between sunlight, melanin, and freckles.

EXTREME SCIENCE

Artificial Skin

Skin acts like a barrier, keeping our insides in and infections out. Nobody can survive without skin. But when a large amount of skin is severely damaged, the body cannot work fast enough to replace it. In some cases there isn't enough undamaged skin left on the body for transplanting. Using skin from another person risks introducing infections or rejection by the body. The answer? Artificial skin.

Here's the Skinny

To make artificial skin, scientists start with cells in a tiny skin sample. Cells from infants are used because infant skin-cell molecules are still developing, and scientists can manipulate the molecules to avoid transplant rejection. The cells from just one small sample of skin can be grown into enough artificial skin to cover 15 basketball courts. Before artificial skin, badly burned victims didn't have much chance to live. Today, 96 out of 100 burn victims survive.

A surgeon lifts a layer of artificial skin. The skin is so thin, a newspaper could be read behind it.

What's Next?

- Scientists are hoping to be able to grow organs using this technology. Someday artificially grown livers, kidneys, and hearts may take the place of transplants and mechanical devices.

- A self-repairing plastic skin that knits itself back together when cracked has been developed. It may someday be used to create organs or even self-repairing rocket and spacecraft parts.

- Artificial polymer "skin" for robots is being developed to help robots do delicate work such as microsurgery or space exploration.

Robot designer David Hanson has developed the K-bot, a lifelike face that uses 24 motors to create expressions.

EXPLORE

1. **COMPARE AND CONTRAST** Detail the advantages and disadvantages of skin transplanted from another place on the body and artificial skin.

2. **CHALLENGE** Artificial skin is being considered for applications beyond those originally envisioned. Research and present a new potential application.

A spray-on polymer creates an artificial outer skin to help heal surface wounds on an arm.

the **BIG** idea

Systems function to transport materials and to defend and protect the body.

CONTENT REVIEW
CLASSZONE.COM

◀ KEY CONCEPTS SUMMARY

3.1 ## The circulatory system transports materials.

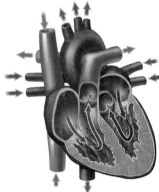

The heart, blood vessels, and blood of the circulatory system work together to transport materials from the digestive and respiratory systems to all cells. The blood exerts pressure on the walls of the blood vessels and keeps the blood moving around the body.

VOCABULARY
circulatory system
  p. 65
blood p. 65
red blood cell p. 67
artery p. 69
vein p. 69
capillary p. 69

3.2 ## The immune system defends the body.

The immune system defends the body from pathogens. White blood cells identify and attack pathogens that find their way inside the body. The immune system responds to attack with inflammation, fever, and development of immunity.

Types of Pathogens	
Disease	**Pathogen**
colds, chicken pox, hepatitis, AIDS, influenza, mumps, measles, rabies	virus
food poisoning, strep throat, tetanus, tuberculosis, acne, ulcers, Lyme disease	bacteria
athlete's foot, thrush, ring worm	fungus
malaria, parasitic pneumonia, pinworm, lice, scabies	parasites

VOCABULARY
pathogen p. 74
immune system p. 75
antibody p. 75
antigen p. 78
immunity p. 80
vaccine p. 80
antibiotic p. 81

3.3 ## The integumentary system shields the body.

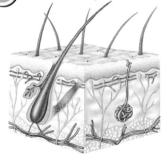

The skin protects the body from harmful materials in the environment, and allows you to sense temperature, pain, touch, and vibration. In most cases the skin is able to heal itself after injury.

VOCABULARY
integumentary system
  p. 83
epidermis p. 84
dermis p. 84

Draw a word triangle for each of the terms below. Write a term and its definition in the bottom section. In the middle section, write a sentence in which you use the term correctly. In the top section, draw a small picture to illustrate the term.

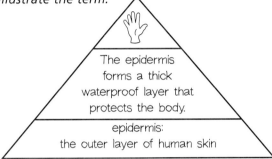

The epidermis forms a thick waterproof layer that protects the body.

epidermis: the outer layer of human skin

1. capillary

2. blood

3. dermis

4. antigen

Write a sentence describing the relationship between each pair of terms.

5. pathogen, antibody

6. artery, vein

7. immunity, vaccine

Reviewing Key Concepts

Multiple Choice *Choose the letter of the best answer.*

8. Which chamber of the heart pumps oxygen-poor blood into the lungs?
   a. right atrium
   b. right ventricle
   c. left atrium
   d. left ventricle

9. Which blood structures carry blood back to the heart?
   a. veins
   b. capillaries
   c. arteries
   d. platelets

10. The structures in the blood that carry oxygen to the cells of the body are the
   a. plasma
   b. platelets
   c. white blood cells
   d. red blood cells

11. High blood pressure is unhealthy because it
   a. does not exert enough pressure on your arteries
   b. causes your heart to work harder
   c. does not allow enough oxygen to get to the cells in your body
   d. causes your veins to collapse

12. Which category of pathogens causes strep throat?
   a. virus
   b. bacteria
   c. fungus
   d. parasite

13. Which of the following is a function of white blood cells?
   a. destroying foreign organisms
   b. providing your body with nutrients
   c. carrying oxygen to the body's cells
   d. forming a blood clot

14. Which makes up the integumentary system?
   a. a network of nerves
   b. white blood cells and antibodies
   c. the brain and spinal cord
   d. the skin, hair, and nails

15. Which structure is found in the epidermis layer of the skin?
   a. pores
   b. sweat glands
   c. surface cells
   d. oil glands

16. The layer of fatty tissue below the dermis protects the body from
   a. cold temperatures
   b. bacteria
   c. sunburn
   d. infection

Short Answer *Write a short answer to each question.*

17. What are platelets? Where are they found?

18. What are antibodies? Where are they found?

19. What special structures are found in the dermis layer of the skin?

20. COMPARE AND CONTRAST How do the functions of the atria and ventricles of the heart differ? How are they alike? Use this diagram of the heart as a guide.

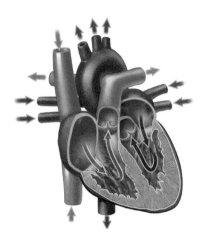

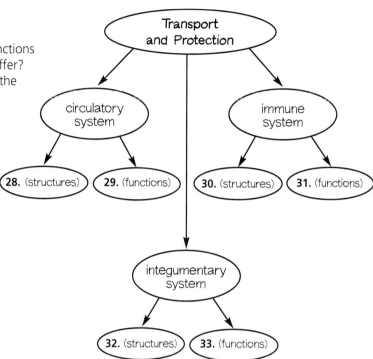

21. APPLY Veins have one-way valves that push the blood back to the heart. Most arteries do not have valves. Explain how these structures help the circulatory system function.

22. PROVIDE EXAMPLES Describe three structures in the body that help prevent harmful foreign substances from entering the body.

23. IDENTIFY CAUSE HIV is a virus that attacks and destroys the body's T cells. Why is a person who is infected with the HIV virus more susceptible to infection and disease?

24. APPLY You fall and scrape your knee. How does the production of histamines aid the healing of this injury?

25. ANALYZE Describe how the structure of the epidermis helps protect the body from disease.

25. SYNTHESIZE Explain how sweat glands, oil glands, and hair help your body maintain homeostasis.

27. HYPOTHESIZE People with greater concentrations of melanin in their skin are less likely to get skin cancer than people who have lesser concentrations of melanin. Write a hypothesis explaining why this is so.

the BIG idea

34. INFER Look again at the picture on pages 62–63. Now that you have finished the chapter, how would you change or add details to your answer to the question on the photograph?

35. SYNTHESIZE Write a paragraph explaining how the integumentary system and the immune system work together to help your body maintain its homeostasis. Underline these terms in your paragraph.

UNIT PROJECTS

If you need to create graphs or other visuals for your project, be sure you have grid paper, poster board, markers, and other supplies.

Analyzing Data

Choose the letter of the best answer.

This chart shows the amount of time a person can stay in the sun without burning, based on skin type and use of a sunscreen with the SPF shown.

Recommended Sun Protection Factors (SPF)					
Skin Type	**1 hr**	**2hr**	**3 hr**	**4hr**	**5hr**
Very Fair/Sensitive	15	30	30	45	45
Fair/Sensitive	15	15	30	30	45
Fair	15	15	15	30	30
Medium	8	8	15	15	30
Dark	4	8	8	15	15

1. What is the least SPF that a person with very fair skin should use while exposed to the sun?

  a. 8
  b. 15
  c. 30
  d. 45

2. If a person with a medium skin type is exposed to the sun for 5 hours, which SPF should be used?

  a. 4
  b. 8
  c. 15
  d. 30

3. Which skin type requires SPF 30 for three hours of sun exposure?

  a. fair/sensitive   **c.** medium
  b. fair   **d.** dark

4. Based on the data in the chart, which statement is a reasonable conclusion?

  a. People with a fair skin type are less prone to UV damage than those with a dark skin type.

  b. The darker the skin type, the more SPF protection a person needs.

  c. A person with a medium skin type does not need as much SPF protection as a person with a fair skin type.

  d. If exposure to the sun is longer, then a person needs a higher SPF for protection.

5. If a person normally burns after 10 minutes with no protection, an SPF 2 would protect that person for 20 minutes. How long would the same person be protected with SPF 15?

  a. 1 hour

  b. $1\frac{1}{2}$ hours

  c. 2 hours

  d. $2\frac{1}{2}$ hours

Extended Response

6. UV index levels are often broadcast with daily weather reports. A UV index of 0 to 2 indicates that it would take an average person about 60 minutes to burn. A UV index level of 10 indicates that it would take the average person about 10 minutes to burn. Write a paragraph describing some variable conditions that would affect this rate. Include both environmental as well as conditions that would apply to an individual.

7. Sun protection factors are numbers on a scale that rate the effectiveness of sunscreen. Without the use of sunscreen, UV rays from the Sun can cause sunburns. People who spend time in the sun without protection, or who get repeated burns are at a higher risk of developing deadly forms of skin cancer. Based on the information in the table and your knowledge of the layers of the skin, design a brochure encouraging people to protect their skin from the sun. Include in your brochure the harmful effects on your skin and ways to protect your skin from harmful UV rays.

SEEING INSIDE the Body

What began as a chance accident in a darkened room was only the beginning. Today, technology allows people to produce clear and complete pictures of the human body. From X-rays to ultrasound to the latest computerized scans, accidental discoveries have enabled us to study and diagnose the inner workings of the human body.

Being able to see inside the body without cutting it open would have seemed unthinkable in the early 1890s. But within a year of the discovery of the X-ray in 1895, doctors were using technology to see through flesh to bones. In the time since then, techniques for making images have advanced to allow doctors to see soft tissue, muscle, and even to see how body systems work in real time. Many modern imaging techniques employ X-ray technology, while others employ sound waves or magnetic fields.

1895

Accidental X-Ray Shows Bones

Working alone in a darkened lab to study electric currents passing through vacuum tubes, William Conrad Roentgen sees a mysterious light. He puts his hand between the tubes and a screen, and an image appears on the screen—a skeletal hand! He names his discovery the X-ray, since the images are produced by rays behaving like none known before them. Roentgen uses photographic paper to take the first X-ray picture, his wife's hand.

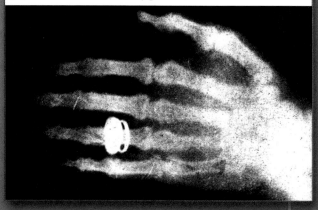

EVENTS

1880   1890

APPLICATIONS AND TECHNOLOGY

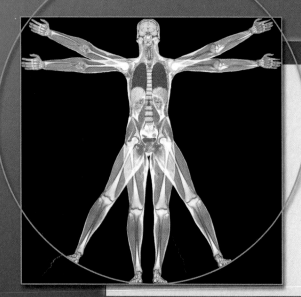

APPLICATION

Doctor Detectives

Within a year of Roentgen's discovery, X-rays were used in medicine for examining patients. By the 1920s, their use was wide-spread. Modern day X-ray tubes are based on the design of William Coolidge. Around 1913, Coolidge developed a new X-ray tube which, unlike the old gas tube, provides consistent exposure and quality. X-ray imaging changed the practice of medicine by allowing doctors to look inside the body without using surgery. Today, X-ray images, and other technologies, like the MRI used to produce the image at the left, show bones, organs, and tissues.

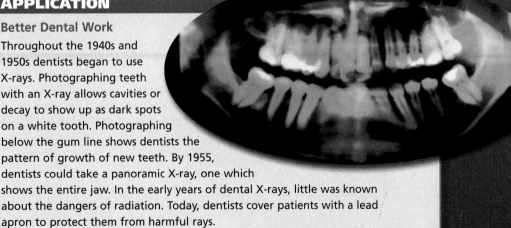

1914–1918

Radiologists in the Trenches

In World War I field hospitals, French physicians use X-ray technology to quickly diagnose war injuries. Marie Curie trains the majority of the female X-ray technicians. Following the War, doctors return to their practices with new expertise.

1898

Radioactivity

Building on the work of Henri Becquerel, who in 1897 discovers "rays" from uranium, physicist, Marie Curie discovers radioactivity. She wins a Nobel Prize in Chemistry in 1911 for her work in radiology.

1955

See-Through Smile

X-ray images of the entire jaw and teeth allow dentist to check the roots of teeth and wisdom teeth growing below the gum line.

1900   1910   1950

APPLICATION

Better Dental Work

Throughout the 1940s and 1950s dentists began to use X-rays. Photographing teeth with an X-ray allows cavities or decay to show up as dark spots on a white tooth. Photographing below the gum line shows dentists the pattern of growth of new teeth. By 1955, dentists could take a panoramic X-ray, one which shows the entire jaw. In the early years of dental X-rays, little was known about the dangers of radiation. Today, dentists cover patients with a lead apron to protect them from harmful rays.

1976

New Scans Show Blood Vessels

The first computerized tomography (CT) systems scan only the head, but whole-body scanners follow by 1976. With the CT scan, doctors see clear details of blood vessels, bones, and soft organs. Instead of sending out a single X-ray, a CT scan sends several beams from different angles. Then a computer joins the images, as shown in this image of a heart.

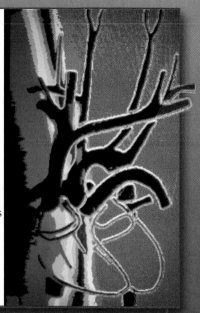

1977

Minus the Radiation

Doctors Raymond Damadian, Larry Minkoff, and Michael Goldsmith, develop the first magnetic resonance imaging (MRI). They nick-name the new machine "The Indomitable," as everyone told them it couldn't be done. MRI allows doctors to "see" soft tissue, like the knee below, in sharp detail without the use of radiation.

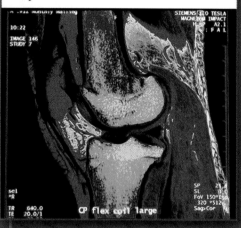

1973

PET Shows What's Working

The first positron emission tomography machine is called PET Scanner 1. It uses small doses of radioactive dye which travel through a patient's bloodstream. A PET scan then shows the distribution of the dye.

1960   **1970**   **1980**

TECHNOLOGY

Ultrasound: Moving Images in Real Time

Since the late 1950s, Ian Donald's team in Scotland had been viewing internal organs on a TV monitor using vibrations faster than sound. In 1961, while examining a female patient, Donald noticed a developing embryo. Following the discovery, ultrasound imaging became widely used to monitor the growth and health of fetuses. Ultrasound captures images in real-time, show-ing movement of internal tissues and organs. Ultrasound uses high frequency sound waves to create images of organs or structures inside the body. Sound waves are bounced back from organs, and a computer converts the sound waves into moving images on a television monitor.

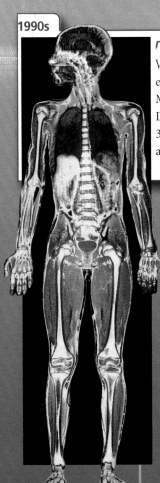

Filmless Images

With digital imaging, everything from X-rays to MRIs is now filmless. Data moves directly into 3D computer programs and shared databases.

2003

Multi-Slice CT

By 2003, 8- and 16-slice CT scanners offer detail and speed. A multi-slice scanner reduces exam time from 45 minutes to under 10 seconds.

 RESOURCE CENTER
CLASSZONE.COM

Find more on advances in medical imaging.

1990   **2000**

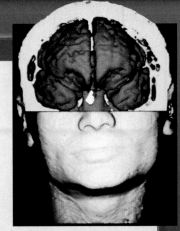

TECHNOLOGY

3-D Images and Brain Surgery

In operating rooms, surgeons are beginning to use another type of 3D ultrasound known as interventional MRI. They watch 3-D images in real time and observe details of tissues while they operate. These integrated technologies now allow scientists to conduct entirely new types of studies. For example, 3-D brain images of many patients with one disease—can now be integrated into a composite image of a "typical" brain of someone with that disease.

INTO THE FUTURE

Although discovered over 100 years ago X-rays are certain to remain a key tool of health workers for many years. What will be different in the future? Dentists have begun the trend to stop using film images, and rely on digital X-rays instead. In the future, all scans may be viewed and stored on computers. Going digital allows doctors across the globe to share images quickly by email.

Magnetic resonance imaging has only been in widespread use for about 20 years. Look for increased brain mapping—ability to scan the brain during a certain task. The greater the collective data on brain-mapping, the better scientists will understand how the brain works. To produce such an image requires thousands of patients and trillions of bytes of computer memory.

Also look for increased speed and mobile MRI scanners, which will be used in emergency rooms and doctor's offices to quickly assess internal damage after an accident or injury.

ACTIVITIES

Writing About Science: Brochure

Make a chart of the different types of medical imaging used to diagnose one body system. Include an explanation of how the technique works and list the pros and cons of using it.

Reliving History

X-rays use radioactivity which can be dangerous. You can use visible light to shine through thin materials that you don't normally see through. Try using a flashlight to illuminate a leaf. Discuss or draw what you see.

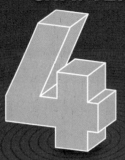

Control and Reproduction

the BIG idea

The nervous and endocrine systems allow the body to respond to internal and external conditions.

Key Concepts

SECTION 4.1
The nervous system responds and controls.
Learn how the senses help the body get information about the environment.

SECTION 4.2
The endocrine system helps regulate body conditions.
Learn the functions of different hormones.

SECTION 4.3
The reproductive system allows the production of offspring.
Learn about the process of reproduction.

Internet Preview

CLASSZONE.COM

Chapter 4 online resources: Content Review, Visualization, three Resource Centers, Math Tutorial, Test Practice

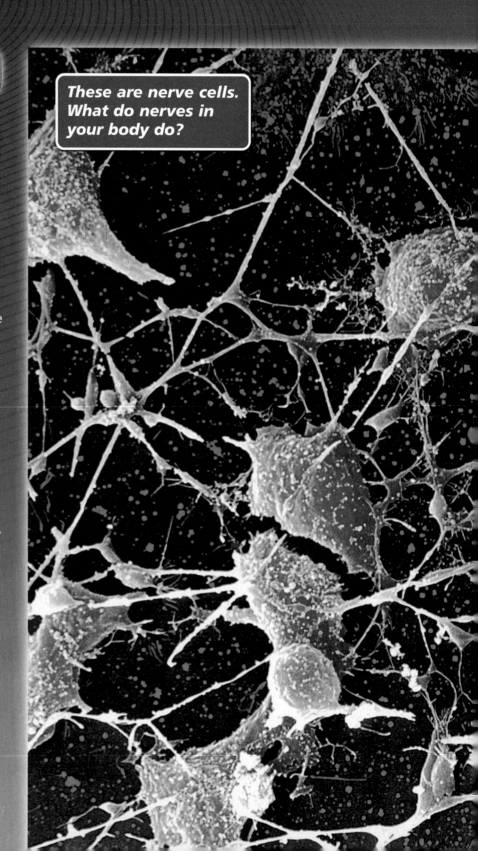

These are nerve cells. What do nerves in your body do?

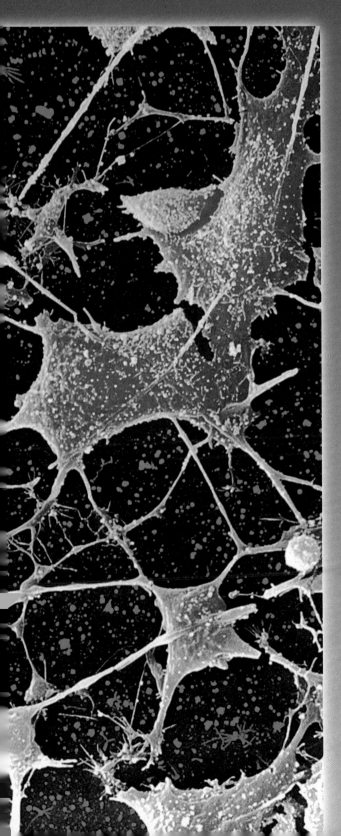

EXPLORE the BIG idea

Color Confusion

Make a list of six colors using a different color marker or colored pencil to write each one. Make sure not to write the color name with the same color marker or pencil. Read the list out loud as fast as you can. Now try quickly saying the color of each word out loud.

Observe and Think Did you notice a difference between reading the words in the list and saying the colors? If so, why do you think that is?

Eggs

Examine a raw chicken egg. Describe the appearance of the outside shell. Break it open into a small dish and note the different parts inside. Wash your hands when you have finished.

Observe and Think If this egg had been fertilized, which part do you think would have served as the food for the growing chicken embryo? Which part would protect the embryo from impact and serve to cushion it?

Internet Activity: The Senses

Go to **ClassZone.com** to learn how the senses allow the body to respond to external conditions. See how each sense sends specific information to the brain.

Observe and Think How do the different senses interact with one another?

NSTA
scilinks.org

SCI
LINKS

Reproductive System **Code: MDL047**

Getting Ready to Learn

CONCEPT REVIEW

- The circulatory system transports materials.
- The immune system responds to foreign materials.
- The integumentary system protects the body.

VOCABULARY REVIEW

homeostasis p. 12

circulatory system p. 65

immune system p. 75

integumentary system p. 83

 CONTENT REVIEW
CLASSZONE.COM
Review concepts and vocabulary.

TAKING NOTES

CHOOSE YOUR OWN STRATEGY

Take notes using one or more of the strategies from earlier chapters—**main idea webs, outlines,** or **main idea and detail notes.** You can also use other note-taking strategies that you might already know.

VOCABULARY STRATEGY

Place each vocabulary term at the center of a **description wheel** diagram. Write some words describing it on the spokes.

See the Note-Taking Handbook on pages R45–R51.

SCIENCE NOTEBOOK

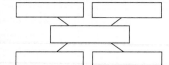
Main Idea Web

Main Idea and Detail Notes

Outline
I. Main Idea
   A. Supporting idea
      1. Detail
      2. Detail
   B. Supporting idea

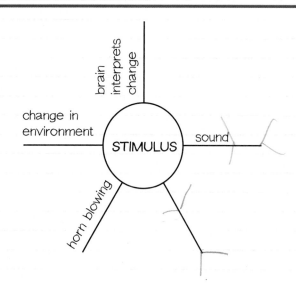

The nervous system responds and controls.

 BEFORE, you learned

- The body can respond to the presence of foreign materials
- The body is defended from harmful materials
- The immune system responds to pathogens in many ways

▶ **NOW, you will learn**

- How the body's senses help monitor the environment
- How the sensory organs respond to stimuli
- How the nervous system works with other body systems

VOCABULARY

stimulus p. 102
central nervous system
  p. 104
neuron p. 105
peripheral nervous
  system p. 106
autonomic nervous
system p. 107
voluntary nervous system
  p. 107

EXPLORE Smell

Can you name the scent?

PROCEDURE

① With a small group, take turns smelling the 3 mystery bags given to you by your teacher.

② In your notebook, write down what you think is inside each bag without showing the people in your group.

③ Compare your answers with those in your group and then look inside the bags.

MATERIALS
three small
paper bags

WHAT DO YOU THINK?
- Did you know what was in the bags before looking inside? If so, how did you know?
- What are some objects that would require more than a sense of smell to identify?

Senses connect the human body to its environment.

CHOOSE YOUR OWN STRATEGY
Use a strategy from an earlier chapter to take notes on the main idea. *Senses connect the human body to its environment.*

To maintain homeostasis and to survive, your body must constantly monitor the environment in which you live. This involves organs that interact so closely with the nervous system that they are often considered extensions of the nervous system. These are your sense organs. They give you the ability to see, smell, touch, hear, and taste.

Each of the senses can detect a specific type of change in the environment. For example, if you have begun to cross the street but suddenly hear a horn blowing, you may stop and step back onto the curb. Your sense of hearing allowed your brain to perceive that a car was coming and thus helped you to protect yourself.

The sound of the horn is a **stimulus.** A stimulus is a change in your environment that you react to, such as a smell, taste, sound, feeling, or sight. Your brain interprets any such change. If it did not, the information perceived by the senses would be meaningless.

Sight

If you have ever tried to find your way in the dark, you know how important light is for seeing. Light is a stimulus. You are able to detect it because your eyes, the sense organs of sight, capture light and help turn it into an image, which is processed by the brain.

Light enters the eye through the lens, a structure made of transparent tissue. Muscles surrounding the lens change its shape so the lens focuses light. Other muscles control the amount of light that enters the eye by altering the size of the pupil, a dark circle in the center of the eye. To reduce the amount of light, the area around the pupil, called the iris, contracts, making the pupil smaller, thus allowing less light to enter. When the iris relaxes, more light can enter the eye.

At the back of the eye, the light strikes a layer called the retina. Among the many cells of the retina are two types of receptors, called rods and cones. Rods detect changes in brightness, while cones are sensitive to color.

Sight

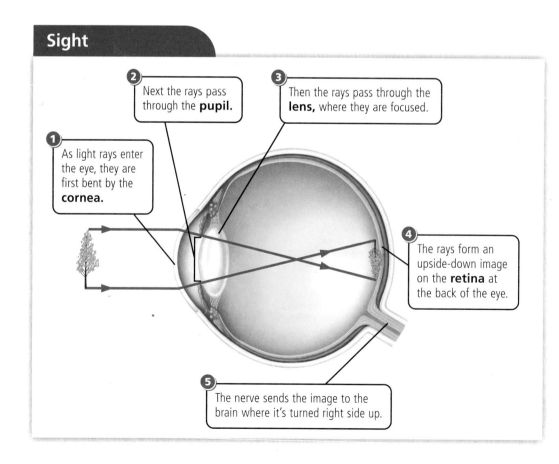

2 Next the rays pass through the **pupil.**

3 Then the rays pass through the **lens,** where they are focused.

1 As light rays enter the eye, they are first bent by the **cornea.**

4 The rays form an upside-down image on the **retina** at the back of the eye.

5 The nerve sends the image to the brain where it's turned right side up.

Hearing

Your eyes perceive light waves, but your ears perceive and interpret a different type of stimulus, sound waves. Sound waves are produced by vibrations. A reed on a clarinet vibrates, and so do your vocal cords. So does a bell after it has been hit by a mallet. The motion causes changes in the air that surrounds the bell. These changes can often be processed by the ear as sound, although many vibrations are too low or high to be heard by humans.

Sound waves enter the ear and are funneled into the auditory canal, a tube-shaped structure that ends at the eardrum. The eardrum vibrates when the sound waves strike it, and it transmits some of the vibrations to a tiny bone called the stirrup. Pressure caused by vibrations from the stirrup causes fluid in the ear to move. The movement of the fluid sends signals to the brain that are interpreted as sound.

 CHECK YOUR READING How are vibrations involved in hearing?

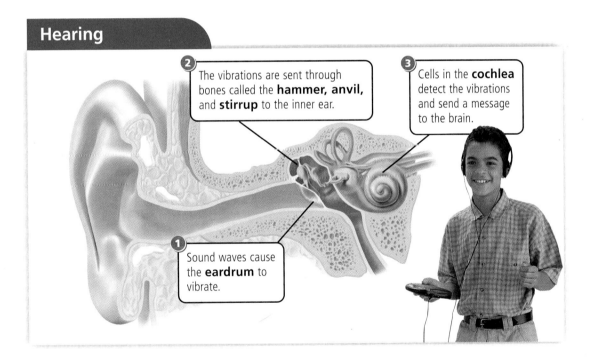

Hearing

2 The vibrations are sent through bones called the **hammer, anvil,** and **stirrup** to the inner ear.

3 Cells in the **cochlea** detect the vibrations and send a message to the brain.

1 Sound waves cause the **eardrum** to vibrate.

Touch

The sense of touch depends on tiny sensory receptors in the skin. Without these you wouldn't be able to feel pressure, temperature, or pain. Nerves in the outer layer of your skin, or epidermis, sense textures, like smooth glass or rough concrete. Nerves deeper in the skin, in the dermis, sense pressure. Receptors also sense how hot or cold an object is and can thus help protect you from burning yourself. The sense of touch is important in alerting your brain to danger. Though you might wish that you couldn't feel pain, it serves a critical purpose. Without it, you could harm your body without realizing it.

Smell

Whereas sight, touch, and hearing involve processing physical information from the environment, the senses of smell and taste involve processing chemical information. Much as taste receptors sense chemicals in food, smelling receptors sense chemicals in the air. High in the back of your nose, a patch of tissue grows hairlike fibers covered in mucus. Scent molecules enter your nose, stick to the mucus, and then bind to receptors in the hairlike fibers. The receptors send an impulse to your brain, and you smell the scent.

Taste

Your tongue is covered with small sensory structures called taste buds, which are also found in the throat and on the roof of the mouth. Each taste bud includes about 100 sensory cells that are specialized to detect sweet, sour, bittter, and salty. The thousands of tastes you experience are due to sense organs in your nose. When you have a cold, your ability to taste decreases.

Taste

Taste receptors on the tongue sense four types of taste: sweet, bitter, sour, and salty.

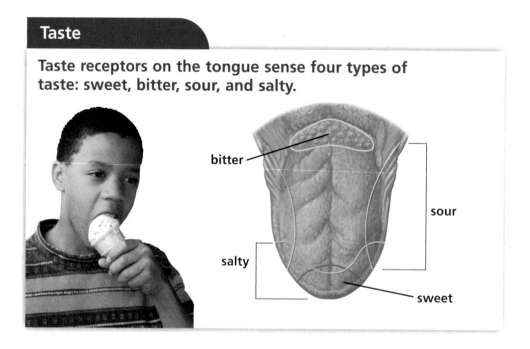

bitter

sour

salty

sweet

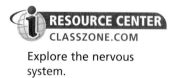

RESOURCE CENTER
CLASSZONE.COM

Explore the nervous system.

The central nervous system controls functions.

The **central nervous system** consists of the brain and spinal cord. The brain is located in and protected by the skull, and the spinal cord is located in and protected by the spine. The central nervous system communicates with the rest of the nervous system through electrical signals sent to and from neurons. Impulses travel very quickly, some as fast as 90 meters (295 ft) per second. That's like running almost the entire length of a soccer field in one second!

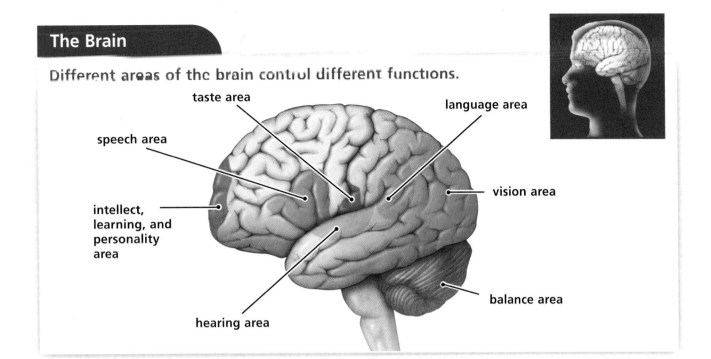

Different areas of the brain control different functions.

taste area

language area

speech area

vision area

intellect,
learning, and
personality
area

balance area

hearing area

Brain

The average adult brain contains nearly 100 billion nerve cells, called **neurons.** The brain directly controls voluntary behavior, such as walking and thinking. It also allows the body to control most involuntary responses such as heartbeat, blood pressure, fluid balance, and posture.

As you can see in the diagram, every area of the brain has a specific function, although many functions may involve more than one area. For example, certain areas in the brain control the senses, while other areas help you stand up straight. The lower part of the brain, called the brain stem, controls activities such as breathing and vomiting.

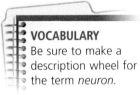

VOCABULARY
Be sure to make a description wheel for the term *neuron*.

Spinal Cord

The spinal cord is about 44 centimeters (17 in.) long and weighs about 35–40 grams (1.25–1.4 oz). It is the main pathway for information, connecting the brain and the nerves throughout your body. The spinal cord is protected and supported by the vertebral column, which is made up of small bones called vertebrae. The spinal cord itself is a double-layered tube with an outer layer of nerve fibers wrapped in tissue, an inner layer of nerve cell bodies, and a central canal that runs the entire length of the cord. Connected to the spinal cord are 31 pairs of nerves, which send sensory impulses into the spinal cord, which in turn sends them to the brain. In a similar way, spinal nerves send impulses to muscles and glands.

 CHECK YOUR READING Describe the functions performed by the central nervous system.

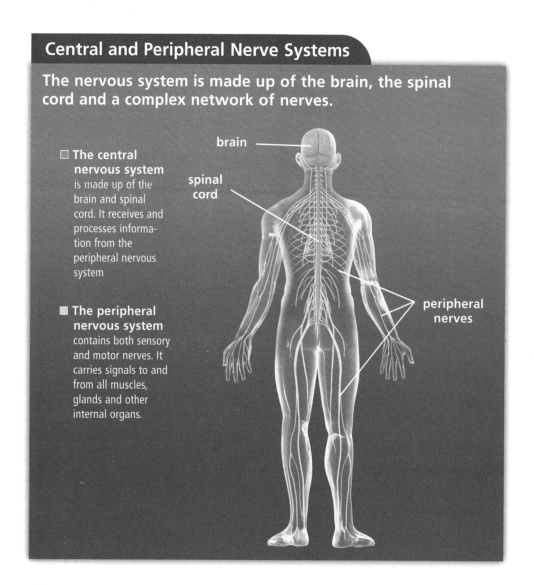

Central and Peripheral Nerve Systems

The nervous system is made up of the brain, the spinal cord and a complex network of nerves.

☐ **The central nervous system** is made up of the brain and spinal cord. It receives and processes information from the peripheral nervous system

■ **The peripheral nervous system** contains both sensory and motor nerves. It carries signals to and from all muscles, glands and other internal organs.

brain

spinal cord

peripheral nerves

The peripheral nervous system is a network of nerves.

Nerves, which are found throughout the body, are often referred to all together as the **peripheral nervous system.** Both sensory and motor nerves are parts of the peripheral nervous system. Sensory nerves receive information from the environment—such as heat or cold—and pass the information to the central nervous system. Motor nerves send signals to your muscles that allow you to move. The peripheral nervous system includes both voluntary motor nerves and involuntary responses.

Another type of motor nerves controls the involuntary responses of the body. In times of danger, there is no time to think. The body must respond immediately. In less stressful situations, the body maintains activities like breathing and digesting food. These functions go on without conscious thought. They are controlled by part of the peripheral nervous system called the autonomic (AW-tuh-NAHM-ihk) nervous system.

The **autonomic nervous system** controls the movement of the heart, the smooth muscles in the stomach, the intestines, and the glands. The autonomic nervous system has two distinct functions: to conserve and store energy and to respond quickly to changes. You can think of the autonomic nervous system as having a division that performs each of these two main functions.

Each division is controlled by different locations on the spinal cord, or within the brain and the brain stem. The cerebellum, which is located at the rear of the brain, coordinates balance and related muscle activity. The brain stem, which lies between the spinal cord and the rest of the brain, controls heartbeat, respiration, and the smooth muscles in the blood vessels.

When you are under stress, one part of the autonomic nervous system causes what is called the "fight or flight response." Rapid changes in your body prepare you either to fight the danger or to take flight and run away from the danger. The response of your nervous system is the same, whether the stress is a real danger, like falling off a skateboard, or a perceived danger, like being worried or embarrassed.

The **voluntary nervous system** monitors movement and functions that can be controlled consciously. Every movement you think about is voluntary. The voluntary nervous system controls the skeletal muscles of the arms, the legs, and the rest of the body. It also controls the muscles that are responsible for speech and the senses.

The autonomic nervous system responds quickly to changes in balance.

 CHECK YOUR READING What is the difference between the voluntary and the autonomic nervous systems?

 **4.1 Review**

KEY CONCEPTS

1. Make a chart of five senses that includes a definition and a stimulus for each sense.

2. Explain the process by which you hear a sound.

3. What are two body systems with which the nervous system interacts? How do these interactions take place?

CRITICAL THINKING

4. **Classify** Determine if the following actions involve the autonomic or the voluntary nervous system: chewing, eye blinking, jumping at a loud noise, and riding a bike.

5. **Apply** Describe what messages are sent by the nervous system when you go outside wearing a sweater on a hot day.

⬥ CHALLENGE

6. **Hypothesize** When people lose their sense of smell, their sense of taste is often affected as well. Why do you think the ability to taste would be decreased by the loss of the ability to smell?

CHAPTER INVESTIGATION

Are You a Supertaster?

OVERVIEW AND PURPOSE Do you think broccoli tastes bitter? If so, you might be extra sensitive to bitter tastes. In this investigation you will

- examine the surface of your tongue to find a possible connection between the bumps you find there and your sensitivity to bitter flavors
- calculate the average number of papillae in your class

Make sure to do this investigation in the cafeteria since you will be placing food coloring on your tongue.

MATERIALS
- blue food coloring
- paper cup
- 1 cotton swab
- 1 reinforcement circle for ring-binder paper
- paper towel or napkin
- 1 sheet of white paper

▶ Problem

How can you tell if you are a supertaster?

▶ Hypothesize

Write a hypothesis to explain how you might tell if you are a supertaster. Your hypothesis should take the form of an "If . . . , then . . . , because . . ." statement.

▶ Procedure

1. Make a data table in your **Science Notebook** like the one shown on page 109.

2. Put a few drops of blue food coloring into a paper cup.

3. Use a paper towel or a napkin to pat your tongue thoroughly dry.

4. Dip the tip of a cotton swab into the blue food coloring, and use it to paint the first 2 centimeters of your tongue.

5　Press a piece of white paper firmly onto the painted surface of your tongue, and then place the paper on your desk.

step 5

6　Place a notebook reinforcement circle on the blue area.

7　You should see white circles in a field of blue. The white circles are the bumps on your tongue called fungiform papillae, which contain taste buds. Count the number of white circles inside the reinforcement circle. There may be many white circles crammed together that vary in size, or just a few. If there are just a few, they may be larger than the ones on someone who has many white circles close together. If there are too many to count, try to count the number in half of the circle and multiply this number by 2. Record your total count in your data table.

▶ Observe and Analyze　[Write It Up]

1. **OBSERVE** What did you observe while looking at the tongue print? Is the surface the same all over your tongue?

2. **CALCULATE** Record the number of papillae within the reinforcement circle of all the students in your class.

AVERAGE Calculate the average number of papillae counted in the class.

$$\text{average} = \frac{\text{sum of papillae in class}}{\text{number of students}}$$

▶ Conclude　[Write It Up]

1. **INTERPRET** How do the number of fungiform papillae on your tongue compare with the number your partner counted?

2. **INFER** Do you think there is a relationship between the number of fungiform papillae and taste? If so, what is it?

3. **IDENTIFY** What foods might a supertaster not like?

4. **APPLY** Do you think that there are other taste perceptions besides bitterness that might be influenced by the number of fungiform papillae that an individual has? Why do you think so?

▶ INVESTIGATE Further

CHALLENGE Calculate the area in square millimeters inside the reinforcement circle, and use this value to express each person's papillae count as a density (number of papillae per square millimeter).

Are You a Supertaster?

Table 1. Papillae

Name	Number of papillae

The endocrine system helps regulate body conditions.

BEFORE, you learned

- Many body systems function without conscious control
- The body systems work automatically to maintain homeostasis
- Homeostasis is important to an organism's survival

NOW, you will learn

- About the role of hormones
- About the functions of glands
- How the body uses feedback mechanisms to help maintain homeostasis

VOCABULARY

endocrine system p.110
hormone p.111
gland p.111

THINK ABOUT

How does your body react to surprise?

In a small group, determine how your body responds to a surprising situation. Have one student in the group pretend he or she is responding to a surprise. The other group members should determine how the body reacts physically to that event. How do your respiratory system, digestive system, circulatory system, muscle system, and skeletal system react?

CHOOSE YOUR OWN STRATEGY
Begin taking notes on the main idea: *Hormones are the body's messengers.* Use a strategy from an earlier chapter or one of your own. Include a definition of *hormone* in your notes.

Hormones are the body's chemical messengers.

Imagine you're seated on a roller coaster climbing to the top of a steep incline. In a matter of moments, your car drops hundreds of feet. You might notice that your heart starts beating faster. You grab the seat and notice that your palms are sweaty. These are normal physical responses to scary situations. The **endocrine system** controls the conditions in your body by making and sending chemicals from one part of the body to another. Most responses of the endocrine system are controlled by the nervous system.

Hormones are chemicals that are made in one organ and travel through the blood to target cells. Target cells respond to the chemical. Many hormones, as you can see in the table below, affect all the cells in the body.

Because hormones are made at one location and function at another, they are often called chemical messengers. When the hormone reaches its target cells, it binds to receptors on the surface of or inside the cells. There the hormone begins the chemical changes that cause the target cells to function in a specific way. All of the functions of the endocrine system work automatically, without your conscious control.

Different types of hormones perform different jobs. Some of these jobs are to control the production of other hormones, to regulate the balance of chemicals such as glucose and salt in your blood, or to produce responses to changes in the environment. Some hormones are made only during specific times in a person's life. For example, hormones that control the development of sexual characteristics are not produced during childhood. When production begins in adolescence, these hormones cause major changes in a person's body.

The individuals on this roller coaster are experiencing a burst of the hormone adrenaline.

 How are hormones like messengers?

Hormones		
Name	**Where produced**	**Travels to**
Growth hormone	pituitary gland	all body cells
Antidiuretic hormone	pituitary gland	kidneys
Thyroxine	thyroid gland	all body cells
Cortisol	adrenal glands	all body cells
Adrenaline	adrenal glands	heart, lungs, stomach, intestines, glands
Insulin	pancreas	all body cells
Testosterone (males)	testes	all body cells
Estrogen (females)	ovaries	all body cells

Glands produce and release hormones.

The main structures of the endocrine system are groups of specialized cells called **glands.** Many glands in the body produce hormones and release them into your circulatory system. As you can see in the illustration on page 113, endocrine glands can be found in many parts of your body. However, all hormones move from the cells in which they are produced to target cells.

RESOURCE CENTER
CLASSZONE.COM

Learn more about the endocrine system.

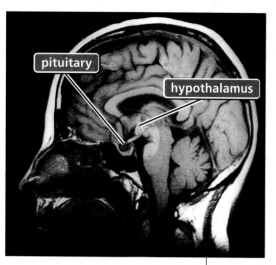

The hypothalamus and the pituitary are important endocrine glands.

Pituitary Gland The pituitary (pih-TOO-ih-TEHR-ee) gland can be thought of as the director of the endocrine system. The pituitary gland is the size of a pea and is located at the base of the brain—right above the roof of your mouth. Many important hormones are produced in the pituitary gland, including hormones that control growth, sexual development, and the absorption of water into the blood by the kidneys.

Hypothalamus The hypothalamus (HY-poh-THAL-uh-muhs) is attached to the pituitary gland and is the primary connection between the nervous and endocrine systems. All of the secretions of the pituitary gland are controlled by the hypothalamus which produces hormones with releasing functions.

Pineal Gland The pineal (PIHN-ee-uhl) gland is a tiny organ about the size of a pea. It is buried deep in the brain. The pineal gland is sensitive to different levels of light and is essential to rhythms such as sleep, body temperature, reproduction, and aging.

Thyroid Gland You can feel your thyroid gland if you place your hand on the part of your throat called the Adam's apple and swallow. What you feel is the cartilage surrounding your thyroid gland. The thyroid releases hormones necessary for growth and metabolism. The tissue of the thyroid is made of millions of tiny pouches, which store the thyroid hormone. The thyroid gland also produces the hormone calcitonin, which is involved in the regulation of calcium in the body.

Thymus The thymus is located in your chest. It is relatively large in the newborn baby and continues to grow until puberty. Following puberty, it gradually decreases in size. The thymus helps the body fight disease by controlling the production of white blood cells called T-cells.

Adrenal Glands The adrenal glands are located on top of your kidneys. The adrenal glands secrete about 30 different hormones that regulate carbohydrate, protein, and fat metabolism and water and salt levels in your body. Some other hormones produced by the adrenal glands help you fight allergies or infections. Roller coaster rides, loud noises, or stress can activate your adrenal glands to produce adrenaline, the hormone that makes your heart beat faster.

Pancreas The pancreas is part of both the digestive and the endocrine systems. The pancreas secretes two hormones, insulin and glucagon. These hormones regulate the level of glucose in your blood. The pancreas sits beneath the stomach and is connected to the small intestine.

Ovaries and Testes The ovaries and testes also secrete hormones that control sexual development.

Other Organs Some organs that are not considered part of the endocrine system do produce important hormones. The kidneys secrete a hormone that regulates the production of red blood cells. This hormone is secreted whenever the oxygen level in your blood decreases. Once the hormone has stimulated the red bone marrow to produce more red blood cells, the oxygen level of the blood increases. The heart produces two hormones that help regulate blood pressure. These hormones, secreted by one of the chambers of the heart, stimulate the kidneys to remove more salt.

Which glands and organs are part of the endocrine system?

Endocrine System

The endocrine system is made of a group of glands. These glands produce and release hormones, or chemical messengers.

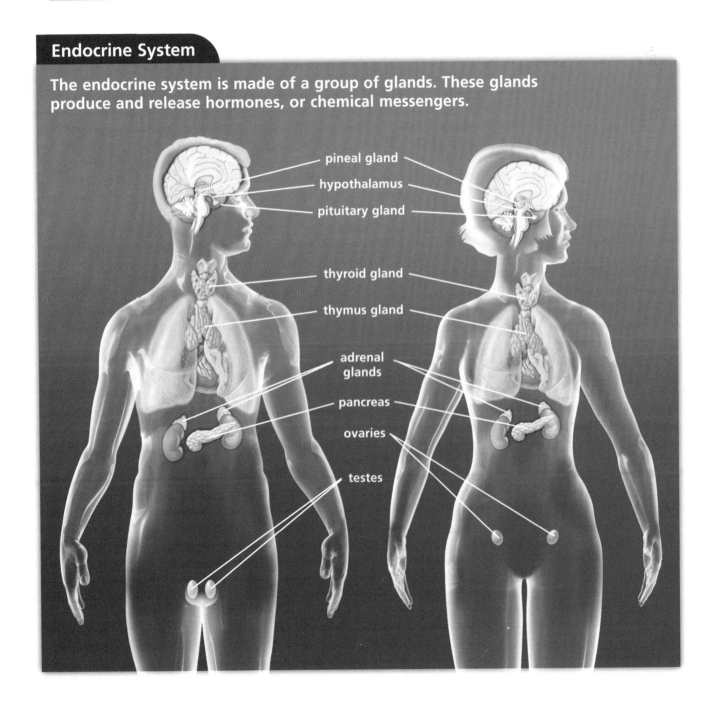

pineal gland
hypothalamus
pituitary gland
thyroid gland
thymus gland
adrenal glands
pancreas
ovaries
testes

INVESTIGATE Response to Exercise

How does your body temperature change when you exercise?

PROCEDURE

1. Working in groups of two, read all the instructions in this activity first. Appoint one person to be the subject and one person to be the timer and note taker. Using a mercury-free thermometer, have the subject take his or her temperature. Record the temperature in your notebook.

2. While staying seated the subject begins to do sitting-down jumping jacks. The subject does the jumping jacks for 1 minute and then immediately takes his or her temperature. Continue this procedure for a total of 3 times, measuring the temperature after each minute of exercise.

WHAT DO YOU THINK?

- How did the subject's temperature change while exercising?

- What factors may contribute to the rate at which the temperature changed in each person?

- How did the subject's physical appearance change from the beginning of the activity to the end?

CHALLENGE Graph the results on a line graph, with temperature on the *x*-axis and time on the *y*-axis.

SKILL FOCUS
Observing

MATERIALS
- stopwatch or timing device
- notebook
- graph paper
- mercury-free thermometer
- rubbing alcohol or plastic thermometer covers

TIME

30 minutes

Control of the endocrine system includes feedback mechanisms.

As you might recall, the cells in the human body function best within a specific set of conditions. Homeostasis (HOH-mee-oh-STAY-sihs) is the process by which the body maintains these internal conditions, even though conditions outside the body may change. The endocrine system is very important in maintaining homeostasis.

 Why is homeostasis important?

Because hormones are powerful chemicals capable of producing dramatic changes, their levels in the body must be carefully regulated. The endocrine system has several levels of control. Most glands are regulated by the pituitary gland, which in turn is controlled by the hypothalamus, part of the brain. The endocrine system helps maintain homeostasis through the action of negative feedback mechanisms.

Negative Feedback

Most feedback mechanisms in the body are called negative mechanisms, because the final effect of the response is to turn off the response. An increase in the amount of a hormone in the body feeds back to inhibit the further production of that hormone.

The production of the hormone thyroxine by the thyroid gland is an example of a negative feedback mechanism. Thyroxine controls the body's metabolism, or the rate at which the cells in the body release energy by cellular respiration. When the body needs energy, the thyroid gland releases thyroxine into the blood to increase cellular respiration. However, the thyroid gland is controlled by the pituitary gland, which in turn is controlled by the hypothalamus. Increased levels of thyroxine in the blood inhibit the signals from the hypothalamus and the pituitary gland to the thyroid gland. Production of thyroxine in the thyroid gland decreases.

Negative and Positive Feedback

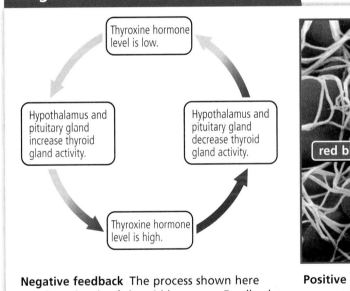

Thyroxine hormone level is low.

Hypothalamus and pituitary gland decrease thyroid gland activity.

Thyroxine hormone level is high.

Hypothalamus and pituitary gland increase thyroid gland activity.

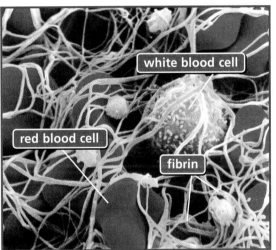

white blood cell

red blood cell

fibrin

Negative feedback The process shown here regulates levels of thyroid hormone. Feedback keeps conditions within a narrow range to maintain homeostasis.

Positive feedback These red blood cells are surrounded by fibrin, a protein that allows them to clot.

Positive Feedback

Some responses of the endocrine system, as well as other body systems, are controlled by positive feedback. The outcome of a positive feedback mechanism is not to maintain homeostasis, but to produce a response that continues to increase. Most positive feedback mechanisms result in extreme responses that are necessary under extreme conditions.

For example, when you cut yourself, the bleeding is controlled by positive feedback. First, the damaged tissue releases a chemical signal.

The signal starts a series of chemical reactions that lead to the formation of threadlike proteins called fibrin. The fibrin causes the blood to clot, filling the injured area. Other examples of positive feedback include fever, the immune response, puberty, and the process of childbirth.

 CHECK YOUR READING What is the difference between negative and positive feedback?

Balanced Hormone Action

In the body, the action of one hormone is often balanced by the action of another. When you ride a bicycle, you are able to ride in a straight line, despite bumps and dips in the road, by making constant steering adjustments. If the bicycle is pulled to the right, you adjust the handlebars by turning a tiny bit to the left.

Some hormones maintain homeostasis in the same way that you steer your bicycle. The pancreas, for example, produces two hormones. One hormone, insulin, decreases the level of sugar in the blood. The other hormone, glucagon, increases sugar levels in the blood. The balance of the levels of these hormones maintains stable blood sugar between meals.

Hormone Imbalance

Because hormones regulate critical functions in the body, too little or too much of any hormone can cause serious disease. When the pancreas produces too little insulin, sugar levels in the blood can rise to dangerous levels. Very high levels of blood sugar can damage the circulatory system and the kidneys. This condition, known as diabetes mellitus, is often treated by injecting synthetic insulin into the body to replace the insulin not being made by the pancreas.

 **Review**

KEY CONCEPTS

1. List three different jobs that hormones perform.

2. Draw an outline of the human body. Add the locations and functions of the pituitary, thyroid, adrenal, and pineal glands to your drawing.

3. What is the function of a negative feedback mechanism?

CRITICAL THINKING

4. **Analyze** Explain why hormones are called chemical messengers.

5. **Analyze** List two sets of hormones that have opposing actions. How do the actions of these hormones help maintain homeostasis?

○ CHALLENGE

6. **Connect** Copy the diagram below and add three more stimuli and the resulting feedback mechanisms.

CONNECTING SCIENCES

Heating and Cooling

The cells in our bodies can survive only within a limited temperature range. The body must maintain a constant core temperature at about 37°C (98.6°F). Body temperature is a measure of the average thermal energy in the body. To keep a constant temperature range, our bodies either lose or gain thermal energy.

Energy cannot be created or destroyed, but it can be transferred from one form or place to another. The major source of thermal energy in our bodies is food. When our bodies break down nutrients, some of the chemical energy is released as thermal energy that heats our bodies. Also, some of the kinetic energy from muscle movement is converted into thermal energy.

Body temperature is controlled by the hypothalamus region of the brain. The hypothalamus controls the rate of nutrient use. The hypothalamus also controls shivering and sweating.

Heat is the flow of energy from a warmer to a cooler object. Heat transfer between the body and its surroundings occurs in four ways.

1. **Evaporation:** When water evaporates, or changes from liquid to gas, energy is required. When perspiration evaporates from the surface of our skin, we lose thermal energy as heat.

2. **Radiation:** Heat transfer also occurs through waves that radiate out from a warm object or area. Sitting in the sunshine warms us because we gain thermal energy from the Sun's radiation. Our warm bodies can also radiate energy into cooler air.

3. **Conduction:** When two objects are in direct contact, heat flows by conduction from the warmer to the cooler object. If you stand barefoot on hot sand, heat quickly flows into your feet by conduction.

4. **Convection:** In convection, heat transfer occurs through the movement of particles in a gas or liquid. Your body loses some thermal energy because of convection in the air around you.

EXPLORE

1. **CONNECT** What are some behaviors that help you lose or gain thermal energy?
2. **CHALLENGE** Choose a behavior that either warms or cools your body. Draw a diagram and label it with the types of heat transfer that are occurring.

4.3

The reproductive system allows the production of offspring.

 BEFORE, you learned

- Some hormones regulate sexual development
- Glands release hormones

 NOW, you will learn

- About specialized cells and organs in male and female reproductive systems
- About fertilization
- About the development of the embryo and fetus during pregnancy

VOCABULARY

menstruation p. 119
fertilization p. 121
embryo p. 121
fetus p. 122

EXPLORE Reproduction

How are sperm and egg cells different?

PROCEDURE

(1) From your teacher, gather slides of egg cells and sperm cells.

(2) Put each slide under a microscope.

(3) Draw a sketch of each cell.

(4) With a partner, discuss the differences that you observed.

MATERIALS

- slides of egg and sperm cells
- microscope
- paper
- pencil

WHAT DO YOU THINK?

- What were the differences that you observed?
- What are the benefits of the different characteristics for each cell?

The reproductive system produces specialized cells.

CHOOSE YOUR OWN STRATEGY
Begin taking notes on the idea that the reproductive system produces specialized cells. You might use an outline or another strategy of your choice.

Like all living organisms, humans reproduce. The reproductive system allows adults to produce offspring. Although males and females have different reproductive systems, both systems share an important characteristic. They both make specialized cells. In any organism or any system, a specialized cell is a cell that takes on a special job.

In the female these specialized cells are called egg cells. In the male they are called sperm cells. In the reproductive system, each specialized cell provides genetic material. Genetic material contains the information that an organism needs to form, develop, and grow.

Both the male and female reproductive systems rely on hormones from the endocrine system. The hormones act as chemical messengers that signal the process of sexual development. Sexual development includes the growth of reproductive organs and the development of sexual characteristics. Once mature, the reproductive organs produce hormones to maintain secondary sexual characteristics.

The Female Reproductive System

The female reproductive system has two functions. The first is to produce egg cells, and the second is to protect and nourish the offspring until birth. The female has two reproductive organs called ovaries. Each ovary contains on average hundreds of egg cells. About every 28 days, the pituitary gland releases a hormone that stimulates some of the eggs to develop and grow. The ovaries then produce hormones that get the uterus ready to receive the egg

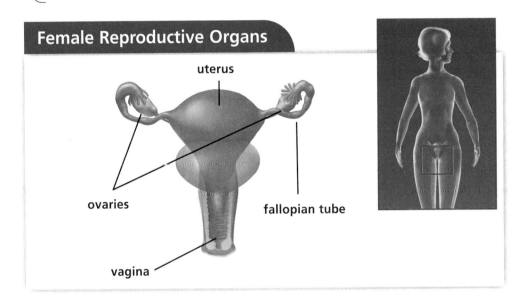

Female Reproductive Organs

uterus

ovaries

fallopian tube

vagina

Menstruation

After an egg cell develops fully, another hormone signals the ovary to release the egg. The egg moves from the ovary into a fallopian tube. Within ten to twelve hours, the egg cell may be fertilized by a sperm cell and move to the uterus. Once inside the thick lining of the uterus, the fertilized egg cell rapidly grows and divides.

However, if fertilization does not occur within 24 hours after the egg cell leaves the ovary, both the egg and the lining of the uterus begin to break down. The muscles in the uterus contract in a process called **menstruation.** Menstruation is the flow of blood and tissue from the body through a canal called the vagina over a period of about five days.

 CHECK YOUR READING Where does the egg travel after it leaves the ovary?

The Male Reproductive System

Testes The organs that produce sperm are called the testes (TEHS-teez). Inside the testes are tiny, coiled tubes hundreds of feet long. Sperm are produced inside these coiled tubes. The testes release a hormone that controls the development of sperm. This hormone is also responsible for the development of physical characteristics in men such as facial hair and a deep voice.

Sperm Sperm cells are the specialized cells of the male reproductive system. Males start producing sperm cells sometime during adolescence. The sperm is a single cell with a head and a tail. The sperm's head is filled with chromosomes, and the tail functions as a whip, making the sperm highly mobile. The sperm travel from the site of production, the testes, through several different structures of the reproductive system. While they travel, the sperm mix with fluids. This fluid is called semen and contains nutrients for the sperm cells. One drop of semen contains up to several million sperm cells.

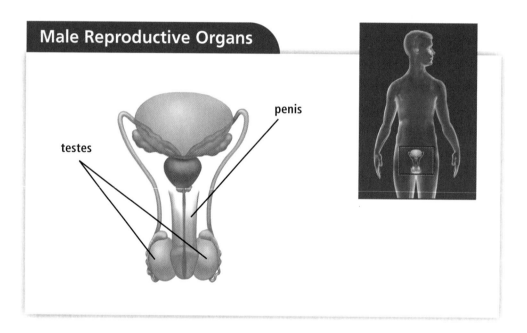

Male Reproductive Organs

penis

testes

The production of offspring includes fertilization, pregnancy, and birth.

Each sperm cell, like each egg cell, has half of the genetic material needed for a human being to grow and develop. During sexual intercourse, millions of sperm cells leave the testes. The sperm cells exit the male's body through the urethra, a tube that leads out of the penis. The sperm cells enter the female's body through the vagina. Next they travel into the uterus and continue on to the fallopian tube.

VISUALIZATION
CLASSZONE.COM

Follow an egg from fertilization to implantation.

Fertilization

Fertilization occurs when one sperm cell joins the egg cell. The fallopian tube is the site of fertilization. Immediately, chemical changes in the egg's surface prevent any more sperm from entering. Once inside the egg, the genetic material from the sperm combines with the genetic material of the egg cell. Fertilization is complete.

The fertilized egg cell then moves down the fallopian tube toward the uterus. You can trace the path of the egg cell in the diagram on this page. It divides into two cells. Each of those cells divides again, to form a total of four cells. Cell division continues, and a ball of cells forms, called an **embryo** (EM-bree-OH). Within a few days, the embryo attaches itself to the thickened, spongy lining of the uterus in a process called implantation.

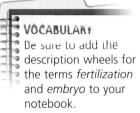

VOCABULARY
Be sure to add the description wheels for the terms *fertilization* and *embryo* to your notebook.

Fertilization

The egg moves down the fallopian tube following fertilization. Its final destination is the uterus.

2 Fertilization occurs.

3 Fertilized egg begins to divide.

4 Dividing egg continues down fallopian tube.

fallopian tube

1 Egg is released from ovary.

ovary

5 Embryo moves towards the uterus.

uterus

6 Embryo implants in lining of uterus.

READING VISUALS Where does fertilization occur?

Pregnancy

The nine months of pregnancy can be divided into three periods of about the same length. Each period marks specific stages of development. In the first week following implantation, the embryo continues to grow rapidly. Both the embryo and the uterus contribute cells to a new, shared organ called the placenta. The placenta has blood vessels that lead from the mother's circulatory system to the embryo through a large tube called the umbilical cord. Oxygen and nutrients from the mother's body will move through the placenta and umbilical cord to the growing embryo.

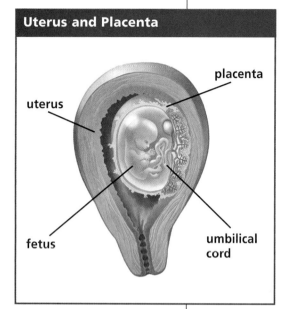

Uterus and Placenta

placenta

uterus

fetus

umbilical cord

Around the eighth week of pregnancy, the developing embryo is called a **fetus.** The fetus begins to have facial features, major organ systems, and the beginnings of a skeleton. The fetus develops the sexual traits that are either male or female. In the twelfth week, the fetus continues to grow and its bones develop further. In the last twelve weeks, the fetus and all of its organ systems develop fully.

 CHECK YOUR READING Describe the development of an embryo and fetus at two weeks, eight weeks, and twelve weeks.

Labor and Delivery

At the end of pregnancy, the fetus is fully developed and is ready to be born. The birth of a fetus is divided into three stages; labor, delivery of the fetus, and delivery of the placenta.

The first stage of birth begins with muscular contractions of the uterus. These contractions initially occur at intervals of 10 to 30 minutes and last about 40 seconds. They happen continually until the muscular contractions are occurring about every 2 minutes.

The second stage of birth is delivery. With each contraction, the opening to the uterus expands until it becomes wide enough for the mother's muscles to push the fetus out. During delivery the fetus is pushed out of the uterus, through the vagina, and out of the body. The fetus is still connected to the mother by the umbilical cord.

The umbilical cord is cut shortly after the fetus is delivered. Within minutes after birth, the placenta separates from the uterine wall and the mother pushes it out with more muscular contractions.

 CHECK YOUR READING What happens during each of the three stages of birth?

Growth of the Fetus

An embryo grows and develops from a cluster of cells to a fully formed fetus.

4-day blastula

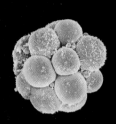

magnification 620x

- Embryo has 16 cells
- Not yet implanted in the uterus

5-week embryo

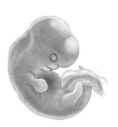

size < 1 cm

- Heart is beating
- Beginning of eyes, arms and legs are visible

8-week fetus

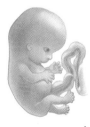

size 2–3 cm

- Embryo is now called a fetus
- Has all basic organs and systems

16-week fetus

size 12 cm

- Can move around in the womb
- Hair, eyelashes and eyebrows are growing

7–8 month fetus shown in this composite image is about 35–40 cm in length and weighs about 1.5–2.3 kg. The fetus usually gains at least 1 kg during the final month of pregnancy.

These twins provide an example of offspring born in a multiple birth.

Multiple Births

Do you have any friends who are twins or triplets? Perhaps you and your brothers or sisters are twins or triplets. The birth of more than one offspring is called a multiple birth. Multiple births are relatively uncommon in humans.

Identical twins are produced when a single fertilized egg divides in half early in embryo development. Each half then forms one complete organism, or twin. Such twins are always of the same sex, look alike, and have identical blood types. Approximately 1 in 29 of twin births, or 4 in every 1000 of all births, is a set of identical twins.

Twins that are not identical are called fraternal twins. Fraternal twins are produced when two eggs are released at the same time and are fertilized by two different sperm. Consequently, fraternal twins may be as similar or different from each other as siblings born at different times. Fraternal twins can be the same sex or different sexes.

 Why are some twins identical and some are not?

 Review

KEY CONCEPTS

1. Describe the function of the male reproductive system and the two main functions of the female reproductive system.

2. Identify two roles hormones play in making egg cells available for fertilization.

3. How is an embryo different from a fetus?

CRITICAL THINKING

4. **Sequence** Describe the sequence of events that occurs between fertilization and the stage called implantation.

5. **Analyze** Detail two examples of hormones interacting with the reproductive system, one involving the male system and one involving the female system.

○ CHALLENGE

6. **Synthesize** Describe the interaction between the endocrine system and the reproductive system.

MATH TUTORIAL
CLASSZONE.COM

Click on Math Tutorial for more help with solving proportions.

Twins and Triplets

Is the number of twins and triplets on the rise? Between 1980 and 1990, twin births in The United States rose from roughly 68,000 to about 105,000. In 1980, there were about 3,600,000 births total. To convert the data to birth rates, you can use proportions. A proportion is an equation. It shows two ratios that are equivalent.

Example

Find the birth rate of twins born in The United States for 1980. The rate is the number of twin births per 1000 births.

(1) Write the ratio of twin births to total births for that year.

$$\frac{68,000 \text{ twin births}}{3,600,000 \text{ total births}}$$

(2) Write a proportion, using x for the number you need to find.

$$\frac{68,000}{3,600,000} = \frac{x}{1000}$$

(3) In a proportion, the cross products are equal, so

$$68,000 \cdot 1000 = x \cdot 3,600,000$$

(4) Solve for x:

$$\frac{68,000,000}{3,600,000} = 18.9$$

ANSWER There were 18.9 twin births for every 1000 births in 1980.

Find the following birth rates.

1. In 1990, there were about 105,000 twin births and about 3,900,000 total births. What was the birth rate of twins?

2. In 1980, about 1,350 sets of triplets were born, and by 1990, this number had risen to about 6,750. What were the birth rates of triplets in 1980 and in 1990?

3. How much did the birth rate increase for twins between 1980 and 1990? for triplets?

4. Find the overall birth rate of twins and triplets in 1980.

5. Find the overall rate of twin and triplet births in 1990. How much did it increase between 1980 and 1990?

CHALLENGE In 1989, there were about 4 million total births, and the rate of triplets born per million births was about 700. How many triplets were born?

Chapter Review

the BIG idea

The nervous and endocrine systems allow the body to respond to internal and external conditions.

CONTENT REVIEW
CLASSZONE.COM

◀ KEY CONCEPTS SUMMARY

4.1 The nervous system responds and controls.

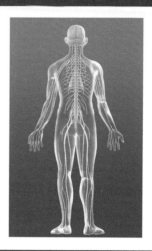

- The nervous system connects the body with its environment using different senses: sight, touch, hearing, smell, and taste. Central nervous system includes the brain, the control center, and the spinal cord.
- The peripheral nervous system includes the autonomic and voluntary systems

VOCABULARY
stimulus p. 102
central nervous system p. 104
neuron p.105
peripheral nervous system p. 106
autonomic nervous system p. 107
voluntary nervous system p. 107

4.2 The endocrine system helps regulate body conditions.

The body has chemical messengers called **hormones** that are regulated by the **endocrine system. Glands** produce and release hormones. The endocrine system includes feedback systems that maintain homeostasis.

Thyroxine hormone level is low.

Hypothalamus and pituitary gland increase thyroid gland activity.

Hypothalamus and pituitary gland decrease thyroid gland activity.

Thyroxine hormone level is high.

VOCABULARY
endocrine system p. 110
hormone p. 111
gland p. 111

4.3 The reproductive system allows the production of offspring.

The female produces eggs, and the male produces sperm. Following **fertilization** the fetus develops over a period of about nine months.

VOCABULARY
menstruation p. 119
fertilization p. 121
embryo p. 121
fetus p. 122

Reviewing Vocabulary

Make a frame for each of the vocabulary words listed. Write the word in the center. Decide what information to frame it with. Use definitions, examples, descriptions, parts, or pictures.

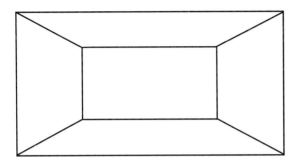

1. stimulus

2. neurons

3. hormones

4. fertilization

5. embryo

Reviewing Key Concepts

Multiple Choice *Choose the letter of the best answer.*

6. Which is a stimulus?
   a. a car horn blowing
   b. jumping at a loud noise
   c. taste buds on the tongue
   d. turning on a lamp

7. Light enters the eye through
   a. the lens
   b. the auditory canal
   c. the olfactory epithelium
   d. the taste buds

8. Which senses allow you to process chemical information?
   a. sight and smell
   b. taste and smell
   c. touch and hearing
   d. hearing and taste

9. What conserves energy and responds quickly to change?
   a. central nervous system
   b. peripheral nervous system
   c. autonomic nervous system
   d. voluntary nervous system

10. Which is <u>not</u> regulated by hormones?
    a. production of red blood cells
    b. physical growth
    c. blood pressure
    d. sexual development

11. Which gland releases hormones that are necessary for growth and metabolism?
    a. thyroid gland   c. adrenal gland
    b. pituitary gland   d. pineal gland

12. Eggs develop in the female reproductive organ called
    a. an ovary   c. a uterus
    b. a fallopian tube   d. a vagina

13. The joining of one sperm cell and one egg cell is an event called
    a. menstruation   c. implantation
    b. fertilization   d. birth

14. A cluster of cells that is formed by fertilization is called the
    a. testes   c. ovary
    b. urethra   d. embryo

15. The period in which a fetus and all of its systems develop fully is the
    a. first three months
    b. second three months
    c. third three months
    d. pregnancy

Short Answer *Write a short answer to each question.*

16. List the parts of the body that are controlled by the autonomic nervous system.

17. What is a negative feedback mechanism? Give an example.

18. How are fertilization and menstruation related?

Thinking Critically

Use the diagram to answer the following two questions.

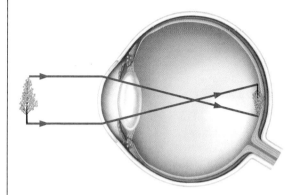

19. SUMMARIZE Use the diagram of the eye to describe how images are formed on the retina.

20. COMPARE AND CONTRAST How is the image that forms on the retina like the object? How is it different? Explain how the viewer interprets the image that forms on the retina.

21. APPLY A person steps on a sharp object with a bare foot and quickly pulls the foot back in pain. Describe the parts of the nervous system that are involved in this action.

22. ANALYZE Explain why positive feedback mechanisms do not help the body maintain homeostasis. Give an example.

23. CONNECT Copy the concept map and add the following terms to the correct box: brain, spinal cord, autonomic.

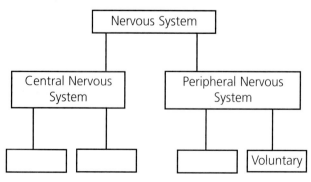

24. DRAW CONCLUSIONS A person who is normally very active begins to notice a significant decrease in energy level. After visiting a doctor, tests results show that one of the endocrine glands is not secreting enough of its hormone. Which gland could this be? Explain your answer.

25. SUMMARIZE Describe the events that occur during the female's 28-day menstrual cycle. Include in your answer how hormones are involved in the cycle.

26. COMPARE AND CONTRAST How are the functions of the ovaries and the testes alike? How are their functions different?

the BIG idea

27. INFER Look again at the picture on pages 98–99. Now that you have finished the chapter, how would you change or add details to your answer to the question on the photograph?

28. SYNTHESIZE How does the nervous system interact with the endocrine and reproductive systems? Give examples that support your answer.

UNIT PROJECTS

If you need to do an experiment for your unit project, gather the materials. Be sure to allow enough time to observe results before the project is due.

Analyzing Data

This chart shows some of the stages of development of a typical fetus.

Week of Pregnancy	Approximate Length of Fetus	Developmental Changes in the Fetus
6	1 cm	Primitive heartbeat
10	3 cm	Face, fingers, and toes are formed
14	8.5 cm	Muscle and bone tissue have developed
18	14 cm	Fetus makes active movements
24	30 cm	Fingerprints and footprints forming
28	37.5 cm	Rapid brain development
36	47.5 cm	Increase in body fat
38	50 cm	Fetus is considered full term

Use the chart to answer the questions below.

1. What is the approximate length the fetus at 10 weeks?

a. 1 cm   **c.** 3 cm

b. 1 in.   **d.** 3 in.

2. At about which week of development does the fetus begin to make active movements?

a. week 10   **c.** week 18

b. week 14   **d.** week 24

3. At about which week of development does the fetus reach a length of about 30 cm?

a. week 18   **c.** week 36

b. week 24   **d.** week 38

4. Which statement is true?

a. Between weeks 28 and 38, the fetus grows at an average of a little over a centimeter per week.

b. The fetus begins to develop fingerprints at about week 28.

c. During week 10, the length of the fetus is about 7.5 cm

d. The fetus is about 12.5 cm long when muscle and bone tissue develop.

5. Between which two weeks of development does the greatest increase in length usually take place?

a. weeks 6 and 10

b. weeks 10 and 14

c. weeks 14 and 18

d. weeks 24 and 28

Extended Response

6. A pregnancy lasts about 42 weeks, roughly 9 months. The development of the fetus can be broken down into three stages, each 14 weeks long. These stages are referred to as trimesters. Briefly describe changes in length and development that occur during each of these stages.

7. The endocrine system and the nervous system have similar functions. Compare and contrast the two systems including the terms in the box. Underline each term in your answer.

homeostasis	autonomic system	hormones
feedback	smooth muscles	

CHAPTER

5 Growth, Development, and Health

the BIG idea

The body develops and maintains itself over time.

How do people change as they grow?

Key Concepts

SECTION

5.1 The human body changes over time.
Learn about the different stages of human development.

SECTION

5.2 Systems in the body function to maintain health.
Learn about what a body needs to be healthy.

SECTION

5.3 Science helps people prevent and treat disease.
Learn how to help prevent the spread of disease.

Internet Preview

CLASSZONE.COM

Chapter 5 online resources:
Content Review,
Visualization, three
Resource Centers, Math
Tutorial, Test Practice

EXPLORE (the BIG idea)

How Much Do You Exercise?

In your notebook, create a chart to keep track of your exercise for a week. Each time you exercise, write down the type of activity and the amount of time you spend. If possible, measure your heart rate during the activity.

Observe and Think How does the exercise affect your heart rate? If you exercised regularly, what would be the effect on your heart rate while you were resting?

How Safe Is Your Food?

Almost all food that you buy in a store is dated for freshness. Look at the labels of various foods including cereal, juice, milk, eggs, cheese, and meats.

Observe and Think Why do you think some foods have a longer freshness period than others? What types of problems could you have from eating food that is past date?

Internet Activity: Human Development

Go to **ClassZone.com** to watch a movie of a person aging.

Observe and Think In what ways does a person's face change as he or she ages?

NSTA
scilinks.org
SCiLINKS

Human Development **Code: MDL048**

Getting Ready to Learn

CONCEPT REVIEW

- The integumentary system protects the body.
- The immune system fights disease.
- A microscope is an instrument used to observe very small objects.

VOCABULARY REVIEW

nutrient p. 45

pathogen p. 74

antibiotic p. 81

hormone p. 111

CONTENT REVIEW
CLASSZONE.COM
Review concepts and vocabulary.

TAKING NOTES

CONTENT FRAME

Make a content frame for each main idea. Include the following columns: *Topic, Definition, Detail,* and *Connection.* In the first column, list topics about the title. In the second column, define the topic. In the third column, include a detail about the topic. In the fourth column, add a sentence that connects that topic to another topic in the chart.

CHOOSE YOUR OWN STRATEGY

For each new vocabulary term, take notes by choosing a strategy from earlier chapters—**four square, magnet word, frame game,** or **description wheel.** Or, use a strategy of your own.

See the Note-Taking Handbook on pages R45–R51.

SCIENCE NOTEBOOK

The human body develops and grows.

Topic	Definition	Detail	Connection
Childhood	Period after infancy and before sexual maturity.	Children depend on parents, but learn to do things for themselves, such as get dressed.	Adults do not have to depend on parents; they are independent and can care for others.

Four Square

Frame Game

Magnet Word

Description Wheel

KEY CONCEPT

The human body changes over time.

◀ **BEFORE, you learned**

- Living things grow and develop
- The digestive system breaks down nutrients in food
- Organ systems interact to keep the body healthy

▶ **NOW, you will learn**

- About four stages of human development
- About the changes that occur as the body develops
- How every body system interacts constantly with other systems to keep the body healthy

VOCABULARY

infancy p. 134
childhood p. 134
adolescence p. 135
adulthood p. 136

EXPLORE Growth

Are there patterns of growth?

PROCEDURE

1. Measure the circumference of your wrist by using the measuring tape as shown. Record the length. Now measure the length from your elbow to the tip of your middle finger. Record the length.

2. Create a table and enter all the data from each person in the class.

WHAT DO YOU THINK?

- How does the distance between the elbow and the fingertip compare with wrist circumference?
- Do you see a pattern between the size of one's wrist and the length of one's forearm?

MATERIALS

- flexible tape measure
- graph paper

CONTENT FRAME
Make a content frame for the first main idea: *The human body develops and grows.* List the red headings in this section in the topics column.

The human body develops and grows.

Have you noticed how rapidly your body has changed over the past few years? Only five years ago you were a young child in grade school. Today you are in middle school. How has your body changed? Growth is both physical and emotional. You are becoming more responsible and socially mature. What are some emotional changes that you have noticed?

Human development is a continuous process. Although humans develop at different rates, there are several stages of development common to human life. In this section we will describe some of the stages, including infancy, childhood, adolescence, and adulthood.

Infancy

The stage of life that begins at birth and ends when a baby begins to walk is called **infancy.** An infant's physical development is rapid. As the infant's body grows larger and stronger, it also learns physical skills. When you were first born, you could not lift your head. But as your muscles developed, you learned to lift your head, to roll over, to sit, to crawl, to stand, and finally to walk. You also learned to use your hands to grasp and hold objects.

Infants also develop thinking skills and social skills. At first, they simply cry when they are uncomfortable. Over time, they learn that people respond to those cries. They begin to expect help when they cry. They learn to recognize the people who care for them. Smiling, cooing, and eventually saying a few words are all part of an infant's social development.

Nearly every body system changes and grows during infancy. For example, as the digestive system matures, an infant becomes able to process solid foods. Changes in the nervous system, including the brain, allow an infant to see more clearly and to control parts of her or his body.

The Apgar score is used to evaluate the newborn's condition after delivery.

Apgar Score			
Quality	0 points	1 point	2 points
Appearance	Completely blue or pale	Good color in body, blue hands or feet	Completely pink or good color
Pulse	No heart rate	<100 beats per minute	>100 beats per minute
Grimace	No response to airway suction	Grimace during suctioning	Grimace, cough/ sneeze with suction
Activity	Limp	Some arm and leg movement	Active motion
Respiration	Not breathing	Weak cry	Good, strong cry

Childhood

The stage called **childhood** lasts for several years. Childhood is the period after infancy and before the beginning of sexual maturity. During childhood children still depend very much upon their parents. As their bodies and body systems grow, children become more able to care for themselves. Although parents still provide food and other needs, children perform tasks such as eating and getting dressed. In addition, children are able to do complex physical tasks such as running, jumping, and riding a bicycle.

Childhood is also a time of mental and social growth. During childhood a human being learns to talk, read, write, and communicate in other ways. Along with the ability to communicate come social skills such as cooperation and sharing. A child learns to interact with others.

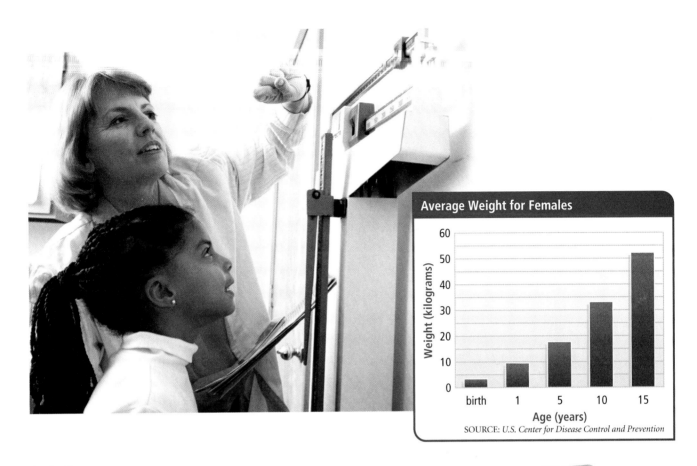

Average Weight for Females

SOURCE: *U.S. Center for Disease Control and Prevention*

Adolescence

The years from puberty to adulthood are called **adolescence** (AD-uhl-EHS-uhns). Childhood ends when the body begins to mature sexually. This process of physical change is called puberty. Not all people reach puberty at the same age. For girls, the changes usually start between ages eight and fourteen; for boys, puberty often begins between ages ten and sixteen.

The human body changes greatly during adolescence. As you learned in Chapter 4, the endocrine system produces chemicals called hormones. During adolescence, hormones signal parts of the reproductive system to mature. At this stage a person's sexual organs become ready for reproduction. These changes are accompanied by other changes. Adolescents develop secondary sexual characteristics. Boys may notice their voices changing. Girls begin developing breasts. Boys and girls both begin growing more body hair.

Probably the change that is the most obvious is a change in height. Boys and girls grow taller by an average of 10 centimeters (3.9 in.) per year during adolescence. Most adolescents eat more as they grow. Food provides materials necessary for growth.

 CHECK YOUR READING What are some of the ways the body changes during adolescence?

VOCABULARY
Choose a strategy from earlier chapters or one of your own to take notes on the term *adolescence.*

Adulthood

When a human body completes its growth and reaches sexual maturity, it enters the stage of life called **adulthood.** An adult's body systems no longer increase in size. They allow the body to function fully, to repair itself, to take care of its own needs, and to produce and care for offspring. Even though a person reaches full height early in adulthood, other physical changes, as well as mental and social development, continue throughout life.

Mental and emotional maturity are important parts of adulthood. To maintain an adult body and an adult lifestyle, an individual needs strong mental and emotional skills.

Later Adulthood

READING **TiP**

You may find it helpful to review the information on the skeletal and muscular system in Chapter 1.

Changes in the body that you might think of as aging begin at about the age of 30. Skin begins to wrinkle and lose its elasticity. Eyesight becomes increasingly poor, hair loss begins, and muscles decrease in strength. After the age of 65, the rate of aging increases. Internal organs become less efficient. Blood vessels become less elastic. The average blood pressure increases and may remain slightly high. Although the rate of breathing usually does not change, lung function decreases slightly. Body temperature is harder to regulate. However, one can slow the process of aging by a lifestyle of exercise and healthy diet.

Systems interact to maintain the human body.

It's easy to observe the external changes to the body during growth and development. Inside the body, every system interacts constantly with other systems to keep the whole person healthy throughout his or her lifetime. For example, the respiratory system constantly sends oxygen to the blood cells of the circulatory system. The circulatory system transports hormones produced by the endocrine system.

Your body systems also interact with the environment outside your body. Your nervous system monitors the outside world through your senses of taste, smell, hearing, vision, and touch. It allows you to respond to your environment. For example, your nervous system allows you to squint if the sun is too bright or to move indoors if the weather is cold. Your endocrine system releases hormones that allow you to have an increased heart rate and send more blood to your muscles if you have to respond to an emergency.

INVESTIGATE Life Expectancy

How has life expectancy changed over time?

In this activity, you will look for trends in the changes in average life expectancy over the past 100 years.

PROCEDURE

(1) Using the following data, create a bar graph to chart changes in life expectancy in the U.S. over the last 100 years.

Life Expectancy 1900–2000

Year	1900	1910	1920	1930	1940	1950	1960	1970	1980	1990	2000
Average Life Expectancy (years)	47.3	50.0	54.1	59.7	62.9	68.2	69.7	70.8	73.7	75.4	76.9

SOURCE: National Center for Health Statistics

(2) Study the graph. Observe any trends that you see. Record them in your notebook.

WHAT DO YOU THINK?

- In general, what do these data demonstrate about life expectancy?
- Between which decades did average life expectancy increase the most?

CHALLENGE Using a computer program, create a table and bar graph to chart the data shown above.

SKILL FOCUS
Graphing

MATERIALS
- graph paper
- computer graphing program

TIME

30 minutes

Every part of your daily life requires interactions among your body systems. Even during sleep body systems cooperate. When you sleep, your nervous system allows your muscular system to keep your heart pumping and your lungs breathing. The heart pumps blood through your circulatory system, which has received oxygen from your respiratory system. All this cooperation takes place even while you are sleeping. Your endocrine system releases growth hormone during your sleep, allowing your bones and muscles to grow. The neurons in your brain change when you fall asleep.

Keeping the body healthy is complex. The digestive and urinary systems eliminate solid and liquid wastes from the body. The circulatory and respiratory systems remove carbon dioxide gas. As you will learn in the next section, a healthy diet and regular exercise help the body to stay strong and function properly.

 CHECK YOUR READING Name three systems that interact as your body grows and maintains itself.

READING VISUALS **COMPARE AND CONTRAST** How do the interactions of your body system change when you are active and when you rest?

When body systems fail to work together, the body can become ill. Stress, for example, can affect all the body systems. Some types of stress, such as fear, can be a healthy response to danger. However, if the body experiences stress over long periods of time, serious health problems such as heart disease, headaches, muscle tension, and depression can arise.

All stages of life include different types of stress. Infants and children face stresses as they learn to become more independent and gain better control over their bodies. Adolescents can be challenged by school, by the changes of puberty, or by being socially accepted by their peers. Adults may encounter stress in their jobs or with their families. The stress of aging can be very difficult for some older adults.

5.1 Review

KEY CONCEPTS

1. Make a development timeline with four sections. Write the names of the stages in order under each section. Include a definition and two details.

2. List a physical characteristic of each stage of development.

3. Give an example of an activity that involves two or more body systems.

CRITICAL THINKING

4. **Compare and Contrast** Make a chart to compare and contrast the infancy and childhood stages of development.

5. **Identify Cause and Effect** How is the endocrine system involved in adolescence?

⬭ CHALLENGE

6. **Synthesis** How does each of the body systems described change as a human being develops from infancy to older adulthood?

STAGE MAKEUP ARTIST

Aging the Face

In a movie, characters may go through development stages of a whole lifetime in just over an hour. An actor playing such a role will need to look both older and younger than he or she really is. Makeup artists have a toolbox full of techniques to make the actor look the part.

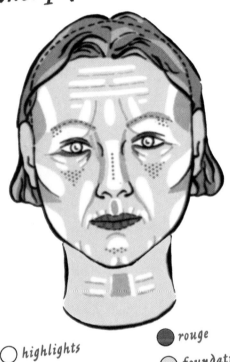

Makeup Guide for Aging

○ highlights
◑ shadows
● rouge
○ foundation

Hair

As humans go through adulthood, their hair may lose the pigments that make it dark. Makeup artists color hair with dyes or even talcum powder. Wigs and bald caps, made of latex rubber, cover an actor's real hair. Eyebrows can be colored or aged by rubbing them with makeup.

Features

For a bigger-looking nose or extra skin around the neck, makeup artists use foam rubber, or layers of liquid rubber, and, sometimes, wads of paper tissue to build up facial features. For example, building up the cheekbones with layers of latex makes the cheeks appear sharper, less rounded, and more hollow.

Skin

To make wrinkles or scars, makeup artists use light-colored makeup for the raised highlights and dark-colored makeup for lower shadows and spots.

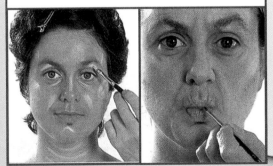

EXPLORE

1. **COMPARE** Look at photos of an older relative at three different stages of life, at about ten years apart. Describe how you might apply makeup to your own face if you were to portray this person's life in three movie scenes. What changes do you need to show?

2. **CHALLENGE** Research to find an image of a character portrayed in a movie by an actor who looked very different in real life. From the picture, describe how the effect was achieved.

Systems in the body function to maintain health.

 BEFORE, you learned

- Human development involves all the body systems
- The human body continues to develop throughout life
- Every body system interacts constantly with other systems to keep the body healthy

▶ **NOW,** you will learn

- About the role of nutrients in health
- Why exercise is needed to keep body systems healthy
- How drug abuse, eating disorders, and addiction can affect the body

VOCABULARY

nutrition p. 140
addiction p. 146

THINK ABOUT

What is health?

If you went online and searched under the word *health,* you would find millions of links. Clearly, health is important to most people. You may be most aware of your health when you aren't feeling well. But you know that clean water, food, exercise, and sleep are all important for health. Preventing illness is also part of staying healthy. How would you define health? What are some ways that you protect your health?

Diet affects the body's health.

What makes a meal healthy? The choices you make about what you eat are important. Nutrients from food are distributed to every cell in your body. You use those nutrients for energy and to maintain and build new body tissues. **Nutrition** is the study of the materials that nourish your body. It also refers to the process in which the different parts of food are used for maintenance, growth, and reproduction. When a vitamin or other nutrient is missing from your diet, illness can occur. Your body's systems can function only when they get the nutrients they need.

VOCABULARY
Choose a strategy from an earlier chapter, such as a magnet word diagram, for taking notes on the term *nutrition.* Or use any strategy that you think works well.

 CHECK YOUR READING   How is nutrition important to health?

This family is enjoying a healthy meal that includes proteins, carbohydrates, and fats.

Getting Nutrients

RESOURCE CENTER
CLASSZONE.COM

Discover more about human health.

In order to eat a healthy diet, you must first understand what good nutrition is. There are six classes of nutrients: carbohydrates, proteins, fats, vitamins, minerals, and water. All of these nutrients are necessary for your body cells to carry out the chemical reactions that sustain life.

Proteins are molecules that build tissues used for growth and repair. Proteins provide the building blocks for many important hormones. Good sources of proteins are poultry, red meat, fish, eggs, nuts, beans, grains, soy, and milk. Protein should make up at least 20 percent of your diet.

Carbohydrates are the body's most important energy source and are found in starch, sugar, and fiber. Fiber provides little energy, but is important for regular elimination. Natural sugars such as those found in fruits and vegetables are the best kinds of sugars for your body. Carbohydrates are found in bread and pasta, fruits, and vegetables. Carbohydrates should make up about 40 to 50 percent of your diet.

Fats are essential for energy and should account for about 10 to 15 percent of your diet. Many people eliminate fats from their diet in order to lose weight. But a certain amount of fat is necessary. Fats made from plants have the greatest health benefits. For example, olive oil is better for you than the oil found in butter.

Vitamins and minerals are needed by your body in small amounts. Vitamins are small molecules that regulate body growth and development. Minerals help build body tissues. While some vitamins can be made by your body, most of them are supplied to the body in food.

Water is necessary for life. A human being could live for about a month without food, but only about one week without water. Water has several functions. Water helps regulate your body temperature through evaporation when you sweat and breathe. Without water, important materials such as vitamins and other nutrients could not be transported around the body. Water helps your body get rid of the waste products that move through the kidneys and pass out of the body in urine. Urine is composed mostly of water.

To make sure your body can function and maintain itself, you need to drink about two and one half liters, or about eight glasses, of water every day. You also get water when you eat foods with water in them, such as fresh fruit and vegetables.

Vitamins and Minerals	
Vitamin or Mineral	**Recommended Daily Allowance**
Vitamin A	0.3 to 1.3 mg
Niacin	6–18 mg
Vitamin B_2	0.5–1.6 mg
Vitamin B_6	0.5–2.0 mg
Vitamin C	15–120 mg
Vitamin E	6–19 mg
Calcium	500–1300 mg
Phosphorus	460–1250 mg
Potassium	1600–2000 mg
Zinc	3–13 mg
Magnesium	80–420 mg
Iron	7–27 mg

Source: National Institutes of Health

Understanding Nutrition

RESOURCE CENTER
CLASSZONE.COM

Examine the basic principles of nutrition.

Ever wonder what the word *lite* really means? What do labels saying that food is fresh or natural or organic mean? Not all advertising about nutrition is reliable. It is important to know what the labels on food really mean. Groups within the government, such as the United States Department of Agriculture, have defined terms that are used to describe food products. For example, if a food label says the food is "all natural," that means it does not contain any artificial flavor, color, or preservative.

Another example is the term *low-fat*. That label means that the food provides no more than 3 grams of fat per serving. The word *organic* means that the produce has been grown using no human-made fertilizers or chemicals that kill pests or weeds. It also means that livestock has been raised on organic feed and has not been given antibiotics or growth hormones. It takes some effort and a lot of reading to stay informed, but the more you know, the better the choices you can make.

What are you eating?

PROCEDURE

1. Gather nutrition labels from the following products: a carbonated soft drink, a bag of fresh carrots, canned spaghetti in sauce, potato chips, plain popcorn kernels, unsweetened applesauce, and fruit juice. Look at the percent of daily values of the major nutrients, as shown on the label for each food.

2. Make a list of ways to evaluate a food for high nutritional value. Include such criteria as nutrient levels and calories per serving.

3. Examine the nutrition labels and compare them with your list. Decide which of these foods would make a healthy snack.

WHAT DO YOU THINK?

- How does serving size affect the way you evaluate a nutritional label?

- What are some ways to snack and get nutrients at the same time?

CHALLENGE Design a full day's food menu that will give you all the nutrients you need. Use snacks as some of the foods that contribute these nutrients.

SKILL FOCUS
Analyzing

MATERIALS
nutrition labels

TIME
30 minutes

Spaghetti
IN TOMATO SAUCE WITH CHEESE

Nutrition Facts
Serving Size: 1 cup (252g)
Servings Per Container: about 2

Amount Per Serving
Calories 210   Calories from Fat 20

	% Daily Value*
Total Fat 2g	3%
Saturated Fat 1g	
Cholesterol 5mg	5%
Sodium 1,020 mg	2%
Total Carbohydrate 41g	43%
Dietary Fiber 3g	14%
Sugars 14g	12%
Protein 7g	

Vitamin A 10%   Vitamin C 0%
Calcium 4%   Iron 10%

* Percent Daily Values are based on a 2,000 calorie diet. Your daily values may be higher or lower depending on your calorie needs.

Exercise is part of a healthy lifestyle.

Regular exercise allows all your body systems to stay strong and healthy. You learned that your lymphatic system doesn't include a structure like the heart to pump its fluid through the body. Instead, it relies on body movement and strong muscles to help it move antibodies and white blood cells. Exercise is good for the lymphatic system.

Exercise

When you exercise, you breathe harder and more quickly. You inhale and exhale more air, which exercises the muscles of your respiratory system and makes them stronger. Exercise also brings in extra oxygen. Oxygen is necessary for cellular respiration, which provides energy to other body systems. The circulatory system is strengthened by exercise. Your heart becomes stronger the more it is used. The skeletal system grows stronger with exercise as well. Studies show that older adults who lift weights have stronger bones than those who do not. In addition, physical activity can flush out skin pores by making you sweat, and it reduces the symptoms of depression.

By eating healthy meals and exercising, you help your body to grow and develop.

Lifestyle

The lifestyles of many people involve regular exercise. Some lifestyles, however, include more sitting still than moving. A lifestyle that is sedentary, associated mostly with sitting down, can harm a person's health. Muscles and bones that are not exercised regularly can begin to break down. Your body stores unused energy from food as fat. The extra weight of body fat can make it harder for you to exercise. Therefore, it is harder to use up energy or to strengthen your skeletal, muscular, and immune systems. Researchers have also made connections between excess body fat and heart disease and diabetes.

 READING How does lifestyle affect health?

CONTENT FRAME
Make a content frame for the main idea: *Drug abuse, addiction, and eating disorders cause serious health problems.*

Drug abuse, addiction, and eating disorders cause serious health problems.

Every day, you make choices that influence your health. Some choices can have more serious health risks, or possibilities for harm, than others. You have the option to make healthy choices for yourself. Making unhealthy decisions about what you put into your body can lead to drug abuse, addiction, or eating disorders.

Drug Abuse

A drug is any chemical substance that you take in to change your body's functions. Doctors use drugs to treat and prevent disease and illness. The use of a drug for any other reason is an abuse of that drug. Abuse can also include using too much of a substance that is not harmful in small amounts. People abuse different drugs for different reasons. Drugs often do allow an individual to feel better for the moment. But they can also cause serious harm to an individual's health.

Tobacco Nicotine, the drug in tobacco, increases heart rate and blood pressure and makes it seem as if the user has more energy. Nicotine is also a poison; in fact, some farmers use it to kill insects. Tobacco smoke contains thousands of chemicals. Tar and carbon monoxide are two harmful chemicals in smoke. Tar is a sticky substance that is commonly used to pave roads. Carbon monoxide is one of the gases that cars release in their exhaust. People who smoke or chew tobacco have a high risk of cancer, and smokers are also at risk for heart disease.

Compounds Found in Unfiltered Tobacco Smoke

Compound	Amount in First-Hand Smoke (per cigarette)	Amount in Second-Hand Smoke (per cigarette)
Nicotine	1–3 mg	2.1–46 mg
Tar	15–40 mg	14–30 mg
Carbon monoxide	14–23 mg	27–61 mg
Benzene	0.012–0.05 mg	0.4 mg
Formaldehyde	0.07–0.1 mg	1.5 mg
Hydrogen cyanide	0.4–0.5 mg	0.014–11 mg
Phenol	0.08–0.16 mg	0.07–0.25 mg

Source: U.S. Department of Health and Human Services

Alcohol Even a small amount of alcohol can affect a person's ability to think and reason. Alcohol can affect behavior and the ability to make decisions. Many people are killed every year, especially in automobile accidents, because of choices they made while drinking alcohol. Alcohol abuse damages the heart, the liver, the nervous system, and the digestive system.

Other Drugs Some drugs, such as cocaine and amphetamines, can make people feel more energetic and even powerful because they stimulate the nervous system and speed up the heart. These drugs are very dangerous. They can cause nervous disorders and heart attacks.

Drugs called narcotics also affect the nervous system. Instead of stimulating it, however, they decrease its activity. Narcotics are prescribed by doctors to relieve pain and to help people sleep. Abuse of narcotics can lead to addiction. More and more narcotics are then needed to gain the same effect. Because narcotics work by decreasing nerve function, large amounts of these drugs can cause the heart and lungs to stop.

Students can be active in protesting drug abuse.

Addiction

Drug abuse can often lead to addiction. **Addiction** is an illness in which a person becomes dependent on a substance or behavior. Repeated use of drugs such as alcohol, tobacco, and narcotics can cause the body to become physically dependent. When a person is dependent on a drug, taking away that drug can cause withdrawal. If affected by withdrawal, a person may become physically ill, sometimes within a very short period of time. Symptoms of withdrawal can include fever, muscle cramps, vomiting, and hallucinations.

Another type of addiction can result from the effect produced by a drug or even a behavior. Although physical dependency may not occur, a person can become emotionally dependent. Gambling, overeating, and risk-taking are some examples of addictive behaviors. With both physical and emotional addictions, increasing amounts of a drug or behavior are necessary to achieve the effects. Someone who suffers from an addiction can be treated and can work to live a healthy life, but most addictions never go away completely.

Eating Disorders

An eating disorder is a condition in which people continually eat too much or too little food. One example of an eating disorder is anorexia nervosa. People with this disorder eat so little and exercise so hard that they become unhealthy. No matter how thin they are, they believe they need to be thinner. People with anorexia do not receive necessary nutrients because they don't eat. When the energy used by the body exceeds the energy taken in from food, tissues in the body are broken down to provide fuel. Bones and muscles, including the heart, can be damaged, and the person can die.

Review

KEY CONCEPTS

1. How do nutrients affect health?

2. Explain the effects of exercise on the respiratory and circulatory systems.

3. Make a chart showing the effects of tobacco, alcohol, and other drugs on the body.

CRITICAL THINKING

4. **Explain** How would you define health? Write your own definition.

5. **Synthesize** Explain how water can be considered a nutrient. Include a definition of *nutrient* in your explanation.

⬤ CHALLENGE

6. **Apply** You have heard about a popular new diet. Most of the foods in the diet are fat-free, and the diet promises fast weight loss. How might this diet affect health? Explain your answer.

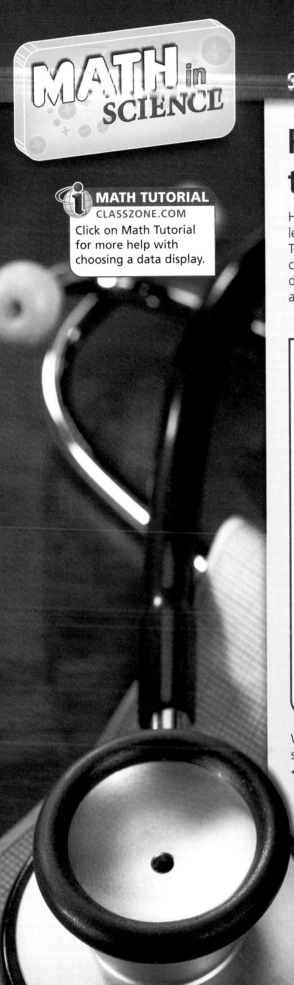

MATH in **SCIENCE**

MATH TUTORIAL
CLASSZONE.COM
Click on Math Tutorial
for more help with
choosing a data display.

Pumping Up the Heart

Heart rates differ with age, level of activity, and fitness. To communicate the differences clearly, you need to display the data visually. Choosing the appropriate display is important.

Example

The fitness trainer at a gym wants to display the following data:

Maximum heart rate while exercising (beats per minute)		
Age 21	Men	197
	Women	194
Age 45	Men	178
	Women	177
Age 65	Men	162
	Women	164

Here are some different displays the trainer could use:

- A bar graph shows how different categories of data compare. Data can be broken into 2 or even 3 bars per category.
- A line graph shows how data changes over time.
- A circle graph represents data as parts of a whole.

ANSWER The fitness trainer wants to show heart rate according to both age and gender, so a double bar graph would be the clearest.

What would be an appropriate way to display data in the following situations?

1. A doctor wants to display how a child's average heart rate changes as the child grows.

2. A doctor wants to display data showing how a person's resting heart rate changes the more the person exercises.

3. A scientist is studying each type of diet that the people in an experiment follow. She will show what percentage of the people with each diet had heart disease.

CHALLENGE Describe a situation in which a double line graph is the most appropriate data display.

Science helps people prevent and treat disease.

 BEFORE, you learned

- Good nutrition and exercise help keep the body healthy
- Drug abuse can endanger health
- Eating disorders can affect the body's health

NOW, you will learn

- About some of the causes of disease
- How diseases can be treated
- How to help prevent the spread of disease

VOCABULARY

microorganism p. 148
bacteria p. 149
virus p. 149
resistance p. 153

EXPLORE The Immune System

How easily do germs spread?

PROCEDURE

1. Early in the day, place a small amount of glitter in the palm of one hand. Rub your hands together to spread the glitter to both palms. Go about your day normally.

2. At the end of the day, examine your environment, including the people around you. Where does the glitter show up?

WHAT DO YOU THINK?
- How easily did the glitter transfer to other people and objects?
- What do you think this might mean about how diseases might spread?

 MATERIALS
glitter

Scientific understanding helps people fight disease.

Disease is a change that disturbs the normal functioning of the body's systems. If you have ever had a cold, you have experienced a disease that affected your respiratory system. What are the causes of disease? Many diseases are classified as infectious diseases, or diseases that can be spread. Viruses, bacteria, and other pathogens cause infectious disease. The organisms that cause sickness are called **microorganisms.**

Before the invention of the microscope, people didn't know about microorganisms that cause disease. They observed that people who lived near each other sometimes caught the same illness, but they didn't understand why. Understanding disease has helped people prevent and treat many illnesses.

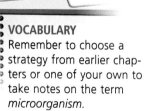

VOCABULARY
Remember to choose a strategy from earlier chapters or one of your own to take notes on the term *microorganism.*

The germ theory describes some causes of disease.

In the 1800s, questions about the causes of some diseases were answered. Scientists showed through experiments that diseases could be caused by very small living things. In 1857, French chemist Louis Pasteur did experiments that showed that microorganisms caused food to decay. Later, Pasteur's work and the work of Robert Koch and Robert Lister contributed to the germ theory. Pasteur's germ theory states that some diseases, called infectious diseases, are caused by germs.

Bacteria and Viruses

Germs are the general name given to organisms that cause disease. **Bacteria** (bak-TEER-ee-uh) are single-celled organisms that live almost everywhere. Within your intestines, bacteria function to digest food. Some bacteria, however, cause disease. Pneumonia (nu-MOHN-yuh), ear infections (ihn-FEHK-shuhnz), and strep throat can be caused by bacteria.

Viruses do not fit all parts of the definition of living things. For example, they must enter and exist inside living cells in order to reproduce. Stomach flu, chicken pox, and colds are sicknesses caused by viruses. Both bacteria and viruses are examples of pathogens, agents that cause disease. The word *pathogen* comes from the Greek *pathos*, which means "suffering." Other pathogens include yeasts, fungi, and protists.

RESOURCE CENTER
CLASSZONE.COM

Explore ways to fight disease.

Treating Infectious Diseases

Diseases caused by bacteria can be treated with medicines that contain antibiotics. An antibiotic is a substance that can destroy bacteria. The first antibiotics were discovered in 1928 when a scientist named Alexander Fleming was performing experiments on bacteria. Fleming found mold growing on his bacteria samples. While most of the petri dish was covered with bacterial colonies, the area around the mold was clear. From this observation, Fleming concluded that a substance in the mold had killed the bacteria.

Fleming had not intended to grow mold in his laboratory, but the accident led to the discovery of penicillin. Since the discovery of penicillin, many antibiotics have been developed. Antibiotics have saved the lives of millions of people.

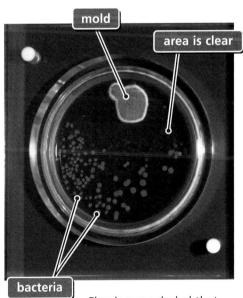

mold

area is clear

bacteria

Fleming concluded that something in the mold had killed the bacteria.

Infectious diseases spread in many ways.

READING TiP

As you read the text on this page, notice how each pathogen shown on p. 151 spreads.

One of the best ways to protect your health is by being informed and by avoiding pathogens. Pathogens can be found in many places, including air, water, and on the surfaces of objects. By knowing how pathogens travel, people are able to limit the spreading of disease.

Food, Air, and Water

Sometimes people get sick when they breathe in pathogens from the air. The viruses that cause colds can travel through air. If you cover your mouth when you sneeze or cough, you can avoid sending pathogens through the air. Pathogens also enter the body in food or water. Washing fruits and vegetables and cooking meats and eggs kills bacteria. Most cities in the United States add substances, such as chlorine, to the supply of public water. These substances kill pathogens. Boiling water also kills pathogens. People sometimes boil water if their community loses power or experiences a flood. Campers need to boil or filter water taken from a stream before they use it.

Contact with Insects and Other Animals

Animals and insects can also carry organisms that cause disease. The animal itself does not cause the illness, but you can become sick if you take in the pathogen that the animal carries. Lyme disease, for example, is caused by bacteria that inhabit ticks. The ticks are not the cause of illness, but if an infected tick bites you, you will get Lyme disease.

A deadly central nervous system infection called rabies can also come from animal contact. The virus that causes rabies is found in the saliva of an infected animal, such as a bat, raccoon, or opossum. If that animal bites you, you may get the disease. A veterinarian can give your pet an injection to prevent rabies. You can get other infections from pets. These infections include worms that enter through your mouth or nose and live in your intestines. You can also get a skin infection called ringworm, which is actually a fungus rather than a worm.

Person-to-Person Contact

Most of the illnesses you have had have probably been passed to you by another person. Even someone who does not feel sick can have pathogens on his or her skin. If you touch that person or if that person touches something and then you touch it, the pathogens will move to your skin. If the pathogens then enter your body through a cut or through your nose, mouth, or eyes, they can infect your body. The simplest way to avoid giving or receiving pathogens is to wash your hands often and well.

Pathogens and Disease

Infectious diseases are caused by microorganisms.

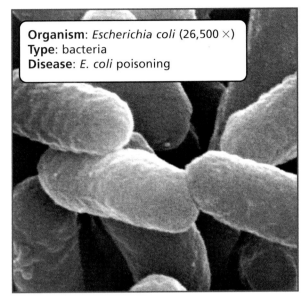

Organism: *Escherichia coli* (26,500 ×)
Type: bacteria
Disease: *E. coli* poisoning

Spread: contaminated food or water

Prevention: handwashing, thoroughly cooking meat, boiling contaminated water, washing fruits and vegetables, drinking only pasteurized milk, juice, or cider

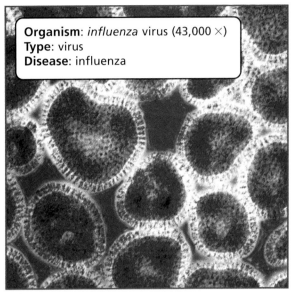

Organism: *influenza* virus (43,000 ×)
Type: virus
Disease: influenza

Spread: inhaling virus from sneezes or coughs of infected person

Prevention: vaccination

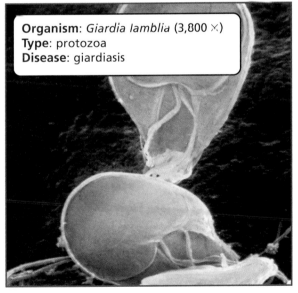

Organism: *Giardia lamblia* (3,800 ×)
Type: protozoa
Disease: giardiasis

Spread: contaminated food or water, close contact with infected person

Prevention: handwashing, thoroughly cooking meat, boiling contaminated water, washing fruits and vegetables, drinking only pasteurized milk, juice, or cider

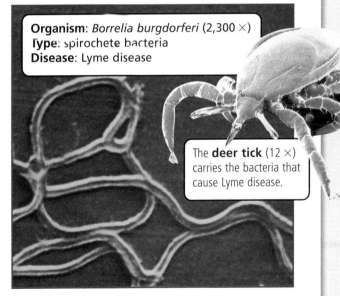

Organism: *Borrelia burgdorferi* (2,300 ×)
Type: spirochete bacteria
Disease: Lyme disease

The **deer tick** (12 ×) carries the bacteria that cause Lyme disease.

Spread: tick bite

Prevention: wear light-colored clothing, tuck pants into socks or shoes, check for ticks after outdoor activities, use repellents containing DEET

READING VISUALS How can people prevent each of these pathogens from spreading?

Noninfectious diseases are not contagious.

Noninfectious diseases are diseases that cannot be spread by pathogens. They are not contagious. People are born with some of these, and others can develop during life.

Diseases Present at Birth

Some diseases present at birth are inherited. Genes, which act as instructions for your cells, are inherited from your parents. Some forms of a gene produce cells that do not function properly. Most genetic disorders are due to recessive forms of a gene, which means that while both parents carry the defective form, neither one has the disorder. Cystic fibrosis and sickle cell disease are diseases inherited this way.

The symptoms of some genetic diseases may not be present immediately at birth. Huntington's disease, even though it is an inherited condition, does not begin to produce symptoms until a person reaches adulthood. Other genes can increase the chances of developing a disease later in life, such as cancer or diabetes, but the pattern of inheritance is complex.

The process of human development is complex. Some diseases present at birth may involve both inherited factors and development. Talipes, a disorder commonly known as clubfoot, is due to the improper development of the bones of the leg and foot. Talipes can be corrected by surgery after birth.

Asthma is a noncontagious disease often present at birth.

Diseases in Later Life

Some diseases, including heart disease, certain forms of cancer, and many respiratory disorders, have much less to do with genetics and more to do with environment and lifestyle. You have learned about the ways in which you can lead a healthy lifestyle. Good nutrition, exercise, and avoiding substances that can damage the body systems not only increase the length of life, but also the quality of life.

While people with family histories of cancer are at higher risk of getting it, environmental factors can influence risk as well. Tar and other chemicals from cigarettes can damage the lungs, in addition to causing cancer. Much is still not known about the causes of cancer.

 CHECK YOUR READING Name a noninfectious disease that is present at birth and one that may occur later in life.

Scientists continue efforts to prevent and treat illness.

In spite of all that scientists have learned, disease is still a problem all over the world. Illnesses such as AIDS and cancer are better understood than they used to be, but researchers must still find ways to cure them.

Even though progress is sometimes slow, it does occur. Better education has led to better nutrition. The use of vaccines has made some diseases nearly extinct. However, new types of illness sometimes appear. AIDS was first identified in the 1980s and spread quickly before it was identified. More recently, the West Nile virus appeared in the United States. This virus is transmitted by infected mosquitoes and can cause the brain to become inflamed. Efforts to control the disease continue.

Scientists work hard to fight disease.

Antibiotics fight pathogens, but they can also lead to changes in them. When an antibiotic is used too often, bacteria can develop **resistance,** or become partially immune, to its effects. This means that the next time those bacteria invade, that particular antibiotic will not stop the infection. For this reason, it is best not to use pathogen-killing drugs unless you really need them.

 CHECK YOUR READING Describe the advantages and disadvantages of using an antibiotic when you are sick.

 **Review**

KEY CONCEPTS

1. Define microorganism and explain how microorganisms can affect health.

2. What is an antibiotic?

3. Make a chart showing ways that infectious diseases spread and ways to keep them from spreading.

CRITICAL THINKING

4. **Connect** Make a list of things you can do to avoid getting Lyme disease or the West Nile virus.

5. **Apply** How does washing your hands before eating help protect your health?

◆ CHALLENGE

6. **Synthesize** How can nutrition help in the prevention of disease? Use these terms in your answer: *nutrients, pathogens,* and *white blood cells.*

CHAPTER INVESTIGATION

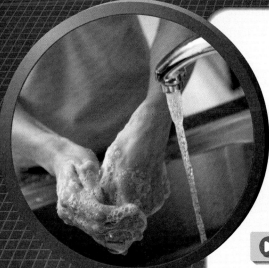

Cleaning Your Hands

OVERVIEW AND PURPOSE Your skin cells produce oils that keep the skin moist. This same layer of oil provides a nutrient surface for bacteria to grow. When you wash your hands with soap, the soap dissolves the oil and the water carries it away, along with the bacteria. In this activity you will
- sample your hands for the presence of bacteria
- test the effectiveness of washing your hands with water compared with washing them with soap and water

▶ Problem

Write It Up

Is soap effective at removing bacteria?

▶ Hypothesize

Write It Up

Write a hypothesis explaining how using soap affects the amount of bacteria on your hands. Your hypothesis should take the form of an "If . . . , then . . . , because . . ." statement.

▶ Procedure

MATERIALS
- 3 covered petri dishes with sterile nutrient agar
- soap
- marker
- tape
- hand lens

1. Make a data table in your **Science Notebook** like the one shown on page 155.

2. Obtain three agar petri dishes. Be careful not to open the dishes accidentally.

3. Remove the lid from one dish and gently press two fingers from your right hand onto the surface of the agar. Close the lid immediately. Tape the dish closed. Mark the tape with the letter *A*. Include your initials and the date.

step 3

4 Wash your hands in water and let them air-dry. Open the second dish with your right hand and press two fingers of your left hand into the agar. Close the lid immediately. Tape and mark the dish B, as in step 3.

5 Wash your hands in soap and water and let them air-dry. Open the third dish with one hand and press two fingers of the other hand into the agar. Close the lid immediately. Tape and mark the dish C, as in step 3.

6 Place the agar plates upside down in a dark, warm place for two to three days. **Caution:** Do not open the dishes. Wash your hands.

▶ Observe and Analyze   Write It Up

1. **OBSERVE** Use a hand lens to observe the amounts of bacterial growth in each dish, and record your observations in Table 1. Which dish has the most bacterial growth? the least growth?

2. **OBSERVE** Is there anything you notice about the bacterial growth in each dish other than the amount of bacterial growth?

3. Return the petri dishes to your teacher for disposal. **Caution:** Do not open the dishes. Wash your hands thoroughly with warm water and soap when you have finished.

▶ Conclude   Write It Up

1. **INFER** Why is it necessary to air-dry your hands instead of using a towel?

2. **INFER** Why is it important to use your right hand in step 3 and your left hand in step 4?

3. **INTERPRET** Compare your results with your hypothesis. Do your observations support your hypothesis?

4. **EVALUATE** Is there much value in washing your hands simply in water?

5. **EVALUATE** How might the temperature of the water you used when you washed your hands affect the results of your experiment?

6. **EVALUATE** Given the setup of your experiment, could you have prepared a fourth sample, for example to test the effectiveness of antibacterial soap?

▶ INVESTIGATE Further

CHALLENGE It is hard to tell which products are best for washing hands without testing them. Design an experiment to determine which cleans your hands best: baby wipes, hand sanitizer, regular soap, or antibacterial soap.

Cleaning Your Hands

Table 1. Observations

Petri Dish	Source	Amount of Bacteria
A	hand	
B	hand washed with water	
C	hand washed with soap and water	

Chapter Review

the BIG idea

The body develops and maintains itself over time.

CONTENT REVIEW
CLASSZONE.COM

KEY CONCEPTS SUMMARY

5.1 **The human body changes over time.**

Your body develops and grows throughout your entire life. Some changes are physical and some are emotional. The stages of life are infancy, childhood, adolescence, adulthood, and later adulthood. All the different systems in the body interact to maintain your health.

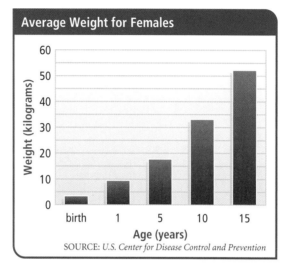

Average Weight for Females

Weight (kilograms) vs Age (years)

SOURCE: U.S. Center for Disease Control and Prevention

VOCABULARY
infancy p. 134
childhood p. 134
adolescence p. 135
adulthood p. 136

5.2 **Systems in the body function to maintain health.**

Your diet affects your health. Important nutrients include proteins, carbohydrates, fats vitamins, minerals, and water. Water is also essential to healthy living. Exercise is the final ingredient to a healthy life. Problems that can interfere with a healthy life are drug abuse, addiction, and eating disorders.

Spaghetti
IN TOMATO SAUCE WITH CHEESE
Nutrition Facts
Serving Size: 1 cup (252g)
Servings Per Container: about 2
Amount Per Serving
Calories 210   Calories from Fat 20
Total Fat 2g   % Daily Value*
   Saturated Fat 1g   3%
Cholesterol 5mg   5%

VOCABULARY
nutrition p. 140
addiction p. 146

5.3 **Science helps people prevent and treat disease.**

• Science helps people fight disease.
• Antibiotics are used to fight diseases caused by bacteria.
• Infectious disease can spread in many ways including food, air, water, insects, animals, and person-to-person contact.
• Noninfectious diseases are not contagious. Some noninfectious diseases are present at birth and others occur in later life.

VOCABULARY
microorganism p. 148
bacteria p. 149
virus p. 149
resistance p. 153

Reviewing Vocabulary

Make a frame for each of the vocabulary words listed below. Write the word in the center. Decide what information to frame it with. Use definitions, examples, descriptions, parts, or pictures.

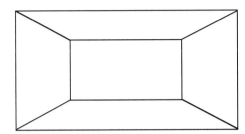

1. infancy
2. childhood
3. adolescence
4. adulthood

Reviewing Key Concepts

Multiple Choice *Choose the letter of the best answer.*

5. The stage of life known as infancy ends when an infant
   a. begins to cry
   b. learns to walk
   c. holds up his head
   d. sees more clearly

6. The process in which the body begins to mature sexually is called
   a. adolescence
   b. adulthood
   c. nutrition
   d. puberty

7. Which nutrients are sources of energy for the body?
   a. fats and carbohydrates
   b. water and protein
   c. fats and proteins
   d. water and carbohydrates

8. Which is *not* a benefit of regular exercise?
   a. flushed-out skin pores
   b. stronger skeletal system
   c. increased body fat
   d. strengthened heart

9. A sedentary life style is associated with
   a. a stronger immune system
   b. more sitting than moving
   c. regular exercise
   d. an eating disorder

10. The chemical found in tobacco that increases heart rate and blood pressure is
    a. cocaine
    c. tar
    b. carbon monoxide
    d. nicotine

11. Which term includes all of the others?
    a. bacteria
    c. virus
    b. germ
    d. pathogen

12. An example of a disease caused by bacteria is
    a. an ear infection
    b. stomach flu
    c. chicken pox
    d. a cold

13. Which statement about viruses is true?
    a. Viruses function to digest food.
    b. Viruses are one-celled organisms.
    c. Viruses need living cells to reproduce.
    d. Examples of viruses are fungi and yeasts.

14. A substance that can destroy bacteria is called
    a. a virus
    c. an antibiotic
    b. a pathogen
    d. a mold

15. Lyme disease is spread through
    a. drinking unfiltered water
    b. uncooked meats
    c. the bite of a dog
    d. the bite of a tick

Short Answer *Write a short answer to each question.*

16. In your own words, define *nutrition.*

17. What are pathogens? Give three examples.

18. Explain what happens if antibiotics are used too often.

Thinking Critically

19. ANALYZE Why do you think crying is an example of a social skill that develops during infancy?

20. ANALYZE Describe one physical, one mental, and one social change that a ten-year-old boy might experience over the next five years.

21. EVALUATE Explain why a diet that doesn't contain any fat would be unhealthly for most people.

22. APPLY Explain why people who live sedentary lifestyles should get more exercise.

23. SYNTHESIZE Discuss why doctors recommend that women avoid alcohol and tobacco use during pregnancy.

24. COMPARE AND CONTRAST How are anorexia and bulimia alike? How do they differ?

25. ANALYZE Explain why the work of Louis Pasteur was important in the understanding of infectious disease.

26. HYPOTHESIZE In 1854 a disease called cholera spread through the city of London. Most of the people who contracted the disease lived near the city's various water pumps. What might you hypothesize about the cause of the disease? How could you prevent people from contracting the disease in the future?

27. PROVIDE EXAMPLES What are some ways that a person can prevent noninfectious diseases such as cancer or diabetes?

the BIG idea

28. INFER Look again at the picture on pages 130–131. Now that you have finished the chapter, how would you change or add details to your answer to the question on the photograph?

29. SUMMARIZE Write one or more paragraphs explaining how lifestyle can lead to a healthy body and a longer life. Include these terms in your description.

nutrition	alcohol
exercise	infectious disease
germs	noninfectious disease
tobacco	

UNIT PROJECTS

Evaluate all the data, results, and information from your project folder. Prepare to present your project.

ⓟ Pump   ⓟ Contaminated pump   • Cholera death

Analyzing Data

The table below presents information about causes of death in the
United States.

Leading Causes of Death in the United States

2000		1900	
Cause of Death	**Percent of Deaths**	**Cause of Death**	**Percent of Deaths**
heart disease	31%	pneumonia*	12%
cancer	23%	tuberculosis*	11%
stroke	9%	diarrhea*	11%
lung disease	5%	heart disease	6%
accident	4%	liver disease	5%
pneumonia*	4%	accident	4%
diabetes	3%	cancer	4%
kidney disease	1%	senility	2%
liver disease	1%	diphtheria*	2%

* infectious disease

Use the table to answer the questions below.

1. What was the leading cause of death in 1900?

   a. heart disease   **c.** pneumonia

   b. cancer   **d.** tuberculosis

2. Which infectious disease was a leading cause of
death both in 1900 and 2000?

   a. tuberculosis   **c.** stroke

   b. diphtheria   **d.** pneumonia

3. Which was the leading noninfectious cause of
death in both 1900 and 2000?

   a. pneumonia   **c.** heart disease

   b. cancer   **d.** accidents

4. Which cause of death showed the greatest
increase between 1900 and 2000?

   a. heart disease   **c.** liver disease

   b. cancer   **d.** pneumonia

5. Which statement is true?

   a. The rate of infectious disease as a leading cause
of death increased from 1900 to 2000.

   b. The rate of infectious disease as a leading cause
of death decreased from 1900 to 2000.

   c. The rate of noninfectious disease as a leading
cause of death decreased from 1900 to 2000.

   d. The rate of noninfectious disease as a leading
cause of death remained the same.

6. How much did the rate of heart disease increase
from 1900 to 2000?

   a. 37%   **c.** 25%

   b. 31%   **d.** 6%

Extended Response

7. Write a paragraph explaining the change in the
number of deaths due to infectious diseases from
1900 to 2000. Use the information in the data and
what you know about infectious disease in your
description. Use the vocabulary words in the box in
your answer.

bacterium	virus	pathogen
antibiotic	resistance	microorganism

8. The spread of infectious disease can be controlled
in many different ways. Write a paragraph describing how the spread of infectious disease may be
limited. Give at least two examples and describe
how these diseases can be prevented or contained.

Student Resource Handbooks

Scientific Thinking Handbook

Making Observations

An **observation** is an act of noting and recording an event, character-istic, behavior, or anything else detected with an instrument or with the senses.

Observations allow you to make informed hypotheses and to gather data for experiments. Careful observations often lead to ideas for new experiments. There are two categories of observations:

- **Quantitative observations** can be expressed in numbers and include records of time, temperature, mass, distance, and volume.

- **Qualitative observations** include descriptions of sights, sounds, smells, and textures.

EXAMPLE

A student dissolved 30 grams of Epsom salts in water, poured the solution into a dish, and let the dish sit out uncovered overnight. The next day, she made the following observations of the Epsom salt crystals that grew in the dish.

Table 1. Observations of Epsom Salt Crystals

To determine the mass, the student found the mass of the dish before and after growing the crystals and then used subtraction to find the difference.

The student measured several crystals and calculated the mean length. (To learn how to calculate the mean of a data set, see page R36.)

Quantitative Observations	Qualitative Observations
• mass = 30 g • mean crystal length = 0.5 cm • longest crystal length = 2 cm	• Crystals are clear. • Crystals are long, thin, and rectangular. • White crust has formed around edge of dish.

Photographs or sketches are useful for recording qualitative observations.

Epsom salt crystals

MORE ABOUT OBSERVING

- Make quantitative observations whenever possible. That way, others will know exactly what you observed and be able to compare their results with yours.

- It is always a good idea to make qualitative observations too. You never know when you might observe something unexpected.

Predicting and Hypothesizing

A **prediction** is an expectation of what will be observed or what will happen. A **hypothesis** is a tentative explanation for an observation or scientific problem that can be tested by further investigation.

EXAMPLE

Suppose you have made two paper airplanes and you wonder why one of them tends to glide farther than the other one.

1. Start by asking a question.

2. Make an educated guess. After examination, you notice that the wings of the airplane that flies farther are slightly larger than the wings of the other airplane.

3. Write a prediction based upon your educated guess, in the form of an "If . . . , then . . ." statement. Write the independent variable after the word *if,* and the dependent variable after the word *then.*

4. To make a hypothesis, explain why you think what you predicted will occur. Write the explanation after the word *because.*

1. Why does one of the paper airplanes glide farther than the other?

2. The size of an airplane's wings may affect how far the airplane will glide.

3. Prediction: If I make a paper airplane with larger wings, then the airplane will glide farther.

> To read about independent and dependent variables, see page R30.

4. Hypothesis: If I make a paper airplane with larger wings, then the airplane will glide farther, because the additional surface area of the wing will produce more lift.

> Notice that the part of the hypothesis after *because* adds an explanation of why the airplane will glide farther.

MORE ABOUT HYPOTHESES

• The results of an experiment cannot prove that a hypothesis is correct. Rather, the results either support or do not support the hypothesis.

• Valuable information is gained even when your hypothesis is not supported by your results. For example, it would be an important discovery to find that wing size is not related to how far an airplane glides.

• In science, a hypothesis is supported only after many scientists have conducted many experiments and produced consistent results.

Inferring

An **inference** is a logical conclusion drawn from the available evidence and prior knowledge. Inferences are often made from observations.

EXAMPLE

A student observing a set of acorns noticed something unexpected about one of them. He noticed a white, soft-bodied insect eating its way out of the acorn.

The student recorded these observations.

Observations

- There is a hole in the acorn, about 0.5 cm in diameter, where the insect crawled out.
- There is a second hole, which is about the size of a pinhole, on the other side of the acorn.
- The inside of the acorn is hollow.

Here are some inferences that can be made on the basis of the observations.

Inferences

- The insect formed from the material inside the acorn, grew to its present size, and ate its way out of the acorn.
- The insect crawled through the smaller hole, ate the inside of the acorn, grew to its present size, and ate its way out of the acorn.
- An egg was laid in the acorn through the smaller hole. The egg hatched into a larva that ate the inside of the acorn, grew to its present size, and ate its way out of the acorn.

When you make inferences, be sure to look at all of the evidence available and combine it with what you already know.

MORE ABOUT INFERENCES

Inferences depend both on observations and on the knowledge of the people making the inferences. Ancient people who did not know that organisms are produced only by similar organisms might have made an inference like the first one. A student today might look at the same observations and make the second inference. A third student might have knowledge about this particular insect and know that it is never small enough to fit through the smaller hole, leading her to the third inference.

Identifying Cause and Effect

In a **cause-and-effect relationship,** one event or characteristic is the result of another. Usually an effect follows its cause in time.

There are many examples of cause-and-effect relationships in everyday life.

Cause	Effect
Turn off a light.	Room gets dark.
Drop a glass.	Glass breaks.
Blow a whistle.	Sound is heard.

Scientists must be careful not to infer a cause-and-effect relationship just because one event happens after another event. When one event occurs after another, you cannot infer a cause-and-effect relationship on the basis of that information alone. You also cannot conclude that one event caused another if there are alternative ways to explain the second event. A scientist must demonstrate through experimentation or continued observation that an event was truly caused by another event.

EXAMPLE

Make an Observation

Suppose you have a few plants growing outside. When the weather starts getting colder, you bring one of the plants indoors. You notice that the plant you brought indoors is growing faster than the others are growing. You cannot conclude from your observation that the change in temperature was the cause of the increased plant growth, because there are alternative explanations for the observation. Some possible explanations are given below.

- The humidity indoors caused the plant to grow faster.

- The level of sunlight indoors caused the plant to grow faster.

- The indoor plant's being noticed more often and watered more often than the outdoor plants caused it to grow faster.

- The plant that was brought indoors was healthier than the other plants to begin with.

To determine which of these factors, if any, caused the indoor plant to grow faster than the outdoor plants, you would need to design and conduct an experiment.

See pages R28–R35 for information about designing experiments.

Recognizing Bias

Television, newspapers, and the Internet are full of experts claiming to have scientific evidence to back up their claims. How do you know whether the claims are really backed up by good science?

Bias is a slanted point of view, or personal prejudice. The goal of scientists is to be as objective as possible and to base their findings on facts instead of opinions. However, bias often affects the conclusions of researchers, and it is important to learn to recognize bias.

When scientific results are reported, you should consider the source of the information as well as the information itself. It is important to critically analyze the information that you see and read.

SOURCES OF BIAS

There are several ways in which a report of scientific information may be biased. Here are some questions that you can ask yourself:

1. **Who is sponsoring the research?**

   Sometimes, the results of an investigation are biased because an organization paying for the research is looking for a specific answer. This type of bias can affect how data are gathered and interpreted.

2. **Is the research sample large enough?**

   Sometimes research does not include enough data. The larger the sample size, the more likely that the results are accurate, assuming a truly random sample.

3. **In a survey, who is answering the questions?**

   The results of a survey or poll can be biased. The people taking part in the survey may have been specifically chosen because of how they would answer. They may have the same ideas or lifestyles. A survey or poll should make use of a random sample of people.

4. **Are the people who take part in a survey biased?**

   People who take part in surveys sometimes try to answer the questions the way they think the researcher wants them to answer. Also, in surveys or polls that ask for personal information, people may be unwilling to answer questions truthfully.

SCIENTIFIC BIAS

It is also important to realize that scientists have their own biases because of the types of research they do and because of their scientific viewpoints. Two scientists may look at the same set of data and come to completely different conclusions because of these biases. However, such disagreements are not necessarily bad. In fact, a critical analysis of disagreements is often responsible for moving science forward.

Identifying Faulty Reasoning

Faulty reasoning is wrong or incorrect thinking. It leads to mistakes and to wrong conclusions. Scientists are careful not to draw unreasonable conclusions from experimental data. Without such caution, the results of scientific investigations may be misleading.

EXAMPLE

Scientists try to make generalizations based on their data to explain as much about nature as possible. If only a small sample of data is looked at, however, a conclusion may be faulty. Suppose a scientist has studied the effects of the El Niño and La Niña weather patterns on flood damage in California from 1989 to 1995. The scientist organized the data in the bar graph below.

The scientist drew the following conclusions:

1. The La Niña weather pattern has no effect on flooding in California.

2. When neither weather pattern occurs, there is almost no flood damage.

3. A weak or moderate El Niño produces a small or moderate amount of flooding.

4. A strong El Niño produces a lot of flooding.

Flood and Storm Damage in California

Weak–moderate El Niño

Strong El Niño

Starting year of season
(July 1–June 30)

SOURCE: *Governor's Office of Emergency Services, California*

For the six-year period of the scientist's investigation, these conclusions may seem to be reasonable. However, a six-year study of weather patterns may be too small of a sample for the conclusions to be supported. Consider the following graph, which shows information that was gathered from 1949 to 1997.

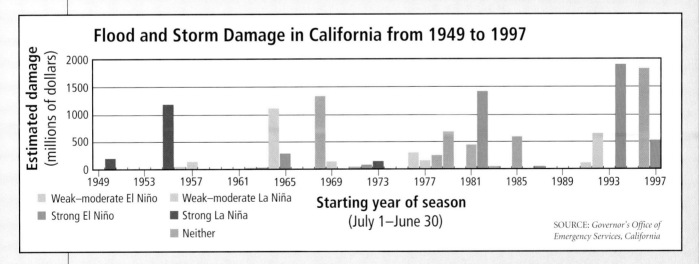

Flood and Storm Damage in California from 1949 to 1997

Weak–moderate El Niño Weak–moderate La Niña
Strong El Niño Strong La Niña
Neither

Starting year of season
(July 1–June 30)

SOURCE: *Governor's Office of Emergency Services, California*

The only one of the conclusions that all of this information supports is number 3: a weak or moderate El Niño produces a small or moderate amount of flooding. By collecting more data, scientists can be more certain of their conclusions and can avoid faulty reasoning.

Analyzing Statements

To **analyze** a statement is to examine its parts carefully. Scientific findings are often reported through media such as television or the Internet. A report that is made public often focuses on only a small part of research. As a result, it is important to question the sources of information.

Evaluate Media Claims

To **evaluate** a statement is to judge it on the basis of criteria you've established. Sometimes evaluating means deciding whether a statement is true.

Reports of scientific research and findings in the media may be misleading or incomplete. When you are exposed to this information, you should ask yourself some questions so that you can make informed judgments about the information.

1. **Does the information come from a credible source?**

   Suppose you learn about a new product and it is stated that scientific evidence proves that the product works. A report from a respected news source may be more believable than an advertisement paid for by the product's manufacturer.

2. **How much evidence supports the claim?**

   Often, it may seem that there is new evidence every day of something in the world that either causes or cures an illness. However, information that is the result of several years of work by several different scientists is more credible than an advertisement that does not even cite the subjects of the experiment.

3. **How much information is being presented?**

   Science cannot solve all questions, and scientific experiments often have flaws. A report that discusses problems in a scientific study may be more believable than a report that addresses only positive experimental findings.

4. **Is scientific evidence being presented by a specific source?**

   Sometimes scientific findings are reported by people who are called experts or leaders in a scientific field. But if their names are not given or their scientific credentials are not reported, their statements may be less credible than those of recognized experts.

Differentiate Between Fact and Opinion

Sometimes information is presented as a fact when it may be an opinion. When scientific conclusions are reported, it is important to recognize whether they are based on solid evidence. Again, you may find it helpful to ask yourself some questions.

1. **What is the difference between a fact and an opinion?**

    A **fact** is a piece of information that can be strictly defined and proved true. An **opinion** is a statement that expresses a belief, value, or feeling. An opinion cannot be proved true or false. For example, a person's age is a fact, but if someone is asked how old they feel, it is impossible to prove the person's answer to be true or false.

2. **Can opinions be measured?**

    Yes, opinions can be measured. In fact, surveys often ask for people's opinions on a topic. But there is no way to know whether or not an opinion is the truth.

HOW TO DIFFERENTIATE FACT FROM OPINION

Human Activities and the Environment

Unfortunately, human use of fossil fuels is one of the most significant developments of the past few centuries. Humans rely on fossil fuels, a non-renewable energy resource, for more than 90 percent of their energy needs.

This careless misuse of our planet's resources has resulted in pollution, global warming, and the destruction of fragile ecosystems. For example, oil pipelines carry more than one million barrels of oil each day across tundra regions. Transporting oil across such areas can only result in oil spills that poison the land for decades.

Opinions
Notice words or phrases that express beliefs or feelings. The words *unfortunately* and *careless* show that opinions are being expressed.

Opinion
Look for statements that speculate about events. These statements are opinions, because they cannot be proved.

Facts
Statements that contain statistics tend to be facts. Writers often use facts to support their opinions.

Lab Handbook

Safety Rules

Before you work in the laboratory, read these safety rules twice. Ask your teacher to explain any rules that you do not completely understand. Refer to these rules later on if you have questions about safety in the science classroom.

Directions

- Read all directions and make sure that you understand them before starting an investigation or lab activity. If you do not understand how to do a procedure or how to use a piece of equipment, ask your teacher.
- Do not begin any investigation or touch any equipment until your teacher has told you to start.
- Never experiment on your own. If you want to try a procedure that the directions do not call for, ask your teacher for permission first.
- If you are hurt or injured in any way, tell your teacher immediately.

Dress Code

goggles

apron

gloves

- Wear goggles when
  — using glassware, sharp objects, or chemicals
  — heating an object
  — working with anything that can easily fly up into the air and hurt someone's eye
- Tie back long hair or hair that hangs in front of your eyes.
- Remove any article of clothing—such as a loose sweater or a scarf—that hangs down and may touch a flame, chemical, or piece of equipment.
- Observe all safety icons calling for the wearing of eye protection, gloves, and aprons.

Heating and Fire Safety

fire safety

heating safety

- Keep your work area neat, clean, and free of extra materials.
- Never reach over a flame or heat source.
- Point objects being heated away from you and others.
- Never heat a substance or an object in a closed container.
- Never touch an object that has been heated. If you are unsure whether something is hot, treat it as though it is. Use oven mitts, clamps, tongs, or a test-tube holder.
- Know where the fire extinguisher and fire blanket are kept in your classroom.
- Do not throw hot substances into the trash. Wait for them to cool or use the container your teacher puts out for disposal.

Electrical Safety

electrical safety

- Never use lamps or other electrical equipment with frayed cords.
- Make sure no cord is lying on the floor where someone can trip over it.
- Do not let a cord hang over the side of a counter or table so that the equipment can easily be pulled or knocked to the floor.
- Never let cords hang into sinks or other places where water can be found.
- Never try to fix electrical problems. Inform your teacher of any problems immediately.
- Unplug an electrical cord by pulling on the plug, not the cord.

Chemical Safety

chemical safety

poison

fumes

Wafting

- If you spill a chemical or get one on your skin or in your eyes, tell your teacher right away.
- Never touch, taste, or sniff any chemicals in the lab. If you need to determine odor, waft. Wafting consists of holding the chemical in its container 15 centimeters (6 in.) away from your nose, and using your fingers to bring fumes from the container to your nose.
- Keep lids on all chemicals you are not using.
- Never put unused chemicals back into the original containers. Throw away extra chemicals where your teacher tells you to.
- Pour chemicals over a sink or your work area, not over the floor.
- If you get a chemical in your eye, use the eyewash right away.
- Always wash your hands after handling chemicals, plants, or soil.

Glassware and Sharp-Object Safety

sharp objects

- If you break glassware, tell your teacher right away.
- Do not use broken or chipped glassware. Give these to your teacher.
- Use knives and other cutting instruments carefully. Always wear eye protection and cut away from you.

Animal Safety

- Never hurt an animal.
- Touch animals only when necessary. Follow your teacher's instructions for handling animals.
- Always wash your hands after working with animals.

Cleanup

disposal

- Follow your teacher's instructions for throwing away or putting away supplies.
- Clean your work area and pick up anything that has dropped to the floor.
- Wash your hands.

Using Lab Equipment

Different experiments require different types of equipment. But even though experiments differ, the ways in which the equipment is used are the same.

Beakers

- Use beakers for holding and pouring liquids.

- Do not use a beaker to measure the volume of a liquid. Use a graduated cylinder instead. (See page R16.)

- Use a beaker that holds about twice as much liquid as you need. For example, if you need 100 milliliters of water, you should use a 200- or 250-milliliter beaker.

Test Tubes

- Use test tubes to hold small amounts of substances.

- Do not use a test tube to measure the volume of a liquid.

- Use a test tube when heating a substance over a flame. Aim the mouth of the tube away from yourself and other people.

- Liquids easily spill or splash from test tubes, so it is important to use only small amounts of liquids.

Test-Tube Holder

- Use a test-tube holder when heating a substance in a test tube.

- Use a test-tube holder if the substance in a test tube is dangerous to touch.

- Make sure the test-tube holder tightly grips the test tube so that the test tube will not slide out of the holder.

- Make sure that the test-tube holder is above the surface of the substance in the test tube so that you can observe the substance.

Test-Tube Rack

- Use a test-tube rack to organize test tubes before, during, and after an experiment.
- Use a test-tube rack to keep test tubes upright so that they do not fall over and spill their contents.
- Use a test-tube rack that is the correct size for the test tubes that you are using. If the rack is too small, a test tube may become stuck. If the rack is too large, a test tube may lean over, and some of its contents may spill or splash.

Forceps

- Use forceps when you need to pick up or hold a very small object that should not be touched with your hands.
- Do not use forceps to hold anything over a flame, because forceps are not long enough to keep your hand safely away from the flame. Plastic forceps will melt, and metal forceps will conduct heat and burn your hand.

Hot Plate

- Use a hot plate when a substance needs to be kept warmer than room temperature for a long period of time.
- Use a hot plate instead of a Bunsen burner or a candle when you need to carefully control temperature.
- Do not use a hot plate when a substance needs to be burned in an experiment.
- Always use "hot hands" safety mitts or oven mitts when handling anything that has been heated on a hot plate.

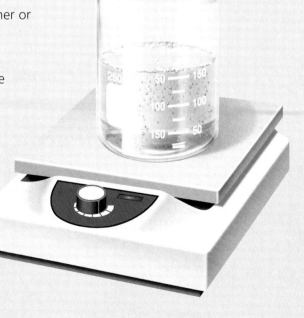

Microscope

Scientists use microscopes to see very small objects that cannot easily be seen with the eye alone. A microscope magnifies the image of an object so that small details may be observed. A microscope that you may use can magnify an object 400 times—the object will appear 400 times larger than its actual size.

Eyepiece Objects are viewed through the eyepiece. The eyepiece contains a lens that commonly magnifies an image 10 times.

Body The body separates the lens in the eyepiece from the objective lenses below.

Coarse Adjustment This knob is used to focus the image of an object when it is viewed through the low-power lens.

Nosepiece The nosepiece holds the objective lenses above the stage and rotates so that all lenses may be used.

Fine Adjustment This knob is used to focus the image of an object when it is viewed through the high-power lens.

High-Power Objective Lens This is the largest lens on the nosepiece. It magnifies an image approximately 40 times.

Low-Power Objective Lens This is the smallest lens on the nosepiece. It magnifies an image approximately 10 times.

Stage The stage supports the object being viewed.

Arm The arm supports the body above the stage. Always carry a microscope by the arm and base.

Diaphragm The diaphragm is used to adjust the amount of light passing through the slide and into an objective lens.

Stage Clip The stage clip holds a slide in place on the stage.

Mirror or Light Source Some microscopes use light that is reflected through the stage by a mirror. Other microscopes have their own light sources.

Base The base supports the microscope.

VIEWING AN OBJECT

1. Use the coarse adjustment knob to raise the body tube.

2. Adjust the diaphragm so that you can see a bright circle of light through the eyepiece.

3. Place the object or slide on the stage. Be sure that it is centered over the hole in the stage.

4. Turn the nosepiece to click the low-power lens into place.

5. Using the coarse adjustment knob, slowly lower the lens and focus on the specimen being viewed. Be sure not to touch the slide or object with the lens.

6. When switching from the low-power lens to the high-power lens, first raise the body tube with the coarse adjustment knob so that the high-power lens will not hit the slide.

7. Turn the nosepiece to click the high-power lens into place.

8. Use the fine adjustment knob to focus on the specimen being viewed. Again, be sure not to touch the slide or object with the lens.

MAKING A SLIDE, OR WET MOUNT

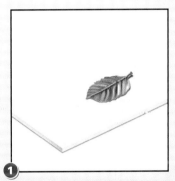

1 Place the specimen in the center of a clean slide.

2 Place a drop of water on the specimen.

3 Place a cover slip on the slide. Put one edge of the cover slip into the drop of water and slowly lower it over the specimen.

4 Remove any air bubbles from under the cover slip by gently tapping the cover slip.

5 Dry any excess water before placing the slide on the microscope stage for viewing.

Spring Scale (Force Meter)

- Use a spring scale to measure a force pulling on the scale.
- Use a spring scale to measure the force of gravity exerted on an object by Earth.
- To measure a force accurately, a spring scale must be zeroed before it is used. The scale is zeroed when no weight is attached and the indicator is positioned at zero.
- Do not attach a weight that is either too heavy or too light to a spring scale. A weight that is too heavy could break the scale or exert too great a force for the scale to measure. A weight that is too light may not exert enough force to be measured accurately.

Graduated Cylinder

- Use a graduated cylinder to measure the volume of a liquid.
- Be sure that the graduated cylinder is on a flat surface so that your measurement will be accurate.
- When reading the scale on a graduated cylinder, be sure to have your eyes at the level of the surface of the liquid.
- The surface of the liquid will be curved in the graduated cylinder. Read the volume of the liquid at the bottom of the curve, or meniscus (muh-NIHS-kuhs).
- You can use a graduated cylinder to find the volume of a solid object by measuring the increase in a liquid's level after you add the object to the cylinder.

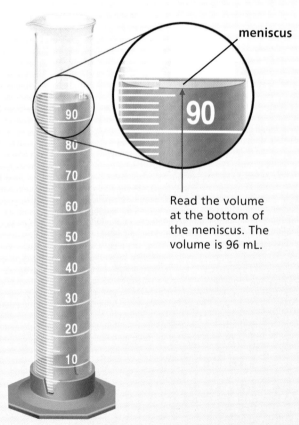

meniscus

Read the volume at the bottom of the meniscus. The volume is 96 mL.

Metric Rulers

- Use metric rulers or meter sticks to measure objects' lengths.

- Do not measure an object from the end of a metric ruler or meter stick, because the end is often imperfect. Instead, measure from the 1-centimeter mark, but remember to subtract a centimeter from the apparent measurement.

- Estimate any lengths that extend between marked units. For example, if a meter stick shows centimeters but not millimeters, you can estimate the length that an object extends between centimeter marks to measure it to the nearest millimeter.

- **Controlling Variables** If you are taking repeated measurements, always measure from the same point each time. For example, if you're measuring how high two different balls bounce when dropped from the same height, measure both bounces at the same point on the balls—either the top or the bottom. Do not measure at the top of one ball and the bottom of the other.

EXAMPLE

How to Measure a Leaf

1. Lay a ruler flat on top of the leaf so that the 1-centimeter mark lines up with one end. Make sure the ruler and the leaf do not move between the time you line them up and the time you take the measurement.

2. Look straight down on the ruler so that you can see exactly how the marks line up with the other end of the leaf.

3. Estimate the length by which the leaf extends beyond a marking. For example, the leaf below extends about halfway between the 4.2-centimeter and 4.3-centimeter marks, so the apparent measurement is about 4.25 centimeters.

4. Remember to subtract 1 centimeter from your apparent measurement, since you started at the 1-centimeter mark on the ruler and not at the end. The leaf is about 3.25 centimeters long (4.25 cm − 1 cm = 3.25 cm).

Triple-Beam Balance

This balance has a pan and three beams with sliding masses, called riders. At one end of the beams is a pointer that indicates whether the mass on the pan is equal to the masses shown on the beams.

1. Make sure the balance is zeroed before measuring the mass of an object. The balance is zeroed if the pointer is at zero when nothing is on the pan and the riders are at their zero points. Use the adjustment knob at the base of the balance to zero it.

2. Place the object to be measured on the pan.

3. Move the riders one notch at a time away from the pan. Begin with the largest rider. If moving the largest rider one notch brings the pointer below zero, begin measuring the mass of the object with the next smaller rider.

4. Change the positions of the riders until they balance the mass on the pan and the pointer is at zero. Then add the readings from the three beams to determine the mass of the object.

300 g	position of largest rider
90 g	position of middle rider
+ 3 g	position of smallest rider
393 g	mass of beaker

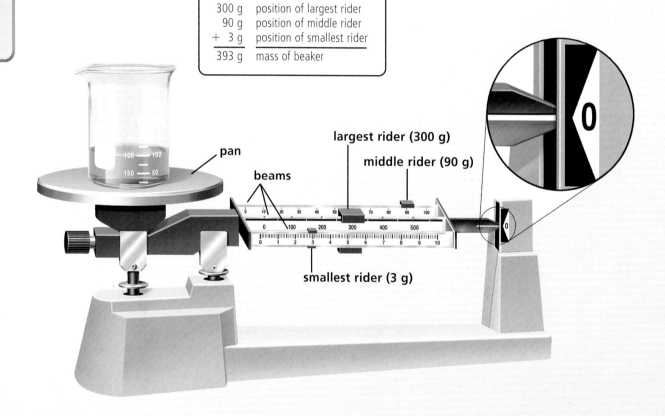

pan

beams

largest rider (300 g)

middle rider (90 g)

smallest rider (3 g)

Double-Pan Balance

This type of balance has two pans. Between the pans is a pointer that indicates whether the masses on the pans are equal.

1. Make sure the balance is zeroed before measuring the mass of an object. The balance is zeroed if the pointer is at zero when there is nothing on either of the pans. Many double-pan balances have sliding knobs that can be used to zero them.

2. Place the object to be measured on one of the pans.

3. Begin adding standard masses to the other pan. Begin with the largest standard mass. If this adds too much mass to the balance, begin measuring the mass of the object with the next smaller standard mass.

4. Add standard masses until the masses on both pans are balanced and the pointer is at zero. Then add the standard masses together to determine the mass of the object being measured.

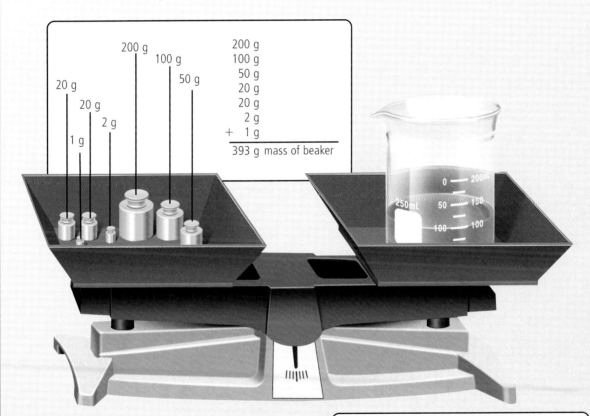

	200 g
	100 g
	50 g
	20 g
	20 g
	2 g
+	1 g
	393 g mass of beaker

Never place chemicals or liquids directly on a pan. Instead, use the following procedure:

1. Determine the mass of an empty container, such as a beaker.

2. Pour the substance into the container, and measure the total mass of the substance and the container.

3. Subtract the mass of the empty container from the total mass to find the mass of the substance.

The Metric System and SI Units

Scientists use International System (SI) units for measurements of distance, volume, mass, and temperature. The International System is based on multiples of ten and the metric system of measurement.

Basic SI Units		
Property	**Name**	**Symbol**
length	meter	m
volume	liter	L
mass	kilogram	kg
temperature	kelvin	K

SI Prefixes		
Prefix	**Symbol**	**Multiple of 10**
kilo-	k	1000
hecto-	h	100
deca-	da	10
deci-	d	$0.1 \left(\frac{1}{10}\right)$
centi-	c	$0.01 \left(\frac{1}{100}\right)$
milli-	m	$0.001 \left(\frac{1}{1000}\right)$

Changing Metric Units

You can change from one unit to another in the metric system by multiplying or dividing by a power of 10.

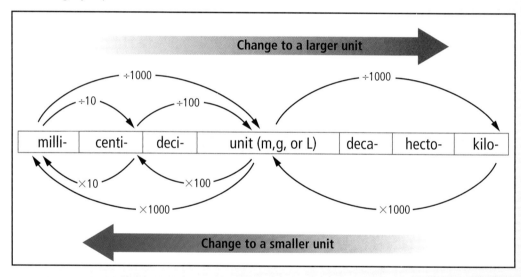

Change to a larger unit

milli- | centi- | deci- | unit (m,g, or L) | deca- | hecto- | kilo-

Change to a smaller unit

Example

Change 0.64 liters to milliliters.

(1) Decide whether to multiply or divide.

(2) Select the power of 10.

ANSWER 0.64 L = 640 mL

Change to a smaller unit by multiplying.

mL ◄——— × 1000 ——— L

0.64 × 1000 = **640.**

Example

Change 23.6 grams to kilograms.

(1) Decide whether to multiply or divide.

(2) Select the power of 10.

ANSWER 23.6 g = 0.0236 kg

Change to a larger unit by dividing.

g ——— ÷ 1000 ——► kg

23.6 ÷ 1000 = **0.0236**

Temperature Conversions

Even though the kelvin is the SI base unit of temperature, the degree Celsius will be the unit you use most often in your science studies. The formulas below show the relationships between temperatures in degrees Fahrenheit (°F), degrees Celsius (°C), and kelvins (K).

$$°C = \frac{5}{9}(°F - 32)$$

$$°F = \frac{9}{5}°C + 32$$

$$K = °C + 273$$

See page R42 for help with using formulas.

Examples of Temperature Conversions		
Condition	**Degrees Celsius**	**Degrees Fahrenheit**
Freezing point of water	0	32
Cool day	10	50
Mild day	20	68
Warm day	30	86
Normal body temperature	37	98.6
Very hot day	40	104
Boiling point of water	100	212

Converting Between SI and U.S. Customary Units

Use the chart below when you need to convert between SI units and U.S. customary units.

SI Unit	From SI to U.S. Customary			From U.S. Customary to SI		
Length	**When you know**	**multiply by**	**to find**	**When you know**	**multiply by**	**to find**
kilometer (km) = 1000 m	kilometers	0.62	miles	miles	1.61	kilometers
meter (m) = 100 cm	meters	3.28	feet	feet	0.3048	meters
centimeter (cm) = 10 mm	centimeters	0.39	inches	inches	2.54	centimeters
millimeter (mm) = 0.1 cm	millimeters	0.04	inches	inches	25.4	millimeters
Area	**When you know**	**multiply by**	**to find**	**When you know**	**multiply by**	**to find**
square kilometer (km^2)	square kilometers	0.39	square miles	square miles	2.59	square kilometers
square meter (m^2)	square meters	1.2	square yards	square yards	0.84	square meters
square centimeter (cm^2)	square centimeters	0.155	square inches	square inches	6.45	square centimeters
Volume	**When you know**	**multiply by**	**to find**	**When you know**	**multiply by**	**to find**
liter (L) = 1000 mL	liters	1.06	quarts	quarts	0.95	liters
	liters	0.26	gallons	gallons	3.79	liters
	liters	4.23	cups	cups	0.24	liters
	liters	2.12	pints	pints	0.47	liters
milliliter (mL) = 0.001 L	milliliters	0.20	teaspoons	teaspoons	4.93	milliliters
	milliliters	0.07	tablespoons	tablespoons	14.79	milliliters
	milliliters	0.03	fluid ounces	fluid ounces	29.57	milliliters
Mass	**When you know**	**multiply by**	**to find**	**When you know**	**multiply by**	**to find**
kilogram (kg) = 1000 g	kilograms	2.2	pounds	pounds	0.45	kilograms
gram (g) = 1000 mg	grams	0.035	ounces	ounces	28.35	grams

Precision and Accuracy

When you do an experiment, it is important that your methods, observations, and data be both precise and accurate.

low precision

precision, but not accuracy

precision and accuracy

Precision

In science, **precision** is the exactness and consistency of measurements. For example, measurements made with a ruler that has both centimeter and millimeter markings would be more precise than measurements made with a ruler that has only centimeter markings. Another indicator of precision is the care taken to make sure that methods and observations are as exact and consistent as possible. Every time a particular experiment is done, the same procedure should be used. Precision is necessary because experiments are repeated several times and if the procedure changes, the results will change.

EXAMPLE

Suppose you are measuring temperatures over a two-week period. Your precision will be greater if you measure each temperature at the same place, at the same time of day, and with the same thermometer than if you change any of these factors from one day to the next.

Accuracy

In science, it is possible to be precise but not accurate. **Accuracy** depends on the difference between a measurement and an actual value. The smaller the difference, the more accurate the measurement.

EXAMPLE

Suppose you look at a stream and estimate that it is about 1 meter wide at a particular place. You decide to check your estimate by measuring the stream with a meter stick, and you determine that the stream is 1.32 meters wide. However, because it is hard to measure the width of a stream with a meter stick, it turns out that you didn't do a very good job. The stream is actually 1.14 meters wide. Therefore, even though your estimate was less precise than your measurement, your estimate was actually more accurate.

Making Data Tables and Graphs

Data tables and graphs are useful tools for both recording and communicating scientific data.

Making Data Tables

You can use a **data table** to organize and record the measurements that you make. Some examples of information that might be recorded in data tables are frequencies, times, and amounts.

EXAMPLE

Suppose you are investigating photosynthesis in two elodea plants. One sits in direct sunlight, and the other sits in a dimly lit room. You measure the rate of photosynthesis by counting the number of bubbles in the jar every ten minutes.

1. Title and number your data table.
2. Decide how you will organize the table into columns and rows.
3. Any units, such as seconds or degrees, should be included in column headings, not in the individual cells.

Table 1. Number of Bubbles from Elodea

Always number and title data tables.

Time (min)	Sunlight	Dim Light
0	0	0
10	15	5
20	25	8
30	32	7
40	41	10
50	47	9
60	42	9

The data in the table above could also be organized in a different way.

Table 1. Number of Bubbles from Elodea

Put units in column heading.

Light Condition	Time (min)						
	0	10	20	30	40	50	60
Sunlight	0	15	25	32	41	47	42
Dim light	0	5	8	7	10	9	9

Making Line Graphs

You can use a **line graph** to show a relationship between variables. Line graphs are particularly useful for showing changes in variables over time.

EXAMPLE

Suppose you are interested in graphing temperature data that you collected over the course of a day.

Table 1. Outside Temperature During the Day on March 7

	Time of Day						
	7:00 A.M.	9:00 A.M.	11:00 A.M.	1:00 P.M.	3:00 P.M.	5:00 P.M.	7:00 P.M.
Temp (°C)	8	9	11	14	12	10	6

1. Use the vertical axis of your line graph for the variable that you are measuring—temperature.

2. Choose scales for both the horizontal axis and the vertical axis of the graph. You should have two points more than you need on the vertical axis, and the horizontal axis should be long enough for all of the data points to fit.

3. Draw and label each axis.

4. Graph each value. First find the appropriate point on the scale of the horizontal axis. Imagine a line that rises vertically from that place on the scale. Then find the corresponding value on the vertical axis, and imagine a line that moves horizontally from that value. The point where these two imaginary lines intersect is where the value should be plotted.

5. Connect the points with straight lines.

Be sure to add a number and a title to your graph.

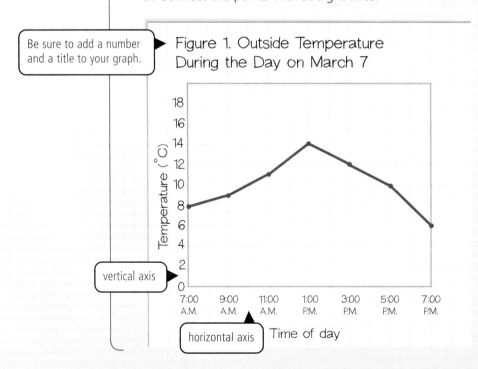

Figure 1. Outside Temperature During the Day on March 7

vertical axis

horizontal axis   Time of day

Making Circle Graphs

You can use a **circle graph,** sometimes called a pie chart, to represent data as parts of a circle. Circle graphs are used only when the data can be expressed as percentages of a whole. The entire circle shown in a circle graph is equal to 100 percent of the data.

EXAMPLE

Suppose you identified the species of each mature tree growing in a small wooded area. You organized your data in a table, but you also want to show the data in a circle graph.

1. To begin, find the total number of mature trees.

$$56 + 34 + 22 + 10 + 28 = 150$$

2. To find the degree measure for each sector of the circle, write a fraction comparing the number of each tree species with the total number of trees. Then multiply the fraction by 360°.

$$\text{Oak: } \frac{56}{150} \times 360° = 134.4°$$

3. Draw a circle. Use a protractor to draw the angle for each sector of the graph.

4. Color and label each sector of the graph.

5. Give the graph a number and title.

Table 1. Tree Species in Wooded Area

Species	Number of Specimens
Oak	56
Maple	34
Birch	22
Willow	10
Pine	28

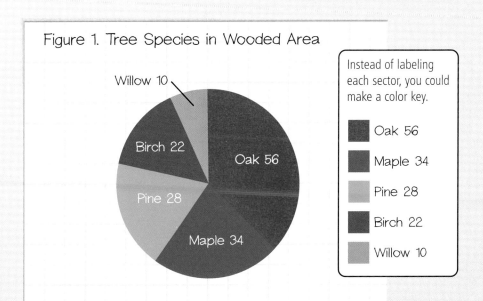

Figure 1. Tree Species in Wooded Area

Willow 10
Birch 22
Pine 28
Oak 56
Maple 34

Instead of labeling each sector, you could make a color key.

- Oak 56
- Maple 34
- Pine 28
- Birch 22
- Willow 10

Bar Graph

A **bar graph** is a type of graph in which the lengths of the bars are used to represent and compare data. A numerical scale is used to determine the lengths of the bars.

EXAMPLE

To determine the effect of water on seed sprouting, three cups were filled with sand, and ten seeds were planted in each. Different amounts of water were added to each cup over a three-day period.

Table 1. Effect of Water on Seed Sprouting

Daily Amount of Water (mL)	Number of Seeds That Sprouted After 3 Days in Sand
0	1
10	4
20	8

1. Choose a numerical scale. The greatest value is 8, so the end of the scale should have a value greater than 8, such as 10. Use equal increments along the scale, such as increments of 2.

2. Draw and label the axes. Mark intervals on the vertical axis according to the scale you chose.

3. Draw a bar for each data value. Use the scale to decide how long to make each bar.

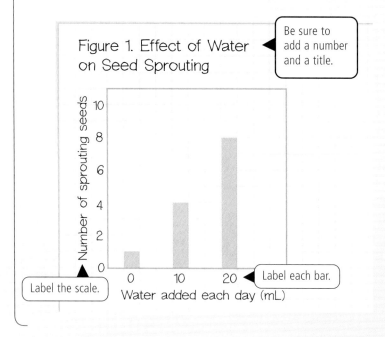

Figure 1. Effect of Water on Seed Sprouting

Be sure to add a number and a title.

Label the scale.

Label each bar.

Double Bar Graph

A **double bar graph** is a bar graph that shows two sets of data. The two bars for each measurement are drawn next to each other.

EXAMPLE

The seed-sprouting experiment was done using both sand and potting soil. The data for sand and potting soil can be plotted on one graph.

1. Draw one set of bars, using the data for sand, as shown below.

2. Draw bars for the potting-soil data next to the bars for the sand data. Shade them a different color. Add a key.

Table 2. Effect of Water and Soil on Seed Sprouting

Daily Amount of Water (mL)	Number of Seeds That Sprouted After 3 Days in Sand	Number of Seeds That Sprouted After 3 Days in Potting Soil
0	1	2
10	4	5
20	8	9

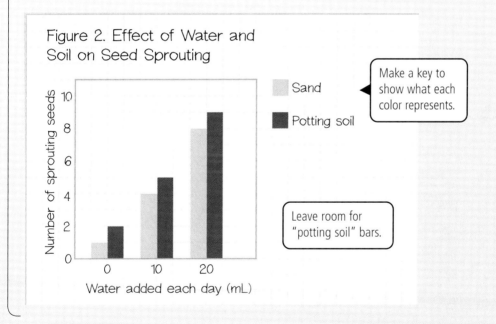

Figure 2. Effect of Water and Soil on Seed Sprouting

Sand

Potting soil

Make a key to show what each color represents.

Leave room for "potting soil" bars.

Designing an Experiment

Use this section when designing or conducting an experiment.

Determining a Purpose

You can find a purpose for an experiment by doing research, by examining the results of a previous experiment, or by observing the world around you. An **experiment** is an organized procedure to study something under controlled conditions.

1. Write the purpose of your experiment as a question or problem that you want to investigate.

2. Write down research questions and begin searching for information that will help you design an experiment. Consult the library, the Internet, and other people as you conduct your research.

> Don't forget to learn as much as possible about your topic before you begin.

EXAMPLE

Middle school students observed an odor near the lake by their school. They also noticed that the water on the side of the lake near the school was greener than the water on the other side of the lake. The students did some research to learn more about their observations. They discovered that the odor and green color in the lake

came from algae. They also discovered that a new fertilizer was being used on a field nearby. The students inferred that the use of the fertilizer might be related to the presence of the algae and designed a controlled experiment to find out whether they were right.

Problem

How does fertilizer affect the presence of algae in a lake?

Research Questions

- Have other experiments been done on this problem? If so, what did those experiments show?
- What kind of fertilizer is used on the field? How much?
- How do algae grow?
- How do people measure algae?
- Can fertilizer and algae be used safely in a lab? How?

> **Research**
> As you research, you may find a topic that is more interesting to you than your original topic, or learn that a procedure you wanted to use is not practical or safe. It is OK to change your purpose as you research.

Writing a Hypothesis

A **hypothesis** is a tentative explanation for an observation or scientific problem that can be tested by further investigation. You can write your hypothesis in the form of an "If . . . , then . . . , because . . ." statement.

Hypothesis

If the amount of fertilizer in lake water is increased, then the amount of algae will also increase, because fertilizers provide nutrients that algae need to grow.

Hypotheses
For help with hypotheses, refer to page R3.

Determining Materials

Make a list of all the materials you will need to do your experiment. Be specific, especially if someone else is helping you obtain the materials. Try to think of everything you will need.

Materials
- 1 large jar or container
- 4 identical smaller containers
- rubber gloves that also cover the arms
- sample of fertilizer-and-water solution
- eyedropper
- clear plastic wrap
- scissors
- masking tape
- marker
- ruler

Determining Variables and Constants

EXPERIMENTAL GROUP AND CONTROL GROUP

An experiment to determine how two factors are related always has two groups—a control group and an experimental group.

1. Design an experimental group. Include as many trials as possible in the experimental group in order to obtain reliable results.
2. Design a control group that is the same as the experimental group in every way possible, except for the factor you wish to test.

Experimental Group: two containers of lake water with one drop of fertilizer solution added to each

Control Group: two containers of lake water with no fertilizer solution added

> Go back to your materials list and make sure you have enough items listed to cover both your experimental group and your control group.

VARIABLES AND CONSTANTS

Identify the variables and constants in your experiment. In a controlled experiment, a **variable** is any factor that can change. **Constants** are all of the factors that are the same in both the experimental group and the control group.

1. Read your hypothesis. The **independent variable** is the factor that you wish to test and that is manipulated or changed so that it can be tested. The independent variable is expressed in your hypothesis after the word *if*. Identify the independent variable in your laboratory report.
2. The **dependent variable** is the factor that you measure to gather results. It is expressed in your hypothesis after the word *then*. Identify the dependent variable in your laboratory report.

Hypothesis
If the amount of fertilizer in lake water is increased, then the amount of algae will also increase, because fertilizers provide nutrients that algae need to grow.

Table 1. Variables and Constants in Algae Experiment

Independent Variable	Dependent Variable	Constants
Amount of fertilizer in lake water	Amount of algae that grow	• Where the lake water is obtained • Type of container used • Light and temperature conditions where water will be stored

> Set up your experiment so that you will test only one variable.

MEASURING THE DEPENDENT VARIABLE

Before starting your experiment, you need to define how you will measure the dependent variable. An **operational definition** is a description of the one particular way in which you will measure the dependent variable.

Your operational definition is important for several reasons. First, in any experiment there are several ways in which a dependent variable can be measured. Second, the procedure of the experiment depends on how you decide to measure the dependent variable. Third, your operational definition makes it possible for other people to evaluate and build on your experiment.

EXAMPLE 1

An operational definition of a dependent variable can be qualitative. That is, your measurement of the dependent variable can simply be an observation of whether a change occurs as a result of a change in the independent variable. This type of operational definition can be thought of as a "yes or no" measurement.

Table 2. Qualitative Operational Definition of Algae Growth

Independent Variable	Dependent Variable	Operational Definition
Amount of fertilizer in lake water	Amount of algae that grow	Algae grow in lake water

A qualitative measurement of a dependent variable is often easy to make and record. However, this type of information does not provide a great deal of detail in your experimental results.

EXAMPLE 2

An operational definition of a dependent variable can be quantitative. That is, your measurement of the dependent variable can be a number that shows how much change occurs as a result of a change in the independent variable.

Table 3. Quantitative Operational Definition of Algae Growth

Independent Variable	Dependent Variable	Operational Definition
Amount of fertilizer in lake water	Amount of algae that grow	Diameter of largest algal growth (in mm)

A quantitative measurement of a dependent variable can be more difficult to make and analyze than a qualitative measurement. However, this type of data provides much more information about your experiment and is often more useful.

Writing a Procedure

Write each step of your procedure. Start each step with a verb, or action word, and keep the steps short. Your procedure should be clear enough for someone else to use as instructions for repeating your experiment.

> If necessary, go back to your materials list and add any materials that you left out.

Controlling Variables
The same amount of fertilizer solution must be added to two of the four containers.

Controlling Variables
All four containers must receive the same amount of light.

Procedure

1. Put on your gloves. Use the large container to obtain a sample of lake water.

2. Divide the sample of lake water equally among the four smaller containers.

3. Use the eyedropper to add one drop of fertilizer solution to two of the containers.

4. Use the masking tape and the marker to label the containers with your initials, the date, and the identifiers "Jar 1 with Fertilizer," "Jar 2 with Fertilizer," "Jar 1 without Fertilizer," and "Jar 2 without Fertilizer."

5. Cover the containers with clear plastic wrap. Use the scissors to punch ten holes in each of the covers.

6. Place all four containers on a window ledge. Make sure that they all receive the same amount of light.

7. Observe the containers every day for one week.

8. Use the ruler to measure the diameter of the largest clump of algae in each container, and record your measurements daily.

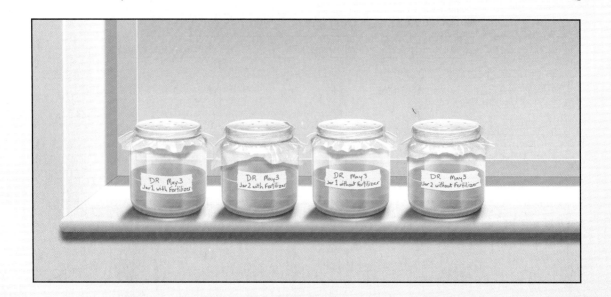

Recording Observations

Once you have obtained all of your materials and your procedure has been approved, you can begin making experimental observations. Gather both quantitative and qualitative data. If something goes wrong during your procedure, make sure you record that too.

Observations
For help with making qualitative and quantitative observations, refer to page R2.

For more examples of data tables, see page R23.

Table 4. Fertilizer and Algae Growth

Date and Time	Experimental Group		Control Group		Observations
	Jar 1 with Fertilizer (diameter of algae in mm)	Jar 2 with Fertilizer (diameter of algae in mm)	Jar 1 without Fertilizer (diameter of algae in mm)	Jar 2 without Fertilizer (diameter of algae in mm)	
5/3 4:00 P.M.	0	0	0	0	condensation in all containers
5/4 4:00 P.M.	0	3	0	0	tiny green blobs in jar 2 with fertilizer
5/5 4:15 P.M.	4	5	0	3	green blobs in jars 1 and 2 with fertilizer and jar 2 without fertilizer
5/6 4:00 P.M.	5	6	0	4	water light green in jar 2 with fertilizer
5/7 4:00 P.M.	8	10	0	6	water light green in jars 1 and 2 with fertilizer and in jar 2 without fertilizer
5/8 3:30 P.M.	10	18	0	6	cover off jar 2 with fertilizer
5/9 3:30 P.M.	14	23	0	8	drew sketches of each container

Notice that on the sixth day, the observer found that the cover was off one of the containers. It is important to record observations of unintended factors because they might affect the results of the experiment.

Use technology, such as a microscope, to help you make observations when possible.

Drawings of Samples Viewed Under Microscope on 5/9 at 100x

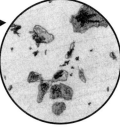

Jar 1 with Fertilizer

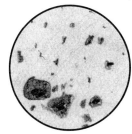

Jar 2 with Fertilizer

Jar 1 without Fertilizer

Jar 2 without Fertilizer

Summarizing Results

To summarize your data, look at all of your observations together. Look for meaningful ways to present your observations. For example, you might average your data or make a graph to look for patterns. When possible, use spreadsheet software to help you analyze and present your data. The two graphs below show the same data.

EXAMPLE 1

Always include a number and a title with a graph.

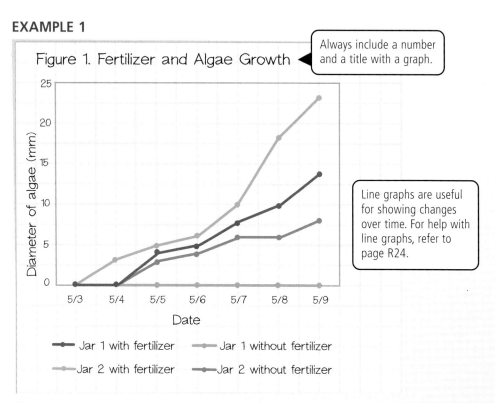

Figure 1. Fertilizer and Algae Growth

Line graphs are useful for showing changes over time. For help with line graphs, refer to page R24.

Bar graphs are useful for comparing different data sets. This bar graph has four bars for each day. Another way to present the data would be to calculate averages for the tests and the controls, and to show one test bar and one control bar for each day.

EXAMPLE 2

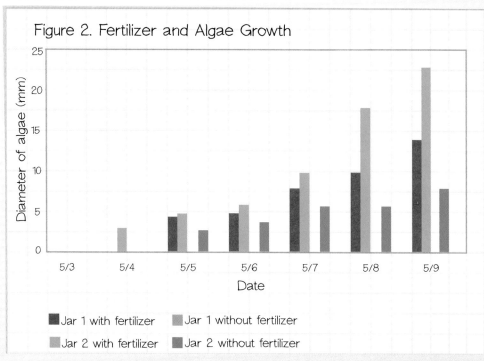

Figure 2. Fertilizer and Algae Growth

LAB HANDBOOK

Drawing Conclusions

RESULTS AND INFERENCES

To draw conclusions from your experiment, first write your results. Then compare your results with your hypothesis. Do your results support your hypothesis? Be careful not to make inferences about factors that you did not test.

For help with making inferences, see page R4.

Results and Inferences

The results of my experiment show that more algae grew in lake water to which fertilizer had been added than in lake water to which no fertilizer had been added. My hypothesis was supported. I infer that it is possible that the growth of algae in the lake was caused by the fertilizer used on the field.

Notice that you cannot conclude from this experiment that the presence of algae in the lake was due only to the fertilizer.

LAB HANDBOOK

QUESTIONS FOR FURTHER RESEARCH

Write a list of questions for further research and investigation. Your ideas may lead you to new experiments and discoveries.

Questions for Further Research

• What is the connection between the amount of fertilizer and algae growth?
• How do different brands of fertilizer affect algae growth?
• How would algae growth in the lake be affected if no fertilizer were used on the field?
• How do algae affect the lake and the other life in and around it?
• How does fertilizer affect the lake and the life in and around it?
• If fertilizer is getting into the lake, how is it getting there?

Math Handbook

Describing a Set of Data

Means, medians, modes, and ranges are important math tools for describing data sets such as the following widths of fossilized clamshells.

13 mm   25 mm   14 mm   21 mm   16 mm   23 mm   14 mm

Mean

The **mean** of a data set is the sum of the values divided by the number of values.

> **Example**
>
> To find the mean of the clamshell data, add the values and then divide the sum by the number of values.
>
> $$\frac{13 \text{ mm} + 25 \text{ mm} + 14 \text{ mm} + 21 \text{ mm} + 16 \text{ mm} + 23 \text{ mm} + 14 \text{ mm}}{7} = \frac{126 \text{ mm}}{7} = 18 \text{ mm}$$
>
> **ANSWER** The mean is 18 mm.

Median

The **median** of a data set is the middle value when the values are written in numerical order. If a data set has an even number of values, the median is the mean of the two middle values.

> **Example**
>
> To find the median of the clamshell data, arrange the values in order from least to greatest. The median is the middle value.
>
> 13 mm   14 mm   14 mm   16 mm   21 mm   23 mm   25 mm
>
> **ANSWER** The median is 16 mm.

Modo

The **modo** of a data set is the value that occurs most often.

Example

To find the mode of the clamshell data, arrange the values in order from least to greatest and determine the value that occurs most often.

13 mm   14 mm   14 mm   16 mm   21 mm   23 mm   25 mm

ANSWER The mode is 14 mm.

A data set can have more than one mode or no mode. For example, the following data set has modes of 2 mm and 4 mm:

2 mm   2 mm   3 mm   4 mm   4 mm

The data set below has no mode, because no value occurs more often than any other.

2 mm   3 mm   4 mm   5 mm

Range

The **range** of a data set is the difference between the greatest value and the least value.

Example

To find the range of the clamshell data, arrange the values in order from least to greatest.

13 mm   14 mm   14 mm   16 mm   21 mm   23 mm   25 mm

Subtract the least value from the greatest value.

13 mm is the least value.
25 mm is the greatest value.

25 mm − 13 mm = 12 mm

ANSWER The range is 12 mm.

Using Ratios, Rates, and Proportions

You can use ratios and rates to compare values in data sets. You can use proportions to find unknown values.

Ratios

A **ratio** uses division to compare two values. The ratio of a value a to a nonzero value b can be written as $\frac{a}{b}$.

Example

The height of one plant is 8 centimeters. The height of another plant is 6 centimeters. To find the ratio of the height of the first plant to the height of the second plant, write a fraction and simplify it.

$$\frac{8 \text{ cm}}{6 \text{ cm}} = \frac{4 \times \overset{1}{\cancel{2}}}{3 \times \underset{1}{\cancel{2}}} = \frac{4}{3}$$

ANSWER The ratio of the plant heights is $\frac{4}{3}$.

You can also write the ratio $\frac{a}{b}$ as "a to b" or as $a:b$. For example, you can write the ratio of the plant heights as "4 to 3" or as $4:3$.

Rates

A **rate** is a ratio of two values expressed in different units. A unit rate is a rate with a denominator of 1 unit.

Example

A plant grew 6 centimeters in 2 days. The plant's rate of growth was $\frac{6 \text{ cm}}{2 \text{ days}}$. To describe the plant's growth in centimeters per day, write a unit rate.

Divide numerator and denominator by 2: $\quad \frac{6 \text{ cm}}{2 \text{ days}} = \frac{6 \text{ cm} \div 2}{2 \text{ days} \div 2}$

> You divide 2 days by 2 to get 1 day, so divide 6 cm by 2 also.

Simplify: $\quad = \frac{3 \text{ cm}}{1 \text{ day}}$

ANSWER The plant's rate of growth is 3 centimeters per day.

Proportions

A **proportion** is an equation stating that two ratios are equivalent. To solve for an unknown value in a proportion, you can use cross products.

Example

If a plant grew 6 centimeters in 2 days, how many centimeters would it grow in 3 days (if its rate of growth is constant)?

$$\text{Write a proportion:} \qquad \frac{6 \text{ cm}}{2 \text{ days}} = \frac{x}{3 \text{ days}}$$

$$\text{Set cross products:} \qquad 6 \text{ cm} \cdot 3 = 2x$$

$$\text{Multiply 6 and 3:} \qquad 18 \text{ cm} = 2x$$

$$\text{Divide each side by 2:} \qquad \frac{18 \text{ cm}}{2} = \frac{2x}{2}$$

$$\text{Simplify:} \qquad 9 \text{ cm} = x$$

ANSWER The plant would grow 9 centimeters in 3 days.

Using Decimals, Fractions, and Percents

Decimals, fractions, and percentages are all ways of recording and representing data.

Decimals

A **decimal** is a number that is written in the base-ten place value system, in which a decimal point separates the ones and tenths digits. The values of each place is ten times that of the place to its right.

Example

A caterpillar traveled from point A to point C along the path shown.

A   **36.9 cm**   B   **52.4 cm**   C

ADDING DECIMALS To find the total distance traveled by the caterpillar, add the distance from A to B and the distance from B to C. Begin by lining up the decimal points. Then add the figures as you would whole numbers and bring down the decimal point.

```
   36.9 cm
 + 52.4 cm
   89.3 cm
```

ANSWER The caterpillar traveled a total distance of 89.3 centimeters.

Example *continued*

SUBTRACTING DECIMALS To find how much farther the caterpillar traveled on the second leg of the journey, subtract the distance from *A* to *B* from the distance from *B* to *C*.

$$\begin{array}{r} 52.4 \text{ cm} \\ -\ 36.9 \text{ cm} \\ \hline 15.5 \text{ cm} \end{array}$$

ANSWER The caterpillar traveled 15.5 centimeters farther on the second leg of the journey.

Example

A caterpillar is traveling from point *D* to point *F* along the path shown. The caterpillar travels at a speed of 9.6 centimeters per minute.

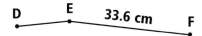

D   E   **33.6 cm**   F

MULTIPLYING DECIMALS You can multiply decimals as you would whole numbers. The number of decimal places in the product is equal to the sum of the number of decimal places in the factors.

For instance, suppose it takes the caterpillar 1.5 minutes to go from *D* to *E*. To find the distance from *D* to *E*, multiply the caterpillar's speed by the time it took.

Align as shown. ▶

$$\begin{array}{rl} 9.6 & \quad 1 \quad \text{decimal place} \\ \times\ 1.5 & +1 \quad \text{decimal place} \\ \hline 480 & \\ 96 & \\ \hline 14.40 & \quad 2 \quad \text{decimal places} \end{array}$$

ANSWER The distance from *D* to *E* is 14.4 centimeters.

DIVIDING DECIMALS When you divide by a decimal, move the decimal points the same number of places in the divisor and the dividend to make the divisor a whole number.

For instance, to find the time it will take the caterpillar to travel from *E* to *F*, divide the distance from *E* to *F* by the caterpillar's speed.

$$9.6\,\overline{)33.6}$$

◀ Move each decimal point one place to the right.

$$\begin{array}{r} 3.5 \\ 96\,\overline{)336.} \\ \underline{288} \\ 480 \\ \underline{480} \\ 0 \end{array}$$

◀ Line up decimal points.

ANSWER The caterpillar will travel from *E* to *F* in 3.5 minutes.

Fractions

A **fraction** is a number in the form $\frac{a}{b}$, where b is not equal to 0. A fraction is in **simplest form** if its numerator and denominator have a greatest common factor (GCF) of 1. To simplify a fraction, divide its numerator and denominator by their GCF.

> ### Example
>
> A caterpillar is 40 millimeters long. The head of the caterpillar is 6 millimeters long. To compare the length of the caterpillar's head with the caterpillar's total length, you can write and simplify a fraction that expresses the ratio of the two lengths.
>
> *Write the ratio of the two lengths:* $\dfrac{\text{Length of head}}{\text{Total length}} = \dfrac{6 \text{ mm}}{40 \text{ mm}}$
>
> *Write numerator and denominator as products of numbers and the GCF:* $= \dfrac{3 \times 2}{20 \times 2}$
>
> *Divide numerator and denominator by the GCF:* $= \dfrac{3 \times \overset{1}{\cancel{2}}}{20 \times \underset{1}{\cancel{2}}}$
>
> *Simplify:* $= \dfrac{3}{20}$
>
> **ANSWER** In simplest form, the ratio of the lengths is $\dfrac{3}{20}$.

Percents

A **percent** is a ratio that compares a number to 100. The word *percent* means "per hundred" or "out of 100." The symbol for *percent* is %.

For instance, suppose 43 out of 100 caterpillars are female. You can represent this ratio as a percent, a decimal, or a fraction.

Percent	Decimal	Fraction
43%	0.43	$\dfrac{43}{100}$

> ### Example
>
> In the preceding example, the ratio of the length of the caterpillar's head to the caterpillar's total length is $\dfrac{3}{20}$. To write this ratio as a percent, write an equivalent fraction that has a denominator of 100.
>
> *Multiply numerator and denominator by 5:* $\dfrac{3}{20} = \dfrac{3 \times 5}{20 \times 5}$
>
> $= \dfrac{15}{100}$
>
> *Write as a percent:* $= 15\%$
>
> **ANSWER** The caterpillar's head represents 15 percent of its total length.

Using Formulas

A **formula** is an equation that shows the general relationship between two or more quantities.

In science, a formula often has a word form and a symbolic form. The formula below expresses Ohm's law.

The term *variable* is also used in science to refer to a factor that can change during an experiment.

Word Form

$$\text{Current} = \frac{\text{voltage}}{\text{resistance}}$$

Symbolic Form

$$I = \frac{V}{R}$$

In this formula, I, V, and R are variables. A mathematical **variable** is a symbol or letter that is used to represent one or more numbers.

Example

Suppose that you measure a voltage of 1.5 volts and a resistance of 15 ohms. You can use the formula for Ohm's law to find the current in amperes.

Write the formula for Ohm's law: $I = \dfrac{V}{R}$

Substitute 1.5 volts for V and 15 ohms for R: $I = \dfrac{1.5 \text{ volts}}{15 \text{ ohms}}$

Simplify: $I = 0.1$ amp

ANSWER The current is 0.1 ampere.

If you know the values of all variables but one in a formula, you can solve for the value of the unknown variable. For instance, Ohm's law can be used to find a voltage if you know the current and the resistance.

Example

Suppose that you know that a current is 0.2 amperes and the resistance is 18 ohms. Use the formula for Ohm's law to find the voltage in volts.

Write the formula for Ohm's law: $I = \dfrac{V}{R}$

Substitute 0.2 amp for I and 18 ohms for R: $0.2 \text{ amp} = \dfrac{V}{18 \text{ ohms}}$

Multiply both sides by 18 ohms: $0.2 \text{ amp} \cdot 18 \text{ ohms} = V$

Simplify: $3.6 \text{ volts} = V$

ANSWER The voltage is 3.6 volts.

Finding Areas

The area of a figure is the amount of surface the figure covers.

Area is measured in square units, such as square meters (m^2) or square centimeters (cm^2). Formulas for the areas of three common geometric figures are shown below.

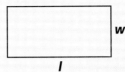

Area = (side length)^2
$A = s^2$

Area = length × width
$A = lw$

Area = $\frac{1}{2}$ × base × height
$A = \frac{1}{2} bh$

Example

Each face of a halite crystal is a square like the one shown. You can find the area of the square by using the steps below.

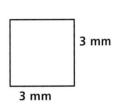

Write the formula for the area of a square:	$A = s^2$
Substitute 3 mm for s:	$= (3 \text{ mm})^2$
Simplify:	$= 9 \text{ mm}^2$

ANSWER The area of the square is 9 square millimeters.

Finding Volumes

The volume of a solid is the amount of space contained by the solid.

Volume is measured in cubic units, such as cubic meters (m^3) or cubic centimeters (cm^3). The volume of a rectangular prism is given by the formula shown below.

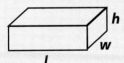

Volume = length × width × height
$V = lwh$

Example

A topaz crystal is a rectangular prism like the one shown. You can find the volume of the prism by using the steps below.

Write the formula for the volume of a rectangular prism:	$V = lwh$
Substitute dimensions:	$= 20 \text{ mm} \times 12 \text{ mm} \times 10 \text{ mm}$
Simplify:	$= 2400 \text{ mm}^3$

ANSWER The volume of the rectangular prism is 2400 cubic millimeters.

Using Significant Figures

The **significant figures** in a decimal are the digits that are warranted by the accuracy of a measuring device.

When you perform a calculation with measurements, the number of significant figures to include in the result depends in part on the number of significant figures in the measurements. When you multiply or divide measurements, your answer should have only as many significant figures as the measurement with the fewest significant figures.

Example

Using a balance and a graduated cylinder filled with water, you determined that a marble has a mass of 8.0 grams and a volume of 3.5 cubic centimeters. To calculate the density of the marble, divide the mass by the volume.

Write the formula for density: $\text{Density} = \dfrac{\text{mass}}{\text{Volume}}$

Substitute measurements: $= \dfrac{8.0 \text{ g}}{3.5 \text{ cm}^3}$

Use a calculator to divide: $\approx 2.285714286 \text{ g/cm}^3$

ANSWER Because the mass and the volume have two significant figures each, give the density to two significant figures. The marble has a density of 2.3 grams per cubic centimeter.

Using Scientific Notation

Scientific notation is a shorthand way to write very large or very small numbers. For example, 73,500,000,000,000,000,000,000 kg is the mass of the Moon. In scientific notation, it is 7.35×10^{22} kg.

Example

You can convert from standard form to scientific notation.

Standard Form	Scientific Notation
720,000	7.2×10^5
5 decimal places left	Exponent is 5.
0.000291	2.91×10^{-4}
4 decimal places right	Exponent is −4.

You can convert from scientific notation to standard form.

Scientific Notation	Standard Form
4.63×10^7	46,300,000
Exponent is 7.	7 decimal places right
1.08×10^{-6}	0.00000108
Exponent is −6.	6 decimal places left

Note-Taking Handbook

Note-Taking Strategies

Taking notes as you read helps you understand the information. The notes you take can also be used as a study guide for later review. This handbook presents several ways to organize your notes.

Content Frame

1. Make a chart in which each column represents a category.
2. Give each column a heading.
3. Write details under the headings.

NAME	GROUP	CHARACTERISTICS	DRAWING
snail	mollusks	mantle, shell	
ant	arthropods	six legs, exoskeleton	
earthworm	segmented worms	segmented body, circulatory and digestive systems	
heartworm	roundworms	digestive system	
sea star	echinoderms	spiny skin, tube feet	
jellyfish	cnidarians	stinging cells	

categories

details

Combination Notes

1. For each new idea or concept, write an informal outline of the information.
2. Make a sketch to illustrate the concept, and label it.

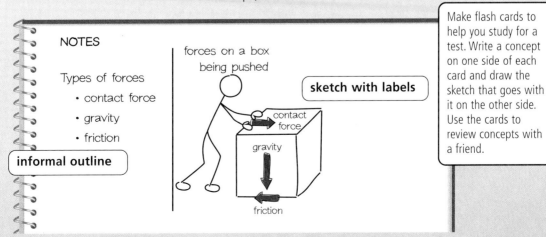

NOTES

Types of forces
- contact force
- gravity
- friction

informal outline

forces on a box being pushed

sketch with labels

contact force

gravity

friction

Make flash cards to help you study for a test. Write a concept on one side of each card and draw the sketch that goes with it on the other side. Use the cards to review concepts with a friend.

Main Idea and Detail Notes

1. In the left-hand column of a two-column chart, list main ideas. The blue headings express main ideas throughout this textbook.

2. In the right-hand column, write details that expand on each main idea.

You can shorten the headings in your chart. Be sure to use the most important words.

When studying for tests, cover up the detail notes column with a sheet of paper. Then use each main idea to form a question—such as "How does latitude affect climate?" Answer the question, and then uncover the detail notes column to check your answer.

MAIN IDEAS	DETAIL NOTES
1. Latitude affects climate. **main idea 1**	1. Places close to the equator are usually warmer than places close to the poles. *details about main idea 1* 1. Latitude has the same effect in both hemispheres.
2. Altitude affects climate. **main idea 2**	2. Temperature decreases with altitude. *details about main idea 2* 2. Altitude can overcome the effect of latitude on temperature.

Main Idea Web

1. Write a main idea in a box.

2. Add boxes around it with related vocabulary terms and important details.

You can find definitions near highlighted terms.

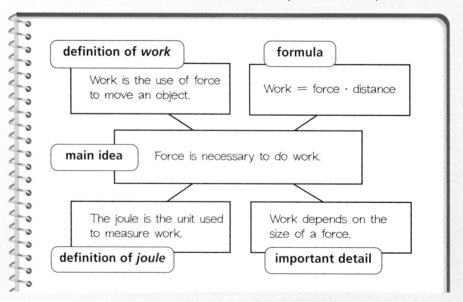

definition of *work*
Work is the use of force to move an object.

formula
Work = force · distance

main idea
Force is necessary to do work.

The joule is the unit used to measure work.
definition of *joule*

Work depends on the size of a force.
important detail

Mind Map

1. Write a main idea in the center.

2. Add details that relate to one another and to the main idea.

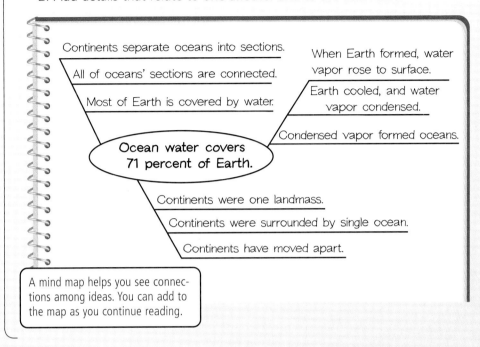

Continents separate oceans into sections.

All of oceans' sections are connected.

Most of Earth is covered by water.

When Earth formed, water vapor rose to surface.

Earth cooled, and water vapor condensed.

Condensed vapor formed oceans.

Ocean water covers 71 percent of Earth.

Continents were one landmass.

Continents were surrounded by single ocean.

Continents have moved apart.

A mind map helps you see connections among ideas. You can add to the map as you continue reading.

Supporting Main Ideas

1. Write a main idea in a box.

2. Add boxes underneath with information—such as reasons, explanations, and examples—that supports the main idea.

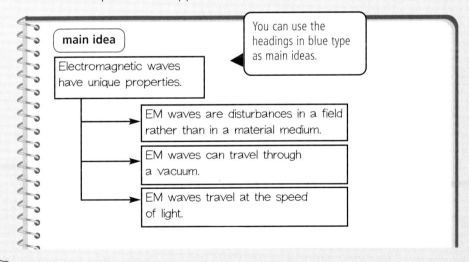

main idea

Electromagnetic waves have unique properties.

You can use the headings in blue type as main ideas.

EM waves are disturbances in a field rather than in a material medium.

EM waves can travel through a vacuum.

EM waves travel at the speed of light.

Outline

1. Copy the chapter title and headings from the book in the form of an outline.

2. Add notes that summarize in your own words what you read.

Cell Processes

1st key idea

I. Cells capture and release energy.

1st subpoint of I

  A. All cells need energy.

2nd subpoint of I

  B. Some cells capture light energy.

1st detail about B

    1. Process of photosynthesis

2nd detail about B

    2. Chloroplasts (site of photosynthesis)

    3. Carbon dioxide and water as raw materials

    4. Glucose and oxygen as products

  C. All cells release energy.

    1. Process of cellular respiration

    2. Fermentation of sugar to carbon dioxide

    3. Bacteria that carry out fermentation

II. Cells transport materials through membranes.

  A. Some materials move by diffusion.

    1. Particle movement from higher to lower concentrations

    2. Movement of water through membrane (osmosis)

  B. Some transport requires energy.

    1. Active transport

    2. Examples of active transport

Correct Outline Form

Include a title.

Arrange key ideas, subpoints, and details as shown.

Indent the divisions of the outline as shown.

Use the same grammatical form for items of the same rank. For example, if A is a sentence, B must also be a sentence.

You must have at least two main ideas or subpoints. That is, every A must be followed by a B, and every 1 must be followed by a 2.

Concept Map

1. Write an important concept in a large oval.
2. Add details related to the concept in smaller ovals.
3. Write linking words on arrows that connect the ovals.

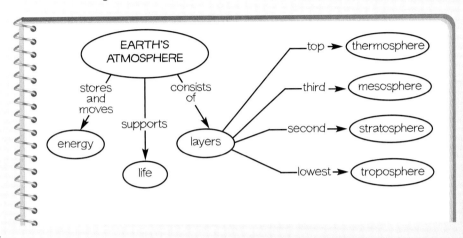

The main ideas or concepts can often be found in the blue headings. An example is "The atmosphere stores and moves energy." Use nouns from these concepts in the ovals, and use the verb or verbs on the lines.

Venn Diagram

1. Draw two overlapping circles, one for each item that you are comparing.
2. In the overlapping section, list the characteristics that are shared by both items.
3. In the outer sections, list the characteristics that are peculiar to each item.
4. Write a summary that describes the information in the Venn diagram.

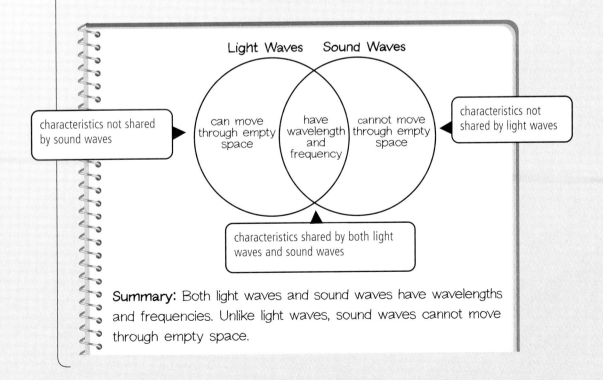

Summary: Both light waves and sound waves have wavelengths and frequencies. Unlike light waves, sound waves cannot move through empty space.

Vocabulary Strategies

Important terms are highlighted in this book. A definition of each term can be found in the sentence or paragraph where the term appears. You can also find definitions in the Glossary. Taking notes about vocabulary terms helps you understand and remember what you read.

Description Wheel

1. Write a term inside a circle.
2. Write words that describe the term on "spokes" attached to the circle.

When studying for a test with a friend, read the phrases on the spokes one at a time until your friend identifies the correct term.

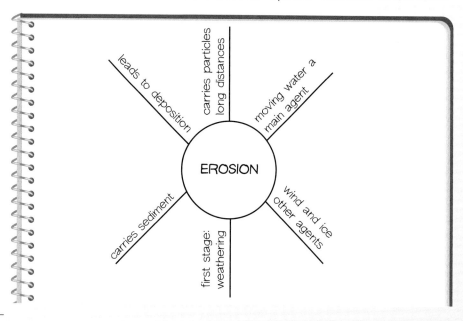

Four Square

1. Write a term in the center.
2. Write details in the four areas around the term.

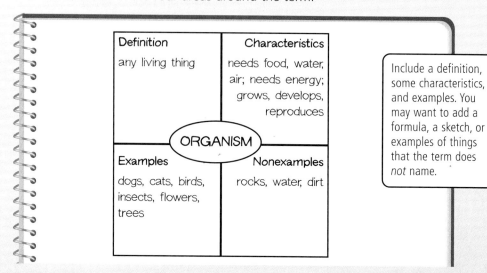

Include a definition, some characteristics, and examples. You may want to add a formula, a sketch, or examples of things that the term does *not* name.

Frame Game

1. Write a term in the center.
2. Frame the term with details.

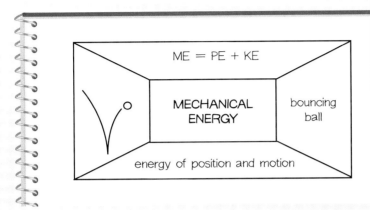

Include examples, descriptions, sketches, or sentences that use the term in context. Change the frame to fit each new term.

Magnet Word

1. Write a term on the magnet.
2. On the lines, add details related to the term.

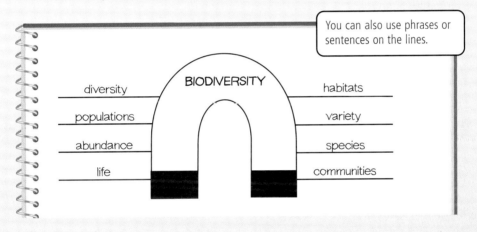

You can also use phrases or sentences on the lines.

Word Triangle

1. Write a term and its definition in the bottom section.
2. In the middle section, write a sentence in which the term is used correctly.
3. In the top section, draw a small picture to illustrate the term.

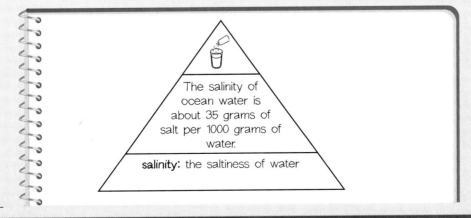

Glossary

GLOSSARY

A

adaptation
A characteristic, a behavior, or any inherited trait that makes a species able to survive and reproduce in a particular environment. (p. xxi)

adaptación Una característica, un comportamiento o cualquier rasgo heredado que permite a una especie sobrevivir o reproducirse en un medio ambiente determinado.

addiction
A physical or psychological need for a habit-forming substance, such as alcohol or drugs. (p. 146)

adicción Una necesidad física o psicológica de una sustancia que forma hábito, como el alcohol o las drogas.

adolescence (AD-uhl-EHS-uhns)
The stage of life from the time a human body begins to mature sexually to adulthood. (p. 135)

adolescencia La etapa de la vida que va desde que el cuerpo humano empieza a madurar sexualmente hasta la edad adulta.

adulthood
The stage of life that begins once a human body completes its growth and reaches sexual maturity. (p. 136)

edad adulta La etapa de la vida que empieza una vez que el cuerpo humano completa su crecimiento y alcanza la madurez sexual.

antibiotic
A medicine that can block the growth and reproduction of bacteria. (p. 81)

antibiótico Una medicina que puede impedir el crecimiento y la reproducción de las bacterias.

antibody
A protein produced by some white blood cells to attack specific foreign materials. (p. 75)

anticuerpo Una proteína producida por algunos glóbulos blancos para atacar materiales extraños específicos.

antigen
A particular substance that the body recognizes as foreign and that stimulates a response. (p. 78)

antígeno Una sustancia que el cuerpo reconoce come extraña y que causa una respuesta.

appendicular skeleton (AP-uhn-DIHK-yuh-luhr)
The bones of the skeleton that function to allow movement, such as arm and leg bones. (p. 16)

esqueleto apendicular Los huesos del esqueleto cuya función es permitir el movimiento, como los huesos del brazo y los huesos de la pierna.

artery
A blood vessel with strong walls that carries blood away from the heart. (p. 69)

arteria Un vaso sanguíneo con paredes fuertes que lleva la sangre del corazón hacia otras partes del cuerpo.

atom
The smallest particle of an element that has the chemical properties of that element.

átomo La partícula más pequeña de un elemento que tiene las propiedades químicas de ese elemento.

autonomic nervous system
The part of the nervous system that controls involuntary action and responses. (p. 107)

sistema nervioso autónomo La parte del sistema nervioso que controla la acción involuntaria y las respuestas.

axial skeleton
The central part of the skeleton, which includes the cranium, the spinal column, and the ribs. (p. 16)

esqueleto axial La parte central del esqueleto que incluye al cráneo, a la columna vertebral y a las costillas.

B

bacteria (bak-TEER-ee-uh)
A large group of one-celled organisms that sometimes cause disease. *Bacteria* is a plural word; the singular is *bacterium.* (p. 149)

bacterias Un grupo grande de organismos unicelulares que algunas veces causan enfermedades.

biodiversity

The number and variety of living things found on Earth or within an ecosystem. (p. xxi)

> **biodiversidad** La cantidad y variedad de organismos vivos que se encuentran en la Tierra o dentro de un ecosistema.

blood

A fluid in the body that delivers oxygen and other materials to cells and removes carbon dioxide and other wastes. (p. 65)

> **sangre** Un fluido en el cuerpo que reparte oxígeno y otras sustancias a las células y elimina dióxido de carbono y otros desechos.

C

capillary

A narrow blood vessel that connects arteries with veins. (p. 69)

> **capilar** Un vaso sanguíneo angosto que conecta a las arterias con las venas.

cardiac muscle

The muscle that makes up the heart. (p. 24)

> **músculo cardiaco** El músculo del cual está compuesto el corazón.

cell

The smallest unit that is able to perform the basic functions of life. (p. xv)

> **célula** La unidad más pequeña capaz de realizar las funciones básicas de la vida.

cellular respiration

A process in which cells use oxygen to release energy stored in sugars. (p. 39)

> **respiración celular** Un proceso en el cual las células usan oxígeno para liberar energía almacenada en las azúcares.

central nervous system

The brain and spinal cord. The central nervous system communicates with the rest of the nervous system through electrical signals sent to and from neurons. (p. 104)

> **sistema nervioso central** El cerebro y la médula espinal. El sistema nervioso central se comunica con el resto del sistema nervioso mediante señales eléctricas enviadas hacia y desde las neuronas.

childhood

The stage of life after infancy and before the beginning of sexual maturity. (p. 134)

> **niñez** La etapa de la vida después de la infancia y antes del comienzo de la madurez sexual.

circulatory system

The group of organs, consisting of the heart and blood vessels, that circulates blood through the body. (p. 65)

> **sistema circulatorio** El grupo de órganos, que consiste del corazón y los vasos sanguíneos, que hace circular la sangre por el cuerpo.

classification

The systematic grouping of different types of organisms by their shared characteristics.

> **clasificación** La agrupación sistemática de diferentes tipos de organismos en base a las características que comparten.

compact bone

The tough, hard outer layer of a bone. (p. 15)

> **hueso compacto** La capa exterior, resistente y dura de un hueso.

compound

A substance made up of two or more different types of atoms bonded together.

> **compuesto** Una sustancia formada por dos o más diferentes tipos de átomos enlazados.

cycle

n. A series of events or actions that repeat themselves regularly; a physical and/or chemical process in which one material continually changes locations and/or forms. Examples include the water cycle, the carbon cycle, and the rock cycle.

v. To move through a repeating series of events or actions.

> **ciclo** Una serie de eventos o acciones que se repiten regularmente; un proceso físico y/o químico en el cual un material cambia continuamente de lugar y/o forma. Ejemplos: el ciclo del agua, el ciclo del carbono y el ciclo de las rocas.

D

data

Information gathered by observation or experimentation that can be used in calculating or reasoning. *Data* is a plural word; the singular is *datum*.

> **datos** Información reunida mediante observación o experimentación y que se puede usar para calcular o para razonar.

density
A property of matter representing the mass per unit volume.

densidad Una propiedad de la materia que representa la masa por unidad de volumen.

dermis
The inner layer of the skin. (p. 84)

dermis La capa interior de la piel.

digestion
The process of breaking down food into usable materials. (p. 46)

digestión El proceso de descomponer el alimento en sustancias utilizables.

digestive system
The structures in the body that work together to transform the energy and materials in food into forms the body can use. (p. 46)

sistema digestivo Las estructuras en el cuerpo que trabajan juntas para transformar la energía y las sustancias en el alimento a formas que el cuerpo puede usar.

DNA
The genetic material found in all living cells that contains the information needed for an organism to grow, maintain itself, and reproduce. Deoxyribonucleic acid (dee-AHK-see-RY-boh-noo-KLEE-ihk).

ADN El material genético que se encuentra en todas las céulas vivas y que contiene la información necesaria para que un organismo crezca, se mantenga a sí mismo y se reproduzca. Ácido desoxiribunucleico.

E

element
A substance that cannot be broken down into a simpler substance by ordinary chemical changes. An element consists of atoms of only one type.

elemento Una sustancia que no puede descomponerse en otra sustancia más simple por medio de cambios químicos normales. Un elemento consta de átomos de un solo tipo.

embryo (EHM-bree-OH)
A multicellular organism, plant or animal, in its earliest stages of development. (p. 121)

embrión Una planta o un animal en su estadio mas temprano de desarrollo.

endocrine system
A group of organs called glands and the hormones they produce that help regulate conditions inside the body. (p. 110)

sistema endocrino Un grupo de órganos llamados glándulas y las hormonas que producen que ayudan a regular las condiciones dentro del cuerpo.

energy
The ability to do work or to cause a change. For example, the energy of a moving bowling ball knocks over pins; energy from food allows animals to move and to grow; and energy from the Sun heats Earth's surface and atmosphere, which causes air to move.

energía La capacidad para trabajar o causar un cambio. Por ejemplo, la energía de una bola de boliche en movimiento tumba los pinos; la energía proveniente de su alimento permite a los animales moverse y crecer; la energía del Sol calienta la superficie y la atmósfera de la Tierra, lo que ocasiona que el aire se mueva.

environment
Everything that surrounds a living thing. An environment is made up of both living and nonliving factors. (p. xix)

medio ambiente Todo lo que rodea a un organismo vivo. Un medio ambiente está compuesto de factores vivos y factores sin vida.

epidermis
The outer layer of the skin. (p. 84)

epidermis La capa exterior de la piel.

experiment
An organized procedure to study something under controlled conditions. (p. xxiv)

experimento Un procedimiento organizado para estudiar algo bajo condiciones controladas.

extinction
The permanent disappearance of a species. (p. xxi)

extinción La desaparición permanente de una especie.

F

fertilization
Part of the process of sexual reproduction in which a male reproductive cell and a female reproductive cell combine to form a new cell that can develop into a new organism. (p. 121)

fertilización El proceso mediante el cual una célula reproductiva masculina y una célula reproductiva femenina se combinan para formar una nueva célula que puede convertirse en un organismo nuevo.

fetus
The developing human embryo from eight weeks to birth. (p. 122)

> **feto** El embrión humano en desarrollo de las ocho semanas al nacimiento.

G

genetic material
The nucleic acid DNA that is present in all living cells and contains the information needed for a cell's growth, maintenance, and reproduction.

> **material genético** El ácido nucleico ADN, ue esta presente en todas las células vivas y que contiene la información necesaria para el crecimiento, el mantenimiento y la reproducción celular.

gland
An organ in the body that produces a specific substance, such as a hormone. (p. 111)

> **glándula** Un órgano en el cuerpo que produce una sustancia específica, como una hormona.

H

homeostasis (HOH-mee-oh-STAY-sihs)
A condition needed for health and functioning in which an organism or cell maintains a relatively stable internal environment. (p. 12)

> **homeostasis** Una condición necesaria para la salud y el funcionamiento en la cual un organismo o una célula mantiene un medio ambiente estable e interna.

hormone
A chemical that is made in one organ and travels through the blood to another organ. (p. 111)

> **hormona** Una sustancia química que se produce en un órgano y viaja por la sangre a otro órgano.

hypothesis
A tentative explanation for an observation or phenomenon. A hypothesis is used to make testable predictions. (p. xxiv)

> **hipótesis** Una explicación provisional de una observación o de un fenómeno. Una hipótesis se usa para hacer predicciones que se pueden probar.

I, J, K

immune system
A group of organs that provides protection against disease-causing agents. (p. 75)

> **sistema immune o inmunológico** Un grupo de órganos que provee protección contra agentes que causan enfermedades.

immunity
Resistance to a disease. Immunity can result from antibodies formed in the body during a previous attack of the same illness. (p. 80)

> **inmunidad** La resistencia a una enfermedad. La inmunidad puede resultar de anticuerpos formados en el cuerpo durante un ataque previo de la misma enfermedad.

infancy
The stage of life that begins at birth and ends when a baby begins to walk. (p. 134)

> **infancia** La etapa de la vida que inicia al nacer y termina cuando el bebe empieza a caminar.

integumentary system (ihn-TEHG-yu-MEHN-tuh-ree)
The body system that includes the skin and its associated structures. (p. 83)

> **sistema tegumentario** El sistema corporal que incluye a la piel y a sus estructuras asociadas.

interaction
The condition of acting or having an influence upon something. Living things in an ecosystem interact with both the living and nonliving parts of their environment. (p. xix)

> **interacción** La condición de actuar o influir sobre algo. Los organismos vivos en un ecosistema interactúan con las partes vivas y las partes sin vida de su medio ambiente.

involuntary muscle
A muscle that moves without conscious control. (p. 24)

> **músculo involuntario** Un músculo que se mueve sin control consciente.

L

law
In science, a rule or principle describing a physical relationship that always works in the same way under the same conditions. The law of conservation of energy is an example.

ley En las ciencias, una regla o un principio que describe una relación física que siempre funciona de la misma manera bajo las mismas condiciones. La ley de la conservación de la energía es un ejemplo.

M

mass
A measure of how much matter an object is made of.

masa Una medida de la cantidad de materia de la que está compuesto un objeto.

matter
Anything that has mass and volume. Matter exists ordinarily as a solid, a liquid, or a gas.

materia Todo lo que tiene masa y volumen. Generalmente la materia existe como sólido, líquido o gas.

menstruation
A period of about five days during which blood and tissue exit the body through the vagina. (p. 119)

menstruación Un período de aproximadamente cinco días durante el cual salen del cuerpo sangre y tejido por la vagina.

microorganism
A very small organism that can be seen only with a microscope. Bacteria are examples of microorganisms. (p. 148)

microorganismo Un organismo muy pequeño que solamente puede verse con un microscopio. Las bacterias son ejemplos de microorganismos.

molecule
A group of atoms that are held together by covalent bonds so that they move as a single unit.

molécula Un grupo de átomos que están unidos mediante enlaces covalentes de tal manera que se mueven como una sola unidad.

muscular system
The muscles of the body that, together with the skeletal system, function to produce movement. (p. 23)

sistema muscular Los músculos del cuerpo que, junto con el sistema óseo, sirven para producir movimiento.

N

neuron
A nerve cell. (p. 105)

neurona Una célula nerviosa.

nutrient (NOO-tree-uhnt)
A substance that an organism needs to live. Examples include water, minerals, and materials that come from the breakdown of food particles. (p. 45)

nutriente Una sustancia que un organismo necesita para vivir. Ejemplos incluyen agua, minerales y sustancias que provienen de la descomposición de partículas de alimento.

nutrition
The study of the materials that nourish the body. (p. 140)

nutrición El estudio de las sustancias que dan sustento al cuerpo.

O

organ
A structure in a plant or animal that is made up of different tissues working together to perform a particular function. (p. 11)

órgano Una estructura en una planta o en un animal compuesta de diferentes tejidos que trabajan juntos para realizar una función determinada.

organism
An individual living thing, made up of one or many cells, that is capable of growing and reproducing.

organismo Un individuo vivo, compuesto de una o muchas células, que es capaz de crecer y reproducirse.

organ system
A group of organs that together perform a function that helps the body meet its needs for energy and materials. (p. 12)

sistema de órganos Un grupo de órganos que juntos realizan una función que ayuda al cuerpo a satisfacer sus necesidades energéticas y de materiales.

P, Q

pathogen
An agent that causes disease. (p. 74)

patógeno Un agente que causa una enfermedad.

peripheral nervous system

The part of the nervous system that lies outside the brain and spinal cord. (p. 106)

sistema nervioso periférico La parte del sistema nervioso que se encuentra fuera del cerebro y la médula espinal.

peristalsis (PEHR-ih-STAWL-sihs)

Wavelike contractions of smooth muscles in the organs of the digestive tract. The contractions move food through the digestive system. (p. 46)

peristalsis Contracciones ondulares de músculos lisos en los órganos del tracto digestivo. Las contracciones mueven el alimento por el sistema digestivo.

R

red blood cell

A type of blood cell that picks up oxygen in the lungs and delivers it to cells throughout the body. (p. 67)

glóbulos rojos Un tipo de célula sanguínea que toma oxígeno en los pulmones y lo transporta a células en todo el cuerpo.

resistance

The ability of an organism to protect itself from a disease or the effects of a substance. (p. 153)

resistencia La habilidad de un organismo para protegerse de una enfermedad o de los efectos de una sustancia.

respiratory system

A system that interacts with the environment and with other body systems to bring oxygen to the body and remove carbon dioxide. (p. 37)

sistema respiratorio Un sistema que interactúa con el medio ambiente y con otros sistemas corporales para traer oxígeno al cuerpo y eliminar dióxido de carbono.

S

skeletal muscle

A muscle that attaches to the skeleton. (p. 24)

músculo esquelético Un músculo que está sujeto al esqueleto.

skeletal system

The framework of bones that supports the body, protects internal organs, and anchors all the body's movement. (p. 14)

sistema óseo El armazón de huesos que sostiene al cuerpo, protege a los órganos internos y sirve de ancla para todo el movimiento del cuerpo.

smooth muscle

Muscle that performs involuntary movement and is found inside certain organs, such as the stomach. (p. 24)

músculo liso Músculos que realizan movimiento involuntario y se encuentran dentro de ciertos órganos, como el estómago.

species

A group of living things that are so closely related that they can breed with one another and produce offspring that can breed as well. (p. xxi)

especie Un grupo de organismos que están tan estrechamente relacionados que pueden aparearse entre sí y producir crías que también pueden aparearse.

spongy bone

Strong, lightweight tissue inside a bone. (p. 15)

hueso esponjoso Tejido fuerte y de peso ligero dentro de un hueso.

stimulus

Something that causes a response in an organism or a part of the body. (p. 102)

estímulo Algo que causa una respuesta en un organismo o en una parte del cuerpo.

system

A group of objects or phenomena that interact. A system can be as simple as a rope, a pulley, and a mass. It also can be as complex as the interaction of energy and matter in the four parts of the Earth system.

sistema Un grupo de objetos o fenómenos que interactúan. Un sistema puede ser algo tan sencillo como una cuerda, una polea y una masa. También puede ser algo tan complejo como la interacción de la energía y la materia en las cuatro partes del sistema de la Tierra.

T

technology

The use of scientific knowledge to solve problems or engineer new products, tools, or processes.

tecnología El uso de conocimientos científicos para resolver problemas o para diseñar nuevos productos, herramientas o procesos.

theory

In science, a set of widely accepted explanations of observations and phenomena. A theory is a well-tested explanation that is consistent with all available evidence.

teoría En las ciencias, un conjunto de explicaciones de observaciones y fenómenos que es ampliamente aceptado. Una teoría es una explicación bien probada que es consecuente con la evidencia disponible.

tissue

A group of similar cells that are organized to do a specific job. (p.10)

tejido Un grupo de células parecidas que juntas realizan una función específica en un organismo.

U

urinary system

A group of organs that filter waste from an organism's blood and excrete it in a liquid called urine. (p. 53)

sistema urinario Un grupo de órganos que filtran desechos de la sangre de un organismo y los excretan en un líquido llamado orina.

urine

Liquid waste that is secreted by the kidneys. (p. 53)

orina El desecho líquido que secretan los riñones.

V, W, X, Y, Z

vaccine

A small amount of a weakened pathogen that is introduced into the body to stimulate the production of antibodies. (p. 80)

vacuna Una pequeña cantidad de un patógeno debilitado que se introduce al cuerpo para estimular la producción de anticuerpos.

variable

Any factor that can change in a controlled experiment, observation, or model. (p. R30)

variable Cualquier factor que puede cambiar en un experimento controlado, en una observación o en un modelo.

vein

A blood vessel that carries blood back to the heart. (p. 69)

vena Un vaso sanguíneo que lleva la sangre de regreso al corazón.

virus

A nonliving, disease-causing particle that uses the materials inside cells to reproduce. A virus consists of genetic material enclosed in a protein coat. (p. 149)

virus Una particular sin vida, que causa enfermedad y que usa los materiales dentro de las células para reproducirse. Un virus consiste de material genético encerrado en una cubierta proteica.

volume

An amount of three-dimensional space, often used to describe the space that an object takes up.

volumen Una cantidad de espacio tridimensional; a menudo se usa este término para describir el espacio que ocupa un objeto.

voluntary muscle

A muscle that can be moved at will. (p. 24)

músculo voluntario Un músculo que puede moverse a voluntad.

voluntary nervous system

The nerves that govern consciously controlled function and movement. (p. 107)

sistema nervioso voluntario Los nervios que gobiernan las funciones y el movimiento cuyo control es consciente.

Index

Page numbers for definitions are printed in **boldface** type.
Page numbers for illustrations, maps, and charts are printed in *italics.*

Acknowledgments

Photography

Cover RNHRD NHS Trust; **iii** *left (top to bottom)* Photograph of James Trefil by Evan Cantwell; Photograph of Rita Ann Calvo by Joseph Calvo; Photograph of Linda Carnine by Amilcar Cifuentes; Photograph of Sam Miller by Samuel Miller; *right (top to bottom)* Photograph of Kenneth Cutler by Kenneth A. Cutler; Photograph of Donald Steely by Marni Stamm; Photograph of Vicky Vachon by Redfern Photographics; **vi** © Larry Dale Gordon/Getty Images; **vii** © Professors P.M. Motta & S. Correr/Photo Researchers, Inc.; **ix** *top* © Gunter Marx Photography/Corbis, *bottom left* Ken O'Donoghue; *bottom right* Frank Siteman; **xiv-xv** © Mark Hambin/Age Fotostock; **xvi-xvii** © Georgette Duowma/Taxi/Getty Images; **xviii-xix** © Ron Sanford/Corbis; **xx-xxi** © Nick Vedros & Assoc./Stone/Getty Images; **xxii** *left* © Michael Gadomski/Animals Animals, *right* © Shin Yoshino/ Minden Pictures; **xxiii** © Laif Elleringmann/Aurora Photos; **xxiv** © Pascal Goetgheluck/Photo Researchers, Inc.; **xxv** *left* © David Parker/Photo Researchers, Inc., *right* James King-Holmes/Photo Researchers, Inc., *bottom* Courtesy, Sinsheimer Labs/University of California, Santa Cruz; **xxvi-xxvii** *background* © Maximillian Stock/Photo Researchers, Inc.; **xxvi** *bottom* Courtesy, John Lair, Jewish Hospital, University of Louisville; **xxvii** *top* © Brand X Pictures/Alamy, *center* Courtesy, AbioMed; **xxxii** *bottom left* Chedd-Angier Production Company; **2–3** © Peter Byron/PhotoEdit; **3** *top right* © ISM/Phototake; **4** *top* © Wellcome Department of Cognitive Neurology/Photo Researchers, Inc., *bottom* Chedd-Angier Production Company; **5** © Myrleen Ferguson Cate/PhotoEdit; **6–7** © Chris Hamilton/Corbis; **7** *top* Frank Siteman, *bottom* Ken O'Donoghue; **9** © SuperStock; **10** Frank Siteman; **11** *left* © Martin Rotker/Phototake; **12** © SW Production/Index Stock Imagery/PictureQuest; **13** *background* © Hulton-Deutsch Collection/Corbis, *center* © Underwood & Underwood/Corbis; **14** Frank Siteman; **15** © Prof. P. Motta/Dept. of Anatomy/University "La Sapienza," Rome/Photo Researchers, Inc.; **16** © Photodisc/Getty Images; **18** *bottom* © Science Photo Library/Photo Researchers, Inc., *bottom left* © Zephyr/Photo Researchers, Inc.; **19** *top* © Zephyr/Photo Researchers, Inc., bottom Frank Siteman; **20** *top left* © Stock Image/SuperStock, *top right* © Science Photo Library/Photo Researchers, Inc.; **21** © Dennis Kunkel/Phototake; **22** Frank Siteman; **23** © Kevin R. Morris/Corbis; **25** *background* © Mary Kate Denny/PhotoEdit, *top* © Martin Rotker/Phototake, *left* © Triarch/Visuals Unlimited, *bottom* © Eric Grave/Phototake; **26** © Ron Frehm/AP Wide World Photos; **27** © Jeff Greenberg/PhotoEdit; **28** *top* © Gunter Marx Photography/Corbis, *bottom, all* Frank Siteman; **30** © Martin Rotker/Phototake; **31** *top* © Stock Image/SuperStock; **34–35** © Larry Dale Gordon/Getty Images; **35** *top* Frank Siteman, *bottom* Ken O'Donoghue; **37** Frank Siteman; **38** © Amos Nachoum/Corbis; **39** Ken O'Donoghue; **41** *bottom left* © Michael Newman/PhotoEdit, *bottom right* © Science Photo Library/Photo Researchers, Inc.; **43** © Kennan Harvey/Getty Images; **44** *background* © Jim Cummins/Getty Images, *center* © Steve Casimiro/Getty Images; **45** Ken O'Donoghue; **47** Ken O'Donoghue; **48** © Professors P. Motta & A. Familiari/University "La Sapienza," Rome/Photo Researchers, Inc.; **49** © David Young-Wolff/PhotoEdit; **50** © Dr. Gladden Willis/Visuals Unlimited; **51** © David Gifford/SPL/Custom Medical Stock Photo; **52** Frank Siteman; **55** © LWA-Dann Tardif/Corbis; **56** *top* © Myrleen Ferguson Cate/PhotoEdit, *bottom left* Ken O'Donoghue, *bottom right* Frank Siteman; **57** Frank Siteman; **62–63** © Professors P.M. Motta & S. Correr/Photo Researchers, Inc.; **63** *both* Frank Siteman; **65** Frank Siteman; **67** © Science Photo Library/Photo Researchers, Inc.; **68** © Myrleen Ferguson Cate/PhotoEdit; **69** © Susumu Nishinaga/Photo Researchers, Inc.; **71** © Journal-Courier/The Image Works; **72** *top left* © Michael Newman/PhotoEdit, *bottom left* Ken O'Donoghue, *center right, bottom right* Frank Siteman; **74** Frank Siteman; **75** *top* © Eddy Gray/Photo Researchers, Inc., *bottom* © Mary Kate Denny/PhotoEdit; **76** © Science Photo Library/Photo Researchers, Inc.; **77** *top* © Dr. P. Marazzi/Photo Researchers, Inc., *top right* © Dr. Jeremy Burgess/Photo Researchers, Inc.; **78** © Science Photo Library/Photo Researchers, Inc.; **79** Frank Siteman; **80** © Bob Daemmrich/The Image Works; **81** © Richard Lord/The Image Works; **82** *background* © SCIMAT/Photo Researchers, Inc., *inset* © Vision/Photo Researchers; **83** Ken O'Donoghue; **84** RMIP/Richard Haynes; **85** Frank Siteman; **86** *top inset* © Dennis Kunkel/Phototake, *bottom inset* © Andrew Syred/Photo Researchers, Inc., *center* © Photodisc/Getty Images; **87** *all* © Eric Schrempp/Photo Researchers, Inc.; **88** © The Image Bank/Getty Images; **89** *background* © James King-Holmes/Photo Researchers, Inc., *top right* © Sygma/Corbis, *bottom right* © David Hanson; **94** *top* © Hulton Archive/Getty Images, *bottom* © Simon Fraser/Photo Researchers, Inc.; **95** *top* © Bettmann/Corbis, *center* © Underwood & Underwood/Corbis, *bottom* © George Bernard/Photo Researchers, Inc.; **96** *top left* © Collection CNRI/Phototake, *top right* © Geoff Tompkinson/ Photo Researchers, Inc., *bottom* © Josh Sher/Photo Researchers, Inc.; **97** *top* © Simon Fraser/Photo Researchers, Inc., *bottom* © GJLP/Photo Researchers, Inc.; **98–99** © Photo Researchers, Inc.; **99** *top* Ken O'Donoghue, *center* © Photospin; **101** Ken O'Donoghue; **103** RMIP/Richard Haynes; **104** © David Young-Wolff/PhotoEdit; **107** © Royalty-Free/Corbis; **108** *top* © Ed Young/Corbis, *bottom* Ken O'Donoghue; **109** *top* Frank Siteman, *bottom* Ken O'Donoghue; **110** © David Young-Wolff/PhotoEdit; **111** © Kwame Zikomo/SuperStock; **112** © ISM/Phototake; **114** Frank Siteman; **115** © CNRI/Photo Researchers, Inc.; **117** *left* © David Young-Wolff/PhotoEdit, *bottom right* © Glenn Oakley/ImageState/PictureQuest; **118** Ken O'Donoghue; **123** *background* © Yoav Levy/Phototake, *top left* © Dr. Yorgos Nikas/ Photo Researchers, Inc.; **124** © David Degnan/Corbis; **125** *left* © Christopher Brown/Stock Boston, Inc./PictureQuest, *right* © Nissim Men/Photonica; **130–131** © Brooklyn Productions/Corbis; **131** top Ken O'Donoghue; **133** Frank Siteman; **134** © Tom Galliher/Corbis; **135** © Tom Stewart/Corbis; **136** © Novastock/Index Stock Imagery, Inc.; **138** *left* © Spencer Grant/PhotoEdit, *right* © Michael Newman/PhotoEdit; **139** *all* from STAGE MAKEUP, STEP BY STEP. Courtesy of Quarto Publishing, Inc.; **140** © Ed Young/Corbis; **141** © Ronnie Kaufman/Corbis; **142** © Photodisc/Getty Images; **144** © Don Smetzer/PhotoEdit; **146** © Brett Coomer/HO/AP Wide World Photos; **147** *left* © Eric Kamp/Index Stock Photography, Inc., *top right* © Ariel Skelley/Corbis; **148** Frank Siteman; **149** © Mediscan/Visuals Unlimited; **151** top left © Dr. Kari Lounatmaa/Science Photo Library/Photo Researchers, Inc., *top right* © Dr. Gopal Murti/Photo Researchers, Inc., *bottom left* © Professors P.M. Motta & F.M. Magliocca/PhotoResearchers, Inc., *bottom right* © Microworks/Phototake, *bottom right inset* © Andrew Spielman/Phototake; **152** © Mary Steinbacher/PhotoEdit; **153** © Srulik Haramary/Phototake; **154** *top left* © Kwame Zikomo/Superstock, bottom left Ken O'Donoghue, *bottom right* Frank Siteman; **155** Ken O'Donoghue; **156** © Mediscan/Visuals Unlimited; **R28** © Photodisc/Getty Images.

Illustration

Debbie Maizels **15, 26, 84, 90, 102, 104, 128**
Linda Nye **11, 30, 46, 66, 70, 90, 92, 119, 120, 121, 122, 123, 126**
Steve Oh/KO Studios **78, 105**
Bart Vallecoccia **11,17, 30, 32, 41, 42, 44, 46, 49, 53, 54, 58, 60, 68, 103, 105, 106, 113, 119, 120, 126**
Dan Stuckenschneider/Uhl Studios **R11-R19, R22, R32**